"Franklin exposes how a generation of American politicians have cynically manipulated the feelings of grief and confusion that still linger from the Vietnam War. . . . A marvel of careful scholarship and clear writing—hard-hitting and absolutely convincing."—Joe Haldeman, author of *The Forever War*

"A calm and thoughtful book on a firestorm of a subject. . . . Intelligent, provocative, and courageous."—*Kirkus Reviews*

"Franklin methodically builds his case . . . and concludes that myth has overshadowed reality, and that Americans over the years have been doubly manipulated: first, by U.S. government officials, . . . second, by the popular media."—*The Christian Science Monitor*

"Franklin reviews the astonishing numbers games the Pentagon and POW/MIA activists have played, . . . analyzes the roles of . . . individuals like Henry Kissinger and H. Ross Perot in developing and sustaining true believers' faith, and reveals the interplay between life and art in POW/MIA books and films."—*Booklist*

D0781722

Books by H. Bruce Franklin

The Wake of the Gods: Melville's Mythology
Future Perfect: American Science Fiction of the 19th Century
Who Should Run the Universities (with John A. Howard)
From the Movement: Toward Revolution
Herman Melville's Mardi (edition)
Herman Melville's The Confidence Man (edition)
Back Where You Came From
The Scarlet Letter *and Hawthorne's Critical Writings* (edition)
The Essential Stalin (edition)
Prison Literature in America: The Victim as Criminal and Artist
Countdown to Midnight
American Prisoners and Ex-Prisoners: An Annotated Bibliography
Robert A. Heinlein: America as Science Fiction
Vietnam and America: A Documented History
   (with Marvin Gettleman, Jane Franklin, and Marilyn Young)
War Stars: The Superweapon and the American Imagination

M.I.A.
or
Mythmaking
In
America

H. BRUCE FRANKLIN

RUTGERS UNIVERSITY PRESS
NEW BRUNSWICK, NEW JERSEY

First published in paperback by Rutgers University Press, 1993
First published in cloth by Lawrence Hill Books, an imprint of
Chicago Review Press, Incorporated, 1992

Library of Congress Cataloging-in-Publication Data

Franklin, H. Bruce (Howard Bruce), 1934–
    M.I.A., or, Mythmaking in America / H. Bruce Franklin.
    p. cm.
    Includes bibliographical references and index.
    ISBN 0-8135-2001-0 (paperback)
    1. Vietnamese Conflict, 1961–1975—Missing in action—
United States. I. Title. II. Title: M.I.A. III. Title: Mythmaking
in America. IV. Title: MIA, or Mythmaking in America.
DS559.8.M5F73   1993
959.704'3373—dc20   93-24778
                                                         CIP

"POW/MIA," copyright 1990 by W. D. Ehrhart, is reprinted from
Just for Laughs, published by Vietnam Generation, Inc., and is used
by permission of W. D. Ehrhart.

Printed in the United States of America

*For all those
who have been trying
for decades to stop
this war*

Contents

Acknowledgments

Many people have helped me create this book. I am grateful to Cora Weiss for giving me unrestricted access to her invaluable Vietnam War archives, to Gloria Coppin and David Burgess for especially helpful interviews, and to Dr. John S. Baky, Acting Director of the Connelly Library of La Salle University, for indispensable aid in utilizing the library's superb special collection on the Vietnam War and American popular culture. Other important assistance in research came from Margaret O. Adams, Archivist of the National Archives' Center for Electronic Records; Dr. Richard J. Sommers, Archivist-Historian of the U.S. Army Military History Institute at Carlisle Barracks; Charles F. Trowbridge, Jr., Deputy Chief of the Special Office for Prisoners of War and Missing in Action of the Defense Intelligence Agency; Betsy Cox, Director of Public Relations of the National League of Families of American Prisoners and Missing in Southeast Asia; Todd Ensign, co-founder of Citizen Soldier; Bob Gardella, a Vietnam veteran imprisoned in America; and Paul Shannon, Editor of *Indochina Newsletter.* The staff of the John Cotton Dana Library provided outstanding assistance; I am particularly indebted to Wanda Gawienoski, Michael Bowman, Marjorie Watson, and Ka-Neng Au. Karen Franklin, Gretchen Franklin, and Robert Franklin each read the entire manuscript and made innumerable excellent suggestions. Shirley Cloyes, Director of Lawrence Hill Books, gave superb guidance and invaluable help through every stage of the book from inception to publication. Barbara Flanagan provided unusually fine copyediting. My greatest debt, as always, is to Jane Morgan Franklin, whose own work on the subject inspired and enriched the book, who participated in every phase of its development, and who contributed in more ways than can ever be acknowledged.

Preface to the Expanded and Updated Edition

Just as the first edition of this book appeared in November 1992, the POW/MIA issue exploded with unprecedented intensity in the American political arena. Suddenly the book became part of its own subject as I was given the role of what one reviewer called "the most visible heretic" of the national POW/MIA religion.

I soon stopped trying to explain that *M.I.A. or Mythmaking In America* is not mainly a polemic disputing the belief that American POWs are being held in Indochina but, rather, a cultural and political history of how and why this belief, contradicted by all evidence and logic, became both the official postwar rationale for continuing hostilities against Vietnam and a national myth profoundly significant to late-twentieth-century American society. On over a hundred TV and radio shows I was cast as the dissident, debating about whether or not there are POWs with such leading characters of the story as Ann Mills Griffiths, Colonel Bo Gritz, Captain Red McDaniel, John LeBoutillier, Jeff Donahue, Senator Charles Grassley, and Senator John Kerry. The major TV networks interviewed me at length—to extract a few seconds of me asserting that there are no POWs. A revealing example came when President George Bush was shouted down at the July 1992 annual meeting of the National League of Families. Interviewed by an NBC-TV team that rushed to my home, I stressed the role of the government, including Bush himself, in perpetuating the belief in live POWs. But on the evening news the two surviving sound bites were so carefully edited that my next-door neighbor joked that the president would certainly call in the morning to thank me for coming to his defense.

From the middle of 1991 into early 1993 the POW/MIA issue kept resurfacing in sensational new forms. Events of this period— such as the Bush administration's 1991 "Road Map" for normalizing relations with Vietnam, the subsequent creation and proceedings of the Senate Select Committee on POW/MIA Affairs, the presidential campaign of Ross Perot, the Clinton administration's early hard-line policy toward Vietnam—have given such dramatic new significance to the POW/MIA myth that it became necessary to add a new chapter to this edition. There I show how these events relate to one another, to the earlier history of the issue, and to the crucial question of finally bringing closure to the Vietnam War.

I have left the original text virtually unchanged, except for a few updates, such as the current number of MIAs. The withering scrutiny of POW/MIA activists and organizations has failed to discover a single error in that text. Though equally hostile to my thesis, the Senate Select Committee in its seventeen-month investigation, conducted at a cost of tens of millions of dollars, unearthed nothing that contradicts any of my evidence and analysis; in fact, it ended up inadvertently corroborating major parts of my argument.

Many people have expressed surprise that the Select Committee did not invite me to testify and indeed adamantly turned down my repeated requests to appear. Perhaps this is not really so surprising. The only true mystery about the POW/MIA issue is who created and perpetuated it, why, and how. Irrefutable evidence proves that the main perpetrators are the two parties to which the senators belong, operating through four Republican and two Democratic administrations. As I show in chapter 6, four of the senators on the

Select Committee personally connived in bamboozling the American people with fraudulent evidence. The why and the how are the main subjects of this book, and the solution to that part of the mystery cuts too deep for comfort into contemporary American politics and culture.

June 18, 1993

Preface

The prevailing conviction in the United States that American prisoners of war are still being held as captives in Indochina may be one of the strangest and most revealing beliefs in the world today. "Bring on Rambo," appropriately commented *The Wall Street Journal* on August 2, 1991, in reporting that 69 percent of Americans surveyed in a *Wall Street Journal*/NBC News poll believed that Americans are still prisoners of war in Southeast Asia and that 52 percent of those surveyed are convinced that the government is not doing enough to get them back.

When I began investigating this belief in live POWs, I intended the results to be only a chapter in a book about how American culture shaped and was reshaped by the Vietnam War. I had little sense of the breadth or depth of the faith, perhaps because it seemed so obviously irrational and related to an issue of such apparently minor significance compared with other effects of the war on both America and the nations of Indochina.

But I soon discovered that this faith was exerting a profound, and even growing, influence in late-twentieth-century America, and I also began to encounter startling facts about its history and evolution. Then a puzzling revelation emerged in people's contradictory responses when they learned what I was working on: some expressed surprise that anyone seriously believed that there are still POWs in Indochina while others expressed equal surprise that anyone would have any doubt that they are there. Before long, I realized that the subject could not possibly be relegated to a chapter, that it demanded a book of its own. Another eyeopener was the discovery that no such book existed, that, except for a handful of articles and a 1979 volume written by an officer of the National War College and published by the National Defense University, virtually all the available literature on the subject consisted of polemical tracts by true believers. So I was now committed to writing a book on what seemed to me the POW/ MIA fantasy.

As I plunged into the literature of true belief, however, I received another shock: it was thoroughly convincing—to anyone unfamiliar with the actual history of the issue and unacquainted with minimal standards of research and documentation. The belief in live POWs was based not just on political rhetoric, rumors, and the POW rescue movies, but also on a sizable body of books, pamphlets, and articles that had promulgated a coherent and superficially plausible pseudohistory compounded of self-deception, amateur research, anecdotes, half-truths, phony evidence, slick political and media manipulation, downright lies, and near-religious fervor. Now I realized that I would have to deal directly with the POW/MIA issue itself, and this, together with its political history, would have to be integrated with my original focus on it as a cultural phenomenon.

I also became convinced that this book should speak not just to scholars of modern America but also to the rest of the people who live in it, and to both those who are unaware of the importance of the POW/MIA belief and those who are unaware that it is an elaborate fraud. Because the subject is so contentious and of such wide interest, I have attempted to write in a way accessible to any literate person concerned with the issue. But being so controversial, the subject also demands meticulous, thorough, and reliable documentation. So while the text itself can be read straight through without consulting the notes, the extensive endnotes are an integral part of the book.

For nonacademic readers, a word about this documentation may be useful. Almost everything previously published on this subject, except for certain congressional and other official documents, has been aimed at proselytizing the POW/MIA creed. Some of these works use documentation to enhance their credibility, but their notes usually turn out to refer almost entirely to secondary sources committed to their own view, hearsay, and other evidence not subject to independent corroboration. Whenever possible I have used primary sources, official documents, interviews, and materials taking views opposed to my own, and I often give multiple sources. This makes it possible for skeptical readers to verify points for themselves and also provides resources for readers who wish to explore aspects of this astonishingly significant subject on their own.

1 PRISONERS OF MYTH

A National Religion?

Only one flag other than the Star-Spangled Banner has ever flown over the White House. There on one day every year since 1982 has fluttered the black and white POW/MIA flag, designed and distributed by the National League of Families of American Prisoners and Missing in Southeast Asia. The endless flow of visitors to the Rotunda of the nation's Capitol streams past an object that may seem somewhat incongruous beneath the epic paintings and amid the heroic statues: the POW/MIA flag, the only flag displayed in the Capitol, given this ongoing position of honor by vote of the Congress of the United States in 1987. This banner thus displays to the world our nation's faith in the flag's central image, the silhouette of a handsome American prisoner of war, his head slightly bowed to reveal behind him the ominous shape of a guard tower. A strand of barbed wire cuts across just below his firm chin. Underneath runs the motto: *You are not forgotten.*

Each year since 1982 the U. S. government has officially declared that it is operating "on the assumption that at least some Americans are still held captive" in Indochina. In 1983, ten years after the last official U.S. combat in Indochina, the president of the United States

3

solemnly pledged that the fate of the POW/MIAs had now become "the highest national priority." The following year, Michael Dukakis, governor of a state that had been in the forefront of the movement against the Vietnam War, signed a decree authorizing that the POW/ MIA flag fly above the State House lawn for a year. Today in Massachusetts, every city and town must fly the POW/MIA flag over at least one municipal building and over all police and fire stations, while all state vehicles must display the POW/MIA logo. This policy is now typical of many states, and the POW/MIA flag is also a familiar sight at rest stops and toll plazas along state highways. Congress and the president every year enact legislation proclaiming National POW/MIA Recognition Day. By 1988, laws mandating observance of this day had been enacted by the legislatures and governors of forty-six states; the last four states fell into line by 1990. In May 1990, Secretary of Defense Dick Cheney sent a directive to the Secretary of each branch of the armed forces and the Chairman of the Joint Chiefs of Staff reminding them of the preeminent importance of "the POW/MIA public awareness program" and specifying that every U.S. military installation should fly the POW/MIA flag, conduct POW/MIA Recognition Day ceremonies, and arrange for materials and presentations from the National League of Families.[1]

Official homage to the Americans still allegedly captive in Southeast Asia is not merely a ritual. It is also a basis—or at least an ostensible basis—for foreign policy. In 1990, the U.S. government boasted that it "has kept the live prisoner issue at the forefront of negotiations" with Vietnam and reiterated its declaration that "the POW/MIA issue" is "a matter of highest national priority" that could be resolved only after "the fullest possible accounting for the missing, the return of all Americans who may still be held in captivity, and the repatriation of all recoverable remains." At the time of this writing, the government still gives as its only official rationale for refusing to recognize and begin normal relations with Vietnam that nation's failure to meet these demands. Beginning in 1982 under the Reagan administration, the Department of Defense has issued annually a *POW-MIA Fact Book*, which states the official rationale for this policy. From 1984 through 1989, the key wording ran: "it would be irresponsible to rule out the possibility that live Americans are being held." In 1990, under the Bush administration, this phrasing was replaced with the less equivocal statement: "the U.S. Government's efforts are predicated on the assumption that some are still alive."[2]

Devotion to American POWs still supposedly enslaved in Indochina is hardly a monopoly of the national, state, and local governments. It permeates the society, running especially strong in the working class. Throughout the nation, particularly in shopping malls and white working-class neighborhoods, the black and white POW/MIA flag often flies beneath or beside the Stars and Stripes. Bumper stickers, buttons, and T-shirts proclaim: *American POW/ MIAs are Alive in Vietnam, Release Our POW/MIAs*, and *POWs Never Have a Nice Day*. A permanent POW/MIA vigil, staffed mainly by Vietnam veterans, is held at the Vietnam Veterans Memorial in Washington. Millions of Americans have worn POW/MIA bracelets, which are still sold by the thousands each year. The POW/MIA flag has waved over the General Motors parts distribution center in Bensalem, Pennsylvania, ever since the United Auto Workers local there threatened to strike if it were not flown every day.[3] Above the New York Stock Exchange, facing the visitors' gallery, hangs a large POW/MIA flag. Video games about POWs have spread from the arcades into homes, as children of all ages play "P.O.W.: Prisoners of War" on Nintendo. A board game dedicated to the POW/MIAs "still alive and being held against their will" is played with 2,477 cards, each inscribed with a different serviceman's "name, rank, branch of service, casualty date, and country where lost or captured." Christmas trees are adorned with POW/MIA ornaments. In the fall of 1990, leather-jacketed bikers staged Operation

Rolling Thunder, a four-thousand-motorcycle cavalcade that roared through New Jersey and Manhattan to demand the release of the American prisoners still held in Southeast Asia.[4] By 1990, the fate of the MIAs had become the most important concern of many Vietnam veterans, displacing their own problems with unemployment, homelessness, Agent Orange, and inadequate medical care.

How could anyone, especially any loyal American, doubt that there are live American prisoners of war still held in Vietnam, Laos, and Cambodia? Hundreds of millions of people around the world have actually seen these forgotten heroes—abandoned by their own government, emaciated, tortured, enslaved but unbowed—on movie and television screens. Their existence proves undeniably the cruelty and inhumanity of the Asian Communists, the fortitude and heroism of the American fighting man, and the noble cause for which the United States fought in Indochina. David Cline, who himself was wounded when his position was overrun in the same time and place as the battle depicted toward the end of the movie *Platoon*, describes one aspect of this phenomenon most succinctly: "Americans want to believe that we were the good guys and those rotten gooks are still making our boys grow rice."[5]

Yet the story also has much deeper meanings. These forsaken heroes have attained the genuine status and total function of myth— indeed an extraordinarily powerful myth—in late-twentieth-century American culture. I use the term *myth* in its fundamental and rigorous sense, to refer to a story of ostensibly historic events or beings crucial to the world view and self-image of a people, a story that, no matter how bizarre it may seem from outside that society or when subjected to rational analysis, appears as essential truth to its believers.

The POW/MIA myth has had a profound political, cultural, and psychological influence in American society, an influence that has continued to deepen into the 1990s, although the likelihood that there are any living POWs wanes with each passing year. Those not possessed by the faith may find it difficult to comprehend its power. As this book will demonstrate, there has yet to be any credible evidence that any prisoners were withheld in Indochina, and even if some had been held, their number could not possibly have been more than a few dozen at the very most. The supposed fate of this conjectural small group therefore might seem to be almost incidental to the catastrophic effects of the war on the ruined nation of Vietnam, whose casualties ran into the millions and whose own MIAs still number over two hundred thousand, as well as to the devastating effects of the war on the United States itself, including the known fate of many tens of thousands of veterans. Indeed, for every missing man who the U.S. government at any time claimed might have been a postwar captive in Indochina there are now probably at least one thousand homeless Vietnam veterans on the streets of the United States, whom some people refer to as "M.I.A: Missing in America." And the saviors such as Gene Hackman, Chuck Norris, Sylvester Stallone, and David Carradine whom Hollywood has pictured on quests to rescue imprisoned Vietnam veterans would have a more realistic chance of success in the United States, where hundreds of thousands are or have been incarcerated in jails and prisons.[6]

The POW myth exerts surprising power on levels of American society from top to bottom. A prudent person would not question the existence of live POWs at a public gathering or in a strange bar, for the belief in their existence, their suffering, and their betrayal often has all the intensity of a religion. Perhaps this faith could be regarded as the closest thing we have to a national religion. Indeed, in the presence of many Americans it would be less offensive to express doubts about the existence of God than about the existence of live POWs in Southeast Asia.

The religious implications of the issue are not just conjectural. That May 1990 directive from Secretary of Defense Cheney to all

U.S. armed forces specified that "Chaplains include a remembrance of our POW/MIAs and their families in each service." Representative Robert Dornan of California asserted in 1989 that the POW/MIA bracelet has achieved recognizability as a symbol "second only to religious symbols such as the cross or Star of David."[7] When pressed by the chairman of a congressional committee for his evidence of live POWs, Colonel James "Bo" Gritz, arguably the single most important figure in vivifying the POW issue in the popular imagination, responded: "I have the same evidence, sir, that might be presented by a clergyman to convince you that God exists."[8]

A good working definition of myth is a story that is the core of someone else's religion. Or, put more bluntly, myth is the essence of a religion in which you don't believe. Indeed, any truly functional myth, or religion, *must* seem essentially implausible and nonrational to nonbelievers, for its powers derive from its defiance and transcendence of perceived reality and ordinary thinking. That is, all myths require faith. If Vietnam announced that it was holding several dozen American prisoners of war until the United States fulfilled some obligation, obviously no such faith would be necessary to believe in their reality. Live POWs could become the basis of a myth *because* Vietnam insists no such beings exist, *because* Vietnam has no plausible reason to hold American prisoners while at the same time denying their existence, *because* it is so unlikely that any could still be alive if they were held in the conditions imagined by believers, and *because* years of espionage, interrogation, spy flights, satellite observation, and even raids on suspected sites have produced not one piece of tangible evidence of their existence.

This last assertion might infuriate many believers, because they are certain of overwhelming evidence. Some could immediately cite a specific example of "tangible evidence"—such as the secret Fort Apache photograph (see page 143)—the existence of which can be denied only because an elaborate government conspiracy has been concealing it from the American public. This elaborate government conspiracy, in turn, has become another crucial component of the myth, and arguments about *its* existence lead in ever widening spirals to the broadest significance of the myth itself.

Recognizing the religious nature of the beliefs explored in this book, one has to ask whether denying the existence of live POWs is an act of cruelty against those family members and friends of missing men who cannot accept their death and even against the millions of strangers who have made faith in living POWs such an important part of their own lives. Denying that these men are alive in Indochinese prison camps might be thought to have psychological effects similar to denying that men who were indisputably killed in action are alive in heaven. But while the belief in live POWs may allow some flicker of hope, it hardly offers comfort, for the missing men are imagined to be in a place much more like hell. The true act of cruelty is preserving false hope, for it condemns all who care about the missing men to what was described in 1975 as "pure hell" by Joan Vinson, former national coordinator of the National League of Families, whose husband was an Air Force colonel missing in action since 1968. Emma Hagerman, whose husband was an Air Force colonel declared missing in action in 1967 and who then became one of the founders of the National League of Families, testified in 1976 that "the MIA disease" turns families into "emotional cripples" who "no longer look for an accounting, but are waiting for a resurrection."9

There are also more critical differences between challenging faith in an afterlife and belief in living captivity, for the first does not have the practical consequences of the second. Whether or not people believe that the dead live in the hereafter has no effect on relations between the United States and Vietnam, or on the political, social, psychological, and cultural responses of the United States to the Vietnam War decades later. But the myth of live POWs does have such effects, and they are profound.

The imagined live POWs have something else in common with

the gods and other mythological beings of all religions: there is no logical way to prove that they do *not* exist. No conceivable search could simultaneously investigate every possible site where they might be concealed in all of Vietnam, Cambodia, and Laos. The non-existence of even a single visible being can be proved only for a single time and at a single place (just because no one has ever seen a purple dragon on your roof doesn't prove that one is never there; it may come only when nobody is looking). Even people generally assumed to be dead make frequent appearances to convinced witnesses; note the common sightings of Adolf Hitler, James Dean, and Elvis Presley. The only logical proof that there are no living American POWs would be irrefutable evidence that every single missing man is dead. But the circumstances in which many of these men disappeared and presumably died make it impossible to discover such evidence.

In any case, although this book reaches the conclusion that there is no plausible basis for believing that there are live American POWs in Indochina, its essential purpose is not to prove their nonexistence, which could be done neither logically nor, of course, to the satisfaction of those whose faith in them is truly religious. Its subject is the ardent faith that there are live POWs and the significance of this faith as a major political, psychological, and cultural feature of late-twentieth-century American life. Because the evidence overwhelmingly indicates virtually no likelihood that there are any American prisoners of the Vietnam War still alive in Indochina, it is appropriate to treat the object of this faith as myth.

Although this myth has been propagated by a vast body of pamphlets, movies, books, TV soaps and documentaries, comic books, presidential proclamations, flags, buttons, bumper stickers, T-shirts, bracelets, and national and state legislation, it has received virtually no serious attention, much less scrutiny, as a prominent and revealing part of modern American culture and history.[10] When did the POW/MIA issue emerge and what made it so potent? What political, economic, and cultural forces have been involved in its propagation? How and why did the issue attain its mythic function in American culture? These are major questions whether or not the nations of Indochina have given a proper accounting of American MIAs and whether or not there is any plausible basis for the belief that some of them are still held in captivity. But one cannot adequately view what the POW/MIA myth reveals about late-twentieth-century America without looking at and seeing through the flimsy, shabby material from which it has been fabricated.

But *Are* There Live POWs?

Counting the Unaccounted For

To keep one's bearings through the thickets that lie ahead, it will be helpful to keep these facts in mind:

- A total of 2,255 Americans are still "unaccounted for" from the war in Indochina.

- Approximately half this total (1,095) were never considered to be either missing in action or prisoners of war. These were *known* at the time of their loss to have been killed in action; they are listed as "unaccounted for" only because their *bodies* have not been recovered.

- Today only one man is still officially listed as either missing in action or a prisoner of war, and he is known to have died more than a quarter of a century ago.

In all major wars, many combatants die without being identified or having their bodies recovered. Approximately 78,750 Americans are still unaccounted for from World War II, and 8,177 are unaccounted for from the Korean War. So the total of 2,255 still unaccounted for in the Indochina War would seem surprisingly small, especially because 81 percent of the missing were airmen mainly lost over the sea, remote mountains, or tropical rain forest, often in planes exploding at supersonic speeds, while most of the rest disappeared amid confused fighting in dense jungle. In fact, the proportion of unaccounted for Americans to the total killed in action is far smaller for the Indochina war than for any previous war in the nation's history, even though this was its longest war, included protracted "secret" wars in Laos and Cambodia whose very existence was denied by the U.S. government, and ended with every battlefield in the possession of the enemy. For World War II, after which the United States was free to explore every battlefield, the 78,750 still unaccounted for represent 19.4 percent of the total 405,399 killed. For the Korean War, more than 15 percent of the dead are still unaccounted for. In contrast, the 2,255 unaccounted for from the Indochina war constitute less than 4 percent of the 58,152 killed.[11]

What is the likelihood of finding and identifying aviators lost under combat conditions? A U.S. Navy study of all fatal non-combat accidents between 1969 and 1975 involving the type of combat aircraft flown in Vietnam showed that in 40 percent of the cases there were insufficient remains for positive identification through autopsy, even though naval investigators arrived on the scene within hours of a crash and the identities of the airmen were already known.[12] Bodies left in Indochina would additionally suffer the ravages of the tropical climate, with its monsoon rains, engulfing mud, and vegetative overgrowth, and would likely be torn apart and scattered by animals.

Speedy recovery even of those bodies that might eventually be found cannot reasonably be expected, given that, despite extensive prior searches, the dead from much earlier wars are still turning up. Almost every year, the remains of Americans killed in World War II are discovered in the European countryside, and crews of at least two American bombers that crashed in New Guinea in the early 1940s were finally found in the 1980s. Although there was never any question as to the actual site of their death, remains of soldiers killed in General Custer's 1876 Battle of the Little Bighorn were still being located in 1985. The skeletons of thirty-two Confederate soldiers killed in the Civil War Battle of Glorieta Pass were unearthed in New Mexico in 1987. The same year, the remains of twenty-eight U.S. soldiers killed during the War of 1812 were discovered in Canada.[13]

Such grim facts highlight a misconception basic to the POW/MIA issue. The total of 2,255 unaccounted for in Indochina is itself quite misleading, because it includes those 1,095 who were originally *known* to have been killed in action in circumstances where their bodies could not be recovered. Their official designation is KIA/BNR—killed in action/body not recovered. Crews of airplanes that exploded in the air or crashed within sight of their aircraft carrier, soldiers machine-gunned to death before the eyes of comrades who were unable to retrieve their bodies, or men blown apart by munitions so thoroughly that there were no retrievable remains—all these are listed in the total of "unaccounted for." This KIA/BNR category was never included with the missing in action during the Vietnam War; it was lumped together with the POW/MIA category only *after* the 1973 Paris Peace Agreement was signed.

So of the 2,255 unaccounted for, only 1,160 were ever actually listed as POW/MIA. But the category "POW/MIA" itself, as we shall see, was an unprecedented invention purposely designed to suggest that each and every missing person might be a prisoner, even though most were lost in circumstances that made capture impossible. Previously, the designation POW applied only to those known or believed to be prisoners. It was quite distinct from the MIA category. While lumping these two designations together in public announcements, the Department of Defense internally maintained them as separate categories throughout the war and its aftermath. The Pentagon listed as a POW anyone reported as a possible prisoner anywhere in Vietnam, Laos, Cambodia, or China at any time from 1963 to 1973, whether or not there was credible evidence of capture and even if there was evidence of subsequent death. After the 1973 Peace Agreement, all but 53 men on this internal list were either released or reported to have died in captivity. In the next three years, intensive analysis of these remaining cases resolved all but a handful (see pages 93–95 for a detailed discussion).

In the ensuing years, exhaustive case-by-case investigation, together with the absence of contradictory evidence, has led the Department of Defense to make a presumptive finding of death for every single person in the combined POW/MIA total except one. This man is Air Force Captain (promoted after his loss to colonel) Charles Shelton, who was shot down over Laos in April 1965; according to the official U.S. position, Shelton is merely "listed as a prisoner of war as a symbolic gesture of the Administration's commitment to this issue."[14] In discussing his case, the Defense Department notes: "Shelton is the only American serviceman the US Government still lists as a POW; this is for symbolic purposes as intelligence reports indicate that he and Hrdlicka [another man whom Laos has not accounted for to the satisfaction of the United States] died in captivity in the mid-1960s."[15] All other known or presumed prisoners of war have been either returned or identified as having died in captivity. So there are officially no longer any MIAs and only one POW—a man who has been dead for more than twenty-five years.

Every responsible investigation conducted since the end of the war has reached the same conclusion: there is no credible evidence that live Americans are being held against their will in Vietnam, Laos, Cambodia, or China. Most telling are those studies initiated from the opposing view.

In the immediate aftermath of the war, one of the principal figures in spreading the notion that Americans were still being held captive in Indochina was conservative Representative Gillespie "Sonny" Montgomery of Mississippi, who was recognized at the time as more convinced and outspoken about this belief "than any other member of Congress."[16] His fervor convinced the House in 1975 to create the Select Committee on Missing Persons in Southeast Asia and to name him as its chair. After fifteen months of investigation, with access to every case file and all classified information, extensive hearings recorded in five volumes, and a major fact-finding trip to Southeast Asia, the Committee issued its final report in 1976 with the unequivocal conclusions that "no Americans are still being held alive as prisoners in Indochina, or elsewhere, as a result of the war in Indochina," and that "because of the nature and circumstances in which many Americans were lost in combat in Indochina, a total accounting by the Indochinese Governments is not possible and should not be expected."[17] Confronted with overwhelming evidence, Montgomery ruefully confessed that his now shattered belief in live prisoners had been "based more on hope than fact and more on rumors than hard evidence," for "like so many others I wanted to believe they were alive, so I did."[18]

Three years later, the National Defense University published a book-length study of the POW/MIA issue and its history written by Navy Captain Douglas L. Clarke of the National War College. A veteran of three hundred combat missions in Indochina, many flown as commander of a carrier-based fighter-bomber squadron, Clarke had close friends among the missing in action and had served for eighteen months in the Office of the Special Assistant for Prisoner of War Matters of the Navy. Captain Clarke found himself not only in agreement with the conclusions of the House Select Committee but also thoroughly convinced that the entire "matter of the missing men has worked against the best interests of the United States in a number of ways" and had even been an offense to the men and their families, as he concludes in his final paragraph:

Whether there will ever be an adequate accounting of the men missing in Southeast Asia is extremely doubtful. There never was one in any previous conflict. The Government did the families—and therefore the lost men—a tragic disservice by encouraging the belief that there would be such an accounting in this war.[19]

For eight years, the administration of President Ronald Reagan kept fomenting the issue of Americans supposedly held in captivity in Indochina. Yet its final report on the matter, jointly prepared by the Department of Defense and the Department of State, released just a few hours before Reagan left office (but never published as a government document), was unable to cite any evidence of unrepatriated live POWs despite intense scrutiny of "several million captured documents"; interrogation of "over one quarter of a million prisoners and defectors" during the war; thorough debriefing of all returning U.S. and allied prisoners; postwar interrogation of tens of thousands of refugees, including "defectors from Vietnam's security services, military and diplomatic corps"; "national technical systems" (satellites, spy flights, and electronic monitoring); and "a special team deployed in Southeast Asia." The report was forced to state outright: "We have yet to find conclusive evidence of the existence of live prisoners, and returnees at Operation Homecoming in 1973 knew of no Americans who were left behind in captivity."[20]

What Does "POW/MIA" Mean?

Before exploring the evolution of the issue, including the arguments and evidence advanced by the crusaders of the faith in live POWs, it may be helpful to introduce a few key questions and concepts. Nothing is more fundamental to the whole POW/MIA question than an understanding of the designation itself, and nothing has been more thoroughly obscured and confused.

Any American serviceperson who does not return from a war or whose remains are not recovered is legally categorized as "unaccounted for." As soon as someone is lost, an investigation is begun to determine in which of three categories to place that person: KIA/ BNR, MIA, or POW. If additional investigation over a lengthy period of time fails to yield any likelihood of life, a "presumptive finding of death" is made through a complex administrative and legal process.

However, during the Vietnam War—for political purposes that will be explored in Chapter 2—the Defense and State departments created a public category that indiscriminately mingled the Pentagon's internal classifications of MIA and POW: "POW/MIA." Because there was already a strong tendency to classify a person as missing unless there was overwhelming evidence of death, the POW/MIA designation created many false hopes by suggesting that any missing person might possibly be a prisoner.

A critical question is how the initial determination is made about whether a missing person is to be regarded as KIA rather than MIA or POW. Each service has its own governing regulations, but each requires "conclusive evidence" of death. The Air Force defines "conclusive evidence," in the absence of remains, to exist when "the available information indicates beyond any reasonable doubt that a missing person could not have survived." The Army's definition of "conclusive evidence of death" is equally stringent: "The facts must be such that death is the only plausible alternative under the circumstances."[21]

Even without subjective elements coming into play, these rigorous definitions lead unavoidably to creating more MIAs than actually exist. And in their application in the Vietnam War, as subsequent investigation has revealed, the overwhelming tendency was to be overoptimistic, thereby turning many of those who should have been classified as KIA/BNR into MIAs and hence into POW/MIAs.

Consider the following situations. Suppose a B-52 with a crew of six fails to return from a bombing raid, and there is little information about its fate. Obviously all six crewmen must be considered MIAs and, therefore, with the new public category, POW/MIAs. Suppose another B-52 is hit by a missile and instantly explodes in a giant fireball, witnessed by other B-52 crews who observe no parachute or other evidence of survivors. Obviously all six crewmen must be considered KIA/BNR. But now suppose still another B-52 is hit by a missile, begins to catch fire, and shortly explodes in a fireball, witnessed by other B-52 crews who do observe one and only one man parachute from the doomed craft. How many POW/MIAs has this third incident produced? Unless the identity of the parachuting man can be established, all six crewmen must, by inescapable logic, be considered POW/MIAs, for he could be any one of the six. So even though five of the men definitely were killed, and the sixth may very well have died, all six must continue to be regarded as POW/MIAs unless and until the parachutist can be identified, for there is no possibility of ever recovering any identifiable remains from the five who died on board.

This kind of situation is not merely hypothetical. In fact, the House Select Committee discovered that such logic had been applied to a number of actual similar cases involving multiengine aircraft with large crews and even more cases involving two-seater jets.[22]

They also learned that far more subjective considerations had led to a considerable inflation of the total number of POW/MIAs:

> In numerous cases, local commanding officers submitted exceptionally optimistic reports or judgments on the incident of loss. Many individuals were placed in MIA status when the circumstances of their loss suggested strongly that they had expired in the incident. For example, in several instances eyewitnesses reported that they believed a fallen comrade had suffered fatal wounds and was dead, but in the absence of their having checked scrupulously for vital signs, reviewing authorities recommended they be classified MIA.[23]

Another common group of cases involved planes lost under conditions in which there was no reasonable hope of survival, but in which subjective sentiment turned the lost aviators into POW/MIAs. A typical example was the case of a Navy pilot lost over water in a thunderstorm after the weather forced his flight leader to cancel their two-plane mission and return to their carrier. Captain Clarke describes the situation and its result:

> When the flight leader finally decided that it was impossible to continue, he initiated a 180-degree turn. It was necessary to take his flight into the lowering clouds during the turn, and when the leader came out of these clouds at the completion of this reversal turn, he was alone. A search disclosed a large oil slick in the immediate area of the wingman's loss.
>
> Many individuals would be tempted to interpret these circumstances as certainly approaching the conclusive evidence required to make a determination of death. The commanding officer involved did not so determine at the time. Whatever his motive or rationale, once he elected not to declare this man dead, that option was effectively denied for virtually the next decade . . . .

In 1975, the United States repeated its previous demands that the Democratic Republic of Vietnam (North Vietnam) and the Provisional Revolutionary Government of South Vietnam account for this missing pilot.[24]

Full Accounting and Live POWs

The main demand made by the U.S. government on the governments of Vietnam, Laos, and Cambodia is that they provide "the fullest possible accounting" for all Americans missing in action during the many years of U.S. warfare in Indochina. The U.S. position, as stated in the lead headline of the 1991 *POW-MIA Fact Book*, is that "THE INDOCHINESE HOLD THE ANSWERS," and that because they refuse to tell the United States everything they know, the United States is justified in acting "ON THE ASSUMPTION THAT AT LEAST SOME AMERICANS ARE STILL HELD CAPTIVE."

This logic confuses the issue of live POWs with the issue of accountability. The thorny question of what constitutes an adequate, acceptable, or "the fullest possible" accounting is rife with debate, ambiguity, and complexity. Many arguments—ethical, political, and legal—could be made on either side of the proposition that the governments of Vietnam, Laos, and Cambodia owe the government of the United States more information than they have provided. One's position on this question might very well be influenced by one's view of the history and justice of America's war against these nations. Laos and Vietnam have returned more than three hundred sets of remains, and both countries have participated with the United States in a number of joint searches of crash sites. Vietnam has issued voluminous diplomatic and public reports documenting what it argues are extraordinary efforts to determine the fate of the missing and to locate and return the remains of Americans who were killed. The United States aggressively disputes these arguments. But, in any case, there is an enormous difference between retaining information and retaining prisoners.

The claim that "THE INDOCHINESE HOLD THE AN-SWERS" is at best disingenuous. How could they possibly know the circumstances of the loss of every missing American? The House Select Committee discovered hundreds of cases for which the United States was demanding an accounting although there was virtually no possibility whatsoever that the Indochinese governments could have any information. Three of the many examples:

On July 7, 1967, two B-52 bombers collided and exploded over the South China Sea. Seven survivors were picked up by U.S. naval forces, whose ships, planes, and helicopters continued to search the entire area for four days. The United States has demanded that Vietnam account for the six missing crewmen.

On June 17, 1966, a C-130E aircraft exploded over the South China Sea east of Nha Trang. The remains of one crewman were recovered by a U.S. Navy gunboat that observed the explosion and the crash of the aircraft in deep water. Three weeks of search and salvage operations turned up no other traces of the remaining crew members and five Air Force personnel riding as passengers, who were all later placed on the list of those for whom Vietnam should give an accounting.

On February 2, 1968, a UH-1H helicopter with five U.S. Army personnel on board crashed into a mountain while making a ground-controlled approach to Danang Air Base, and exploded into flames. A thoroughly trained Army crash investigation team concluded that "everyone perished in the crash." The handful of charred and fractured bone fragments that they could collect were determined to be useless for identification by the Army mortuary, which therefore disposed of them by incineration. The five crewmen were classified as MIA, and the Vietnamese were asked to account for each of them.

The committee concluded that listing such cases "for which no accounting can be expected" may have convinced "the Indochinese leaders that the United States has deliberately requested information which they cannot furnish in order to embarrass them or to prevent meaningful talks."[25]

It is not even safe to assume that any of the Indochinese governments have complete and accurate information about all those cases that were reported to them. Does the United States still maintain complete and accurate records of every single Vietnamese, Laotian, and Cambodian captured or known to have been killed by U.S. forces and its allies during the entire war? What is the likelihood that whatever records the Indochinese once did have contained no errors, survived the years of combat, and have not since been partially lost, misfiled, or destroyed? A number of the remains that they have returned have been shown by advanced forensic tests to be of Asians, indicating that they certainly do not have anything approaching U.S. technical facilities and personnel for identification of decades-old parts of human bodies. Indeed, even with all the effort and expertise that Americans have applied, neither U.S. records nor U.S. identifications are free from error. The Reagan administration's final report on the POW/MIA issue was forced to concede: "While most of the data maintained by the USG [U.S. government] involving details surrounding each loss incident are generally reliable, certain inconsistencies exist due to circumstances prevalent in a wartime environment. This would be true of Indochinese records as well."[26]

In fact, there are cases that suggest that some of the answers may lie closer to home. Private First Class Alan Barton, for example, was reported as missing on July 28, 1970, from his base near the central coastal village of An Khe in South Vietnam. Thirty-two days later, his mother, Dorothy Vogelaar, was notified by her son's commanding officer that he had been "classified as a deserter." On March 28, 1972, some skeletal remains were found on the perimeter of the base; embedded in them were steel pellets from the mine or booby trap that had killed the man. Found with these remains were various personal belongings, but the army lost all of them except a fragment of an envelope postmarked from Private Barton's hometown in Michigan. The remains were sent to the center in Honolulu responsible for identifying the war dead. There they lay for almost eleven years until a comparison of dental records indicated that the remains were those of Alan Barton. The final cruel irony is that his mother had been so tormented by the images of American prisoners of war projected on movie and TV screens, wasting away for years in the hands of the Asian Communists, that she was actually relieved to learn that this was not her son's reality:

> "At least he died quickly," Mrs. Vogelaar says. "He didn't suffer in a prisoner-of-war camp. I had visions of him behind wire—a thin rack of bones—hardly any teeth."[27]

Even if one agrees that some or all of the Indochinese governments have not given an adequate accounting, one cannot then leap to the conclusion that this proves they are holding Americans captive. By conflating the questions of accounting and imprisonment, the U.S. government has built a firm foundation for the widespread belief that there are indeed live POWs.

Certainly without this conflation it would be hard to imagine much concern or passion about the POW/MIA issue. Those citizens who display POW/MIA flags and bumper stickers, those thousands of bikers who have staged thunderous demonstrations, those veterans maintaining a POW/MIA vigil at the Wall, those GM workers who threatened to strike if the POW/MIA flag were not flown over their workplace, and those moviegoers who cheer Rambo are not moved by the abstract question of "the fullest possible accounting." They believe that Asian Communists are still holding Americans as prisoners, and they want them freed before they die in captivity.

Prisoners or Deserters?

One problem implicit in the demand for "the fullest possible accounting" is that there is one category of person listed as missing in action that the present governments of Indochina might believe they should not report on to the United States. For to do so would be a betrayal of those they call "ralliers," whom the U. S. government would regard as "deserters" and "traitors," possibly liable to extreme legal punishment.

Few people today are aware of the enormous numbers of deserters during the Vietnam War. Some sense of the dimensions of this phenomenon can be gathered by comparison with the widely publicized problem of draft evasion and resistance. According to the Department of Defense, which most analysts believe was understating the problem, there were 503,926 "incidents of desertion" between July 1, 1966, and December 31, 1973. From 1963 through 1973 (a period almost half again as long) there were, according to the Justice Department, only 191,840 cases of men who failed to answer draft board notices (and of these, 80 percent responded to second or third notices). A month before the amnesty for desertion and draft evasion was issued in September 1974, there were 4,400 draft violators "at large." At the same time, the admitted number of deserters still "at large" was 28,661—six and a half times the number of draft evaders and resisters and twelve times the number of missing in action.[28] Desertion among the troops deployed in Indochina was so prevalent that it played a major role in what a leading military analyst called "the collapse of the armed forces."[29] It was not uncommon for deserting soldiers to begin new lives and form families in Vietnamese villages and even in sections of Saigon. Some deserters became heavily involved in illegal activities such as the black market and drug trafficking. A few may have even joined the other side and helped to lead attacks on U.S. forces. Needless to say, such acts were not covered by the 1974 amnesty, and those suspected of committing them would still be subject to prosecution.

Some of these men may very well have stayed in Laos and Vietnam after the U.S. troop withdrawal. Reports of their existence continue to surface today, almost two decades later. The one and only MIA from the Indochina war who has actually turned up is Robert Garwood, who was convicted of collaborating with the enemy and who was the person observed in approximately 250 reported live sightings.[30] Not every sighting of a person believed to be American is evidence of a live prisoner, for live deserters are more likely and plausible than live prisoners.

The French Experience

If there are American ex-soldiers living voluntarily in Indochina, they are reenacting one of the sequels to the French war there. This aspect of the French experience has been radically falsified to fit into the pseudohistory constructed to support the plausibility of live POWs. While working on this book, I kept encountering people who know very little about the actual history of the Vietnam War but who are thoroughly familiar with this pseudohistory. For example, many are convinced that Vietnam has been holding hundreds of American prisoners for years after the war because they believe that Vietnam held hundreds of French prisoners for years after the French war against Vietnam.

This misrepresentation of the French experience actually dates back to the creation of the POW/MIA issue during the Vietnam War, and its wide dissemination testifies to the vast network, largely informal, that diffuses the POW myth. By 1971, the French foreign minister found it necessary to declare to the National Assembly that, despite all allegations to the contrary, the Democratic Republic of Vietnam (DRV) had not kept French prisoners against their will after the war. Yet the claim was made again by President Richard Nixon in a July 1972 news conference, prompting another vigorous denial from the French government and this formal statement from the first secretary of the French embassy in Washington:

> According to the figures known by the French Government, North Vietnam, at the end of 1954, had returned to the French authorities 12,900 prisoners from the French Expeditionary Corps in Indochina. . . . We consider that the last French prisoners have been returned by the North Vietnamese less than three months after the conclusion of the Geneva agreements in 1954. We therefore consider this question as definitely settled. To the best of our knowledge, there does not exist any member of the French Expeditionary Corps in the Far East unwillingly kept in North Vietnam.[31]

The main source cited in support of the legend of French POWs enslaved for years by the Vietnamese is Anita Lauve, a U.S. Foreign Service officer for fifteen years whose research on the French experience was performed under a Defense Department contract. However, Lauve in fact makes no such claim; indeed she states outright: "The only French nationals from Metropolitan France who are known to have been belatedly returned to French authorities were 40 enlisted men who were released in 1962 and flown to France with their Vietnamese families. Some, if not all of the men, were reportedly tried in France as deserters."[32]

It has been easy to distort this part of history because so few Americans are aware that the great majority of those fighting under French command were not French but Vietnamese conscripts, Foreign Legionnaires (many of whom were Germans, including tens of thousands of Nazi soldiers captured at the end of World War II), and troops from the French colonies in Africa, especially Algeria, Morocco, and Senegal, forced to fight against an anticolonialist insurgency with which many were beginning to identify. Among all these, only the Algerians had French citizenship (except for those few Foreign Legionnaires who had served the five years requisite for acquiring citizenship); with the Algerian war for independence about to explode, as it did within a few months of the 1954 Geneva Agreement between France and the DRV, many Algerians asked not to be repatriated to France. Well over a thousand Foreign Legionnaires from Eastern Europe and Germany were repatriated, under the aegis of the International Control Commission, through China to their country of origin.

Ironically, some of these included the only POWs from the French forces who actually had been enslaved after the end of a war. At Yalta in 1945, Churchill, Stalin, and Roosevelt had formally agreed not to release German POWs, as they were obliged to do under Article 75 of the 1929 Geneva POW Convention, but to use them as forced laborers in a program called "reparations in kind." General Dwight D. Eisenhower in April 1945 explicitly stripped all captured German soldiers of their rights as prisoners of war by consigning them to a new classification he called "Disarmed Enemy Forces" (DEF). Of the DEF under U.S. jurisdiction, 140,000 were transferred to the Soviet Union, which repatriated the last survivors in 1956; 400,000 were shipped to Great Britain, which used them as slave laborers until July 1948; and 740,000 were given to France, where many of them starved to death. It has been argued that this starvation was a deliberate policy designed to force the prisoners to choose the only available escape: enlistment in the French Foreign Legion, whose ranks were being swelled so that France could reoccupy its colonies in Indochina. So tens of thousands of German POWs, actually U.S. prisoners illegally handed over to France, ended up as one of the main forces fighting from 1946 to 1954 to destroy the Democratic Republic of Vietnam and reduce Vietnam once again to colonial status.[33] The survivors of this last group were actually freed by the Vietnamese victors.

A collateral argument alleges that the long delay and costs associated with exhuming and repatriating remains buried in Vietnam by the French demonstrate the cruelty and inhumanity of the Vietnamese Communists as well as their urge to "ransom" bodies. This argument conveniently ignores the fact that Vietnam was at war with the United States and its proxies during this protracted process, and the difficulty of transporting these remains during wartime is what led the French to bury them in Vietnam in the first place.

"Discrepancies"

The term "discrepancies" is applied to those men who have been at some time listed by the United States as known or believed to have been captured and who were neither released nor listed by Vietnam, Laos, Cambodia, or China as having died in captivity. There is undeniably strong evidence that a small number of men—twenty at the very most—were captured but not included in any final accounting. A few of these cases—certainly no more than five—were men whose capture was actually announced; all of these were prisoners of guerrilla forces. Given the conditions of wartime in Indochina, one might expect that some men would die in captivity without the postwar governments having any record of their identity and fate. In Laos, Cambodia, and South Vietnam, the insurgent fighters were under constant attack, ravaged by disease and malnutrition, and rarely able to provide long-term, uninterrupted, organized administration of large regions. As might be expected, the bulk of the discrepancies pertain to men known or believed to have been captured by guerrilla forces in South Vietnam and Laos. Even in North Vietnam, an impoverished land subjected to one of the most devastating air assaults in history, where downed airmen often had to be rescued by soldiers from villagers enraged by the deaths of their loved ones and where some prisoners did manage to escape into the countryside, it would not be too surprising if the central government did not have a record of the fate of each and every man captured by somebody.

The most glaring discrepancies are singled out for publication each year by the Defense Department in its *POW-MIA Fact Book* in a section entitled "Evidence of Capture of U.S. Personnel." These are not merely representative examples; they are the strongest cases to be offered by the U.S. government as part of its "public awareness" campaign. Since the persuasiveness of the whole issue depends so heavily on these cases, it is quite instructive to examine each one presented in the 1989, 1990, and 1991 editions. For readers unfamiliar with the kinds of arguments and evidence involved, looking at each of these cases may provide a useful introduction to the entire question of live POWs.

The 1990 and 1991 editions cite nine cases, which are presented immediately after a page headlined ARE AMERICANS STILL HELD CAPTIVE IN INDOCHINA? and featuring a half-page replica of the logo on the POW/MIA flag. These nine plus one other make up the examples in the 1989 edition. Eight of the ten have been featured cases in each edition since 1985; these eight constituted every case cited in the 1987 edition. So these must be regarded as the most compelling examples the government can offer and therefore the most solid foundation for its POW/MIA policy. What follows is a case-by-case analysis of each of the ten, using only the Pentagon's own evidence and arguments plus readily available published material.

Only one of these men, Air Force Colonel Robert Anderson, who was shot down in 1972, could possibly have been captured in North Vietnam. The evidence that he might have been taken prisoner consists merely of a radio message he made while parachuting, stating that he was "in good shape and can see no enemy forces on the ground," and a broadcast by Radio Hanoi made that day claiming the capture of "a number of U.S. pilots," though the United

States claims to have lost only one plane on the day of the broadcast. The "back seater" of Anderson's F-4 aircraft "was immediately captured and released during 'Operation Homecoming' the following year." The Pentagon's attempt to use Hanoi's broadcast as evidence that Anderson was captured is misleading and exposes the flimsiness of its case. First, U.S. military officials have repeatedly asserted that the Vietnamese often claimed to have shot down many more planes than they actually downed and wildly overstated the number of crewmen they captured. But whichever side was usually more honest, in this case the truth of the Vietnamese broadcast was proved during Operation Homecoming, with the release of at least four crewmen from other aircraft shot down over North Vietnam during the twenty-four hours that included the loss of Colonel Anderson's plane (John H. Alpers, Jr., back seater of another F-4; James D. Latham and Richard L. Bates, pilot and back seater of another F-4; and Keith H. Lewis, pilot of still another plane). The fact that Colonel Anderson saw no enemy troops on the ground hardly makes his capture by them more likely, and his failure to send any further message suggests the possibility that he may not have survived his parachute landing. Furthermore, his back seater (George F. Latella), who was extensively debriefed like all the others repatriated in Operation Homecoming and who presumably would have made some effort to discover Colonel Anderson's fate, had no evidence whatsoever that he had been captured. Finally, why would the Vietnamese acknowledge the capture of five airmen shot down during this twenty-four-hour period and release them, while concealing the capture of one in order to keep him?

Three of the cases in the *POW-MIA Fact Book* pertain to men who were lost in Laos, and there is clear evidence that all three were indeed captured. Two of these are Air Force Colonels Charles Shelton and David Hrdlicka, who, as noted earlier, were reported by U.S. intelligence sources "to have died in captivity in the mid-1960s." The third is Eugene DeBruin, identified only as a "civilian" captured by Pathet Lao guerrillas in September 1963. In 1966, two fellow prisoners escaped and "provided information"—what information the *POW-MIA Fact Book* does not say—about DeBruin. The 1991 edition concludes the account of his case by stating that the government of Laos has "pledged to furnish the U.S. with a written report regarding his fate, but they have yet to provide that information." However, the 1985 edition had stated explicitly that "the Lao Government recently indicated that he was killed in an escape attempt." So the only real issue about DeBruin evidently is the present Laotian government's unwillingness or inability to furnish a detailed written report on the circumstances of his death during his escape attempt a quarter of a century ago. No edition of the *POW-MIA Fact Book* reveals the following facts, all readily available perhaps not in Laos but in any major library in the United States: DeBruin was a CIA employee engaged as a "kicker" (an air drop handler) on an Air America plane illegally and covertly supplying right-wing guerrillas in Laos when it was shot down; the Pathet Lao promptly reported the capture of DeBruin and four other mercenaries on his crew as well as the names of the two pilots who were killed in the crash; DeBruin received mail, including at least one package; he attempted to escape several times prior to 1966; in that escape attempt, at least one Laotian guard was killed, several others were severely wounded, and DeBruin was last seen by one of the successful escapees holding a Thompson submachine gun; the other successful escapee reported that he left DeBruin on an isolated mountain; so the last available evidence on DeBruin is that he was no longer a prisoner of the Pathet Lao, who may or may not have recaptured him and may or may not know precisely how he died.[34]

The remaining six men in the *POW-MIA Fact Book* were all lost to insurgent forces in South Vietnam. Even according to the Defense Department's account, each seems either to have been killed in combat or to have died in captivity.

Major Lawrence Holland's F-100D aircraft was downed in June

1965 by guerrilla ground fire, which also drove off a rescue helicopter, whose crew members "did see his limp body being dragged away." Later intelligence information revealed that "Holland was killed by Viet Cong soldiers after he opened fire on them," and "he was reportedly buried in the immediate vicinity of the incident." The only issue is that "the Vietnamese have furnished no information on him."

Specialist 5 Philip Terrill and Master Sergeant James Salley were evidently captured in March 1971 by guerrillas, and "former U.S. POWs" reported that "both men died after capture." "Salley was on the Viet Cong 'Died in Captivity' list, but Terrill was not," reports the 1990 *POW-MIA Fact Book*, whose main complaint is that the present government of Vietnam "has yet to provide substantive information or the remains of either man."

Private First Class Donald Sparks was evidently captured in June 1969 after being wounded in the foot. Letters from him, indicating he had not seen another American in ten months of captivity, were found on a dead guerrilla in April 1970. Nothing further is known about his fate, though three former POWs reported: "in the spring of 1970, while en route to a new camp in the same province where Sparks was lost, a Vietnamese guard mentioned that a POW named 'Don' was moving slowly because of a wounded foot, but would soon join them. 'Don' never arrived at the camp." From the Defense Department's own account, it seems that Donald Sparks died in the extremely dangerous conditions he shared with his guerrilla captors. In any event, what motive would the Vietnamese have for releasing three other prisoners held in this province while keeping Private Sparks?

The *POW-MIA Fact Book*'s account of the ninth man, Marine Warrant Officer Solomon Godwin, which is here quoted in full (from the 1990 edition, a text repeated almost verbatim in the 1991 edition), speaks for itself:

WO1 Godwin was captured in Hue on February 5, 1968, during the beginning of the Tet offensive. Godwin was detained in the hills outside Hue until July 1968, when he and another American POW, who returned during "Operation Homecoming" in 1973, began their journey to North Vietnam. Godwin's health deteriorated and he died during the march northward. The returned POW was told to sign a document verifying that Godwin died on July 25, 1968. The place of death was also recorded on the document, although it was illegible to the surviving American.

There is no uncertainty about Warrant Officer Godwin's death. The only issue here seems to be an unstated but implied accusation that because there was at one time a document substantiating his death, the present government of Vietnam is obliged to report it to the United States. This dubious issue becomes even more suspect in the light of the case of John Graf.

Here is the *POW-MIA Fact Book*'s complete account of the case of Navy Lieutenant Commander John Graf (from the 1989 edition; this is the only 1989 example not included in the 1990 and 1991 editions):

LCDR Graf successfully ejected from his aircraft on 15 November 1969. Intelligence reporting confirmed his capture by the Viet Cong. Also captured with LCDR Graf was his crewmember, a PW who returned during Operation Homecoming in 1973. Viet Cong inter-rogation reports of LCDR Graf and the returned PW, dated December 1969, were found in an enemy camp in December 1970. The returned PW reported that LCDR Graf escaped several months after capture. Other captured documents stated that he died during the escape attempt and was buried. The Vietnamese Government has not furnished any information concerning the fate of LCDR Graf.

The 1985 edition provides one additional piece of information gleaned from "intelligence": "Graf drowned in his escape attempt."

Thoughtful consideration of this case reveals the illogic and arrogance fundamental to the U.S. position. The United States sends John Graf to bomb people in the countryside of South Vietnam. They capture him. They are forced by devastating attacks to be continually on the run, as proved by the seizure of documents from a site they evidently abandoned in haste before it was overrun by U.S. forces. Nevertheless, they do their best to keep Graf alive, as demonstrated by their successful efforts to preserve the life of his crew member for more than three years until his repatriation in 1973. Graf tries to escape and dies in the attempt, evidently by drowning. The guerrillas attempt to keep careful records of his capture and death. The United States, however, captures these documents and then later denounces the government of Vietnam for failing to provide the information that is now in the possession of the United States rather than Vietnam. The only accurate term for this may be chutzpah, which has been defined as the attitude of a man who murders his parents and then throws himself on the mercy of the court because he is an orphan.

The Graf case also illustrates a fallacy in the underlying assumption that "the communist governments of Indochina" have all the information necessary to provide an accounting of MIAs acceptable to the United States. In Warrant Officer Godwin's case, the existence more than two decades ago of a document certifying his death is offered as evidence of Indochinese intransigence today. Yet Lieutenant Commander Graf's case demonstrates that the governments of Indochina do not currently possess all the documents that once existed. A careful scrutiny of the ten cases in the 1989 through 1991 editions of the *POW-MIA Fact Book* suggests that for the group as a whole the United States may have more complete and accurate information than the Indochinese governments, and that not much more can ever be expected from any source.

And what is demonstrated by these ten cases, selected and repeated over the years by the Defense Department as its best examples of possibly living prisoners? Six definitely or almost certainly died in captivity (Hrdlicka, Shelton, DeBruin, Salley, Terrill, Godwin). One in all probability died in captivity (Sparks). One definitely died while attempting to escape (Graf). One was killed in combat while resisting capture (Holland). One disappeared without a trace after parachuting from a crippled plane (Anderson). If these are the cases that argue most strongly for the existence of live American prisoners in Indochina today, widespread devout belief in such beings needs to be explored as myth.

Government Conspiracy

Yet there is another possible explanation for the obvious weakness of the case for live POWs presented in government publications: the U.S. government is just pretending. Strange as it may seem, this explanation is one that is accepted by both those who are most thoroughly convinced that there are no live POWs and those who most fervently believe in their existence. The two groups differ, of course, about what it is that the government is pretending and why. But both would agree that one of the most important lessons of the Vietnam War is that the U.S. government routinely and systematically lies to the American people.

To nonbelievers the issue of live POWs seems contrived and even blatantly absurd. Seeing neither credible evidence nor cogent arguments to support it, they tend to think that the government must have ulterior motives for keeping the issue alive. What motives? Stimulating militarism, shifting the onus of the Vietnam War from Washington to Hanoi, distracting attention from the fate of actual Vietnam veterans in America, and, most of all, providing a virtuous rationale for economic and political war against Vietnam—all seem obvious and sufficient motives for the government to keep pretending that there are live POWs in Indochina.

The most committed believers, on the other hand, are familiar with evidence and arguments they find infinitely more convincing than anything the government presents. For them, the government is just pretending to be concerned about the POWs, who it knows full well are there but whom it keeps abandoning. Underlying this belief is another position that may be shared by those with many conflicting points of view.

Indeed, it is hard for any reasoning person to escape the conclusion that if there are live POWs, the U.S. government, or at least the various U.S. intelligence agencies responsible for investigating the question, must have definite evidence of their existence. The United States has an intricate intelligence network operating in Indochina, has interrogated many tens of thousands of refugees (including numerous defectors from military and intelligence services), has organized several cross-border raids to photograph suspected POW camps, and constantly monitors the area with satellites and high-altitude reconnaissance aircraft reputedly capable of photographing the letters on a license plate. So partisans on opposite sides can agree: if there are any live POWs, the government would know about them. While nonbelievers interpret this deduction as powerful evidence that there are no live POWs, fervent believers conclude that the government must be engaged in an elaborate conspiracy to conceal its own evidence of live POWs. For what motives? The answer to this question lies near the heart of the significance of the POW/MIA myth in America today, for this government conspiracy has become a crucial part of the story. But to comprehend the meaning of the myth and its role in postwar America, one must first examine the genesis of the POW/MIA issue, its evolution, and the now almost forgotten part it played in the Vietnam War.

2 ■ PRISONERS OF THE WAR

The Matrix of the POW/MIA Issue

For the first fifteen years of U.S. combat in Indochina—that is, from 1954 to 1969—there was no "POW/MIA issue." Indeed, prisoners of war and missing in action were considered, as in previous wars, to be two quite separate categories.

The first U.S. military personnel taken prisoner in the Vietnam War were five Air Force men captured by the Democratic Republic of Vietnam in 1954; they were released to the French in strict compliance with the timetable established by the 1954 Geneva Agreement.[1] In the spring of 1961, eight American soldiers and airmen were reported as missing in action in Laos; the U.S. government has never claimed that any of these were prisoners. Two U.S. Army servicemen and three civilians were actually captured in Laos in 1961; they were released within the thirty-day period stipulated in the Geneva Agreement of 1962.[2] In September 1963, the Pathet Lao shot down a CIA contract airplane that was illegally supplying a right-wing guerrilla unit and within seven weeks released the names of the U.S. pilot and co-pilot, who had both been killed in the crash, and the five captured crewmen, including CIA employee Eugene DeBruin.[3] Before the end of that year, the Army, Navy, Marines, Air

Force, and CIA all had missing personnel, though officially the United States still was not waging war in Indochina. On March 26, 1964, a U.S. Army Special Forces officer serving as a combat "adviser" became the first American military prisoner of war in Vietnam. Then year after year the number of both missing and prisoners kept mounting, matching the rate of escalation as the United States climbed ever more overtly and ruinously into the longest war in its history. Yet the fate of American prisoners did not become a major public issue until the spring of 1969, at which time the missing also became thoroughly jumbled with the prisoners.

Why then? Made in America by Americans, and manifesting the most ingenious expertise of American design and production, the POW/MIA issue filled desperate emerging needs of certain forces within American society and politics. Neither the original issue nor the myth into which it evolved can be comprehended without understanding the historical matrix in which it was created.

During the eight years that had passed since Americans started becoming MIAs in Indochina, the escalation of the war had also been matched by American opposition to it. The opposition was intensified by ever increasing knowledge about the history of the war and about the falsification of that history. By 1969, millions of Americans had learned that they had been deceived about when, why, and how the war had begun, who was fighting on each side, and even who was winning. They had discovered that the war had begun not as an invasion of a nation called South Vietnam by another nation called North Vietnam, but as an insurgency against a dictatorship that had been established covertly in 1954 by the United States in direct violation of the Geneva Agreements that had concluded the war between France and the Democratic Republic of Vietnam. They had learned that these agreements recognized that Vietnam was a single nation, that the United States had prevented this nation from holding its agreed-upon elections because President Eisenhower believed that the Communists would win at least 80 percent of the vote, that "President" Ngo Dinh Diem had been handpicked by Washington and installed as head of a new puppet government in Saigon even before the conclusion of the Geneva Agreements, that U.S. military and intelligence agents had then immediately begun a campaign of sabotage against the DRV in 1954, and that President John F. Kennedy and U.S. Ambassador Henry Cabot Lodge had directly conspired to have Diem overthrown in 1963 because his tyranny had incited almost every part of the population of "South Vietnam" to rise in rebellion. They then saw a parade of generals, paid and commanded by the United States, play a seemingly endless game of musical chairs to succeed Diem; some even learned that most of these generals who claimed to be the legitimate heads of the government of South Vietnam were actually north Vietnamese who had fought for the French against Vietnam's struggle for independence. They found out that in 1964 President Lyndon B. Johnson's administration had concocted naval battles in the Gulf of Tonkin to legitimize air attacks on North Vietnam and to stampede Congress into signing a blank check to make war; that the destroyer involved in the first Gulf of Tonkin "incident" had actually been participating as an intelligence resource for U.S. mercenary assaults on North Vietnamese coastal defenses as part of a covert air, land, and sea offensive against the Hanoi government and had opened fire first on three PT boats long before they could have attacked it; that the second "incident" consisted of two U.S. destroyers blazing away at purely imaginary PT boats for four hours; and that some of the pilots captured in the "retaliatory" raids were aware of the fabrication. This was merely the prehistory of the war that began in February 1965, when President Johnson, who had just won an electoral landslide partly on his oft-repeated promise "never to send American boys to Asia to do the job that Asian boys should do," sent the first officially acknowledged U.S. combat troops into Vietnam, allegedly to protect a major air base from which U.S. planes were bombing North Vietnam.[4]

Americans did not need to read about that prehistory to see the grotesque features of the war it had unleashed. Those who were not fighting it could, and often did, watch it on their TVs. This is why the media have been charged with helping to destroy the nation's will to win, for when the American people caught a few glimpses of the war's reality many were released from the spell of the official slogans, abstractions, and promises of victory essential to motivate them.

From February 1965 until the end of January 1968—a period just eight months shorter than the United States was at war during World War II—the war became ever more consuming and popular resistance grew ever more potent. By November 1967, the need to convince the public that victory was imminent had become so urgent that President Johnson summoned home General William Westmoreland, head of the 1.4 million troops under U.S. command in Vietnam, to do public relations. In a major address to the National-al Press Club, General Westmoreland told the nation's leading opinion makers that "the enemy's hopes are bankrupt," his forces were "declining at a steady rate," "he can fight only at the edges of his sanctuaries" in other countries, and the United States had entered the phase "when the end begins to come into view," a time when the South Vietnamese army would "take charge of the final mopping up of the Vietcong." In the issue of *The New York Times* that reported this speech, James Reston echoed the official assertions that "the Vietcong now control only 2,500,000 people," little more than half the number they had controlled in 1965, and "it is now merely a matter of time until this trend forces the enemy not to negotiate but to fade away into the jungle."[5] But then came the Tet Offensive.

On January 30, 1968, insurgent fighters simultaneously attacked in every part of South Vietnam, hitting the forces of the United States and the Saigon regime in five of the six major cities, thirty-six provincial capitals, sixty-four district capitals, and almost every military base. Many U.S. airfields, ammunition dumps, and supply centers were devastated, and some were overrun, providing the insurgents with vast quantities of modern arms. Most of the infrastructure of the rural pacification program was wiped out, leaving three-fourths of the countryside under rebel control. U.S. and Saigon forces were driven into a defensive posture around the cities and principal bases of the south. Possibly as many as 200,000 prisoners were freed. Vietnam's old capital city of Hue was overwhelmed in hours and was held for weeks against all-out U.S. air, sea, and ground attacks. Sections of Saigon itself were seized, forcing the United States to bomb and strafe the capital with fighter-bombers and helicopter gunships. U.S. authorities then claimed that they had won a "major victory" in Saigon by recapturing the American embassy compound, repulsing an assault on the Presidential Palace, and driving insurgent forces back to the perimeter of Tan Son Nhut, the city's main military air base, though fighting was to go on in Saigon for months, while sections of the capital and its surrounding suburbs would remain rebel strongholds for the rest of the war. Standing amid dead bodies and demolished buildings on the grounds of the American embassy, with explosions in the background, General Westmoreland declared on national television that the whole offensive was merely a diversion from a planned invasion from the north.[6]

Whether the Tet Offensive was a decisive military victory for the insurgents or merely, as publicly asserted by General Westmoreland and President Johnson, "a military defeat, but a political victory," it certainly succeeded in convincing the vast majority of the American people that victory for the United States was not a feasible outcome of the war. As for the Pentagon, it was secretly recognizing that the situation might be as "grim" as in "1954 or 1965," but "we should at least strive to make it appear otherwise."[7] The underlying logic of the war now seemed to be expressed by the U.S. officer who ordered the destruction of Ben Tre, capital of Ben Tre province, in response to the city's capture by the insurgent forces: "It was necessary to destroy the town in order to save it."

The effects of the Tet Offensive could soon be measured in the aftershocks rocking American society. On March 12, peace candidate Eugene McCarthy came close to defeating the incumbent president in the New Hampshire Democratic primary, and four days later Robert Kennedy entered the presidential race, also as a peace candidate. General Westmoreland was relieved of his command on March 22. On March 31, President Johnson announced that he was offering peace talks, curtailing the bombing of North Vietnam, and withdrawing his candidacy for reelection. The Paris peace talks began on May 10.

The president's decision was based in part on the Defense Department's analysis of the Tet Offensive's devastating effects on the U.S. position within Vietnam and its potentially calamitous consequences at home. In recommending rejection of General Westmoreland's desperate request for an additional 206,000 troops to blunt the offensive, the Pentagon issued this dire top-secret warning:

> It will be difficult to convince critics that we are not simply destroying South Viet Nam in order to "save" it and that we genuinely want peace talks. This growing disaffection accompanied, as it certainly will be, by increased defiance of the draft and growing unrest in the cities because of the belief that we are neglecting domestic problems, runs great risks of provoking a domestic crisis of unprecedented proportions.[8]

This prophecy seemed borne out just over a month later in responses to the April 4 assassination of Dr. Martin Luther King, Jr., who had denounced the war in one of his most powerful speeches exactly one year earlier. Between April 4 and 11, rebellions erupted in 125 U.S. towns and cities; they were suppressed only after 55,000 troops were deployed to aid the often overwhelmed police forces. Television viewers around the world saw Washington itself defended by federal combat troops, while towering above the Capitol rose columns of black smoke from burning buildings. No sooner had the urban rebellions been put down than the campuses erupted. Between April 23 and May 6, militant protest demonstrations, often linked directly to issues raised by the people suffering the gravest economic consequences of the war, swept public and private universities and colleges across the country. Many of these campus demonstrations now included Vietnam veterans and even active-duty GIs, who by the fall were on some campuses actually leading the anti-war movement.[9]

The Democratic primaries were swept by McCarthy and Kennedy, the two peace candidates, who together polled 69 percent of the total popular vote (winning between them 83 percent in Pennsylvania, 63 percent in Wisconsin, 78 percent in Massachusetts, 63 percent in the District of Columbia, 69 percent in Indiana, 83 percent in Nebraska, 82 percent in Oregon, 67 percent in New Jersey, 70 percent in South Dakota, 72 percent in Illinois, and 88 percent in California). Slates of electors representing Vice President Humphrey, who stood for a continuation of the administration's Vietnam policy, garnered a mere 2.2 percent. But on June 4, Robert Kennedy was assassinated. Somehow, by the time the Democratic convention opened in Chicago at the end of August, a majority of the delegates were pledged to Hubert Humphrey. Outside, thousands of anti-war demonstrators and supporters of Eugene McCarthy, confronted by six thousand federal troops, six thousand National Guardsmen, one thousand Secret Service agents, and twelve thousand Chicago police, were teargassed and beaten before the television cameras of the world. When soldiers from Fort Hood, Texas, were ordered to Chicago, forty-three GIs had to be arrested for refusing to oppose the demonstrators.[10]

So there was now only one peace candidate: Richard Nixon, who at the Republican convention in early August had promised secret "new approaches" to "the quest for peace."[11] Outside that convention in Miami Beach, a line of tanks had sealed off the entire peninsula from Miami itself, where police and National Guard units fought rebelling African-Americans in what a Miami police spokesman called "firefights like in Vietnam."[12] In his acceptance speech, after noting that "as we look at America, we see cities enveloped in smoke and flame," Nixon vowed that "if the war is not ended when the people choose in November," "I pledge to you tonight that the first priority foreign policy objective of our next Administration will be to bring an honorable end to the war in Vietnam."[13]

How many people living in this America in 1968 could have predicted that Richard Nixon would be able to keep the United States openly at war in Indochina into 1973? Perhaps even fewer than those who remembered that back in 1954 he had been one of the key figures in engineering the situation that led to the war in the first place.[14] And who could possibly have predicted that to succeed in sustaining the war he would rely on a brand-new issue: the fate of American prisoners of war and missing in action?

Disturbing questions had indeed already emerged about prisoners in Vietnam, but these concerned mainly people captured by the United States and Saigon, not those held by Hanoi and the southern guerrillas. In fact, the fate of Saigon's prisoners had been one of the root causes of the insurgency against the Diem government, whose infamous Law 10/59, promulgated in May 1959, branded members of the forces that had fought for independence against France as "Communists, traitors, and agents of Russia and China" and decreed the "sentence of death" for any person actively resisting Diem's rule.[15] The ensuing wholesale arrest, torture, and execution of hundreds of thousands, featuring portable guillotines and displays of victims' heads and intestines on stakes, helped lead in 1960 to the outbreak of organized armed struggle and the formation of the National Liberation Front of South Vietnam (NLF), contemptuously labeled the "Viet Cong" by Saigon and Washington.[16] As the war developed, anyone even suspected of loyalty to the Viet Cong, whether armed or unarmed, was subject to torture and summary execution. Only after the Hanoi government in 1966 announced that it did not regard its captured U.S. fliers as prisoners of war and that it might try them as war criminals for bombing its schools and hospitals was any semblance of prisoner of war status conferred on captured insurgent fighters in the south. And soon the American public began to learn something about their actual treatment.

Among the many disturbing books that appeared in early 1968 were two that exposed the barbaric treatment of prisoners by the United States and the government it had established in Saigon. Twenty-nine prominent American clergymen published *In the Name of America*, a documentary chronicle of U.S. war crimes in Vietnam, with several sections devoted to the torture, mutilation, and murder of combatant and civilian prisoners. Next came *Against the Crime of Silence*, the proceedings of the War Crimes Tribunal held during 1967 in Stockholm and Copenhagen, with extended testimony by American veterans about their own participation in the systematic torture and execution of prisoners by both U.S. and Saigon soldiers and officials.

In February, the issue exploded into the consciousness of tens of millions of Americans in the form of an excruciating series of images as they actually watched, in their own homes, the chief of the Saigon national police execute a manacled Viet Cong prisoner. In a perfectly framed sequence, General Nguyen Ngoc Loan unholsters a snub-nosed revolver and places its muzzle to the prisoner's right temple. The prisoner's head jolts, a sudden spurt of blood gushes straight out of his left temple, and he collapses in death. A decade later this image, with its roles reversed, would be transformed into the central metaphor of a Hollywood production crucial to reimaging the history of the Vietnam War and its prisoners of war: *The Deer Hunter*. And yet the original image would remain so potent in the popular imagination that further conscious efforts to reverse it would continue at least through the 1980s.[17]

With increasing horror, Americans were soon to witness even worse pictures and accounts of U.S. and Saigon soldiers torturing and slaughtering prisoners, both combatants captured in battle and civilians rounded up in sweeps through hamlets and villages. As early as May 1968 came the first published descriptions of the My Lai massacre of March, in which U.S. soldiers had killed hundreds of villagers, after raping and sodomizing the young women and using babies for target practice; the full story, including horrifying photographs taken by one of the GIs, would not appear in the general U.S. media until late 1969.[18] The CIA's Phoenix program, designed to wipe out the insurgent infrastructure by rounding up, imprisoning, and assassinating tens of thousands of suspects, was launched in mid 1968. By the end of the year Nguyen Van Thieu, head of the Saigon regime, boasted that Phoenix had already killed 18,393 cadre; U.S. intelligence officers attached to Phoenix later testified that they never saw any of its prisoners survive interrogation.[19] Enemy soldiers captured by U.S. forces were, in direct violation of the 1949 Geneva Convention Relative to the Treatment of Prisoners of War, turned over to the Saigon government, whose appalling prison camps were gradually being exposed to American readers and viewers. The American public even got to see photographs of the notorious tiger cages of Con Son Island, where the few survivors were almost all permanently disfigured and severely crippled by torture.[20]

It was in this context that the incoming Nixon administration decided to make the American prisoners and missing a major issue. Five days after Richard Nixon's inauguration, his representative introduced it into the Paris peace talks. A month later, the Defense and State departments began laying the groundwork for a massive campaign at home. Although one possible benefit of this new controversy might be to neutralize some of the outrage about what was being done to Vietnamese prisoners, this was not its main purpose. Throughout President Nixon's first term, the issue of POWs and MIAs would serve mainly as an indispensable device for continuing the war, functioning on the domestic front as a potent counterforce to the anti-war movement while providing an ingenious tool for building insurmountable roadblocks within the peace talks. And then the issue would be transmuted into a major obstacle to normalized relations for more than eighteen years after the 1973 peace accords.

Domestically, the issue was a masterful stroke. After all, how else could any deeply emotional support for the war be generated? Certainly not by holding out the old discredited promises of military victory. While in the early stages of the war, sentiment could be aroused to defend the "democracy" of Ngo Dinh Diem, who would be willing to fight and die for the notoriously corrupt generals ruling Saigon? But supporting their own prisoners of war and missing in action was something no loyal Americans could oppose. It also seemed easy to understand, requiring no knowledge of the history of Vietnam and the war. One measure of the campaign's success was the sale of more than fifty million POW/MIA bumper stickers in the next four years.[21] And once infused with this intense domestic support, the issue could be presented as a purely "humanitarian" question to transform the peace negotiations into a stage for displaying the inhuman features of the enemy.

The "Go Public" Campaign

The Nixon administration's "go public" campaign, designed explicitly to "marshal public opinion" for "the prompt release of all American prisoners of war," was initiated on March 1, 1969, and officially launched on May 19 in a press conference held by Defense Secretary Melvin Laird.[22] It was immediately and enthusiastically promoted by the media, which, in the relatively restrained language of *The New York Times* editorial staff, denounced "the Communist side" as "inhuman," asserted that "at least half of the 1,300 Americans missing in action in Vietnam are believed to be alive," and insisted that "the prisoner-of-war question is a humanitarian, not a political issue."[23]

By the fall, the POW/MIA campaign was already receiving media attention and exerting political influence far out of proportion to its small number of participants, especially in comparison with the millions taking part in the anti-war movement. The campaign was promoted by a medley of astute publicity schemes staged by the Nixon White House, POW family organizations, Congress, and Texas multimillionaire H. Ross Perot (a director of the Richard M. Nixon Foundation).

In September and October, the national media spotlighted three small delegations of wives and parents of missing men who flew to Paris to demand meetings with the negotiators from the DRV and NLF. On November 6, Congress unanimously passed and President Nixon signed a bill declaring November 9 a National Day of Prayer for U.S. prisoners of war in Vietnam. Right on schedule, United We Stand, an organization formed and chaired by H. Ross Perot, on November 9 ran full-page advertisements featuring the picture of two small children praying "Bring our Daddy home safe, sound and soon." Headlined *The Majority Speaks: Release the Prisoners*, the ads demanded that the "North Vietnamese and Viet Cong . . . Release the prisoners now." On November 13 and 14, the House Subcommittee on National Security Policy of the Committee on Foreign Affairs held hearings to denounce "the ruthlessness and cruelty of North Vietnam" and to provide a pep rally for a congressional resolution demanding the release of American POWs; not one person with a dissenting view was allowed to testify.[24] In mid-December, the resolution, which had previously received unanimous endorsement from the Senate, passed the House by a vote of 405–0 and was immediately exploited by U.S. negotiators in Paris.[25] A few days later, Perot had 152 wives and children flown to Paris, while his own chartered jetliner laden with Christmas presents for the POWs and filled with reporters aborted its mission in the capital of Laos, where it was used to stage a major media event.

During the campaign's formative first few months in 1969, Richard G. Capen, Laird's assistant secretary of defense for public affairs, and other officials from the State and Defense departments had visited forty-five sites to conduct unpublicized meetings with families of the missing men, thus shrewdly building foundations among those who could most readily win heartfelt support from the American people. "We brought them together for the first time," Capen later boasted of this whirlwind national trip to organize the families.[26]

The most productive meeting was arranged at the Coronado Naval Officers' Club near San Diego, where on March 26 the State and Defense departments' representatives conferred with selected wives from the Los Angeles area and a San Diego area group of wives organized by Sybil Stockdale, whose husband was the highest ranking naval officer imprisoned in Vietnam and who herself had been working closely with Naval Intelligence since May 1966.[27] By June, Stockdale had made herself the national coordinator of an organization she christened the National League of Families of American Prisoners in Southeast Asia, linking groups of POW wives from several parts of the country.[28] The following month she and several other selected POW family members huddled with Secretary of Defense Laird, and in December she and four other POW wives met with President Nixon, who pledged in their joint press conference that "this Government will do everything that it possibly can to separate out the prisoner issue and have it handled as it should be, as a separate issue on a humane basis."[29]

In the spring of 1970, Sybil Stockdale received a phone call from Republican Senator Robert Dole, who asked whether she could "deliver 1,000 family members" to a POW/MIA "extravaganza" he was planning for May 1 in Constitution Hall if he were to arrange government transportation for them. Dole pledged to orchestrate political support, putting Vice President Spiro Agnew and a bipartisan lineup of senators and representatives on the stage, and having Democratic Representative Clement Zablocki turn his Subcommittee on National Security Policy into a publicity forum just prior to the event.[30] Dole, Stockdale, and Perot collaborated in organizing the festivities, aided by a host of senators and representatives including such prominent Democrats as Senate Majority Leader Mike Mansfield and Senator Edmund Muskie.[31]

The Zablocki committee's hearings, held from April 29 through May 6, heard South Carolina Representative Mendel Rivers, chairman of the House Armed Services Committee, explain how Congress would assist in making sure that "the issue of POW's will be the prime discussion having priority over all other discussions" at the Paris peace negotiations.[32] The first two days of hearings were devoted mainly to doing publicity work for Senator Dole's May 1 POW/MIA rally, as exemplified by this exchange:

TV ARRANGEMENTS FOR RALLY

MR. ZABLOCKI. Just a final question, Senator Dole. What arrangements are being made for national television coverage, which could be used, then, worldwide?

SENATOR DOLE. We are contacting the networks, and there will be press conferences Friday with Mrs. Stockdale and Mr. Perot and others. I will be on the "Today Show" tomorrow with reference to this program. . . . We have talked to Peter Kenney at NBC, he is working on it; we have talked to Mr. Galbraith of CBS, and ABC has been most helpful, and generally they are coming around.[33]

The real stars of the Zablocki show were selected POW wives, especially Sybil Stockdale. Needless to say, the rally itself was a smashing success.

The following day, Stockdale presided in Washington over the constitutional convention that transformed her network into the National League of Families of American Prisoners and Missing in Southeast Asia. Its structure and bylaws had been defined three days earlier by Stockdale, a handful of wives chosen by her, and attorney Charles Havens, with whom she had worked when he was in the Office of International Security Affairs. Within three weeks of its incorporation, the National League received its IRS tax-exempt status as a "non-partisan, humanitarian" organization, free long-distance WATS telephone service provided by the White House, and office space donated by the Reserve Officers Association.[34]

From then until now, the National League of Families would play changing but always crucial roles in the dramatization and evolution of the POW/MIA issue. Almost all its principal organizers and activists were wives or parents of career officers, not draftees, mainly because the vast majority of missing and captured men were flight officers, and the politics of the organization were dominated by their outlook, especially during the war. Receiving in its early years direct and indirect material support from the White House, the Department of Defense, and the Republican National Committee,[35] the League (as it is known to activists in the movement) would have dramatically shifting relations with the government until it became, in the 1980s, the main official liaison between the Department of Defense and the American public on all POW/MIA matters, a function it still serves today.

Promoting the National League of Families was not the only accomplishment of the Zablocki committee. It gave Perot a podium from which to instruct the media about its duties in the POW/MIA campaign in a lengthy lecture preceded by this exchange:

HELP FROM THE MASS MEDIA

MR. ZABLOCKI. Mr. Perot, I am sure you are aware that we have with us today some of the finest ladies and men in the field of communication, newspapers, radio and TV. . . . Do you have a word for them?

MR. PEROT. I sure do.[36]

Perot also issued marching orders to Congress about its role in the media campaign, instructions that the committee obediently agreed to implement. Its immediate task, he explained, would be to set up as a display in the Capitol itself a POW exhibit that he had designed and would finance.[37]

On June 4, 1970, House Speaker John McCormack was the featured speaker during the televised ceremony inaugurating this display in the Capitol, generously donated by H. Ross Perot. The exhibit was designed "to arouse public opinion in behalf of the release of American prisoners of war" and "to encourage the thousands of tourists" who would see it each day to raise this demand "in letters to North Vietnamese leaders and members of Congress." At its center were the figures of two American prisoners: "One sits in the corner of a bare cell, staring bleakly at an empty bowl and chopsticks on which a huge cockroach is perched. On the floor are other cockroaches and a large rat. The other figure lies in a bamboo cage, ankles shackled."[38] By the end of the year, this tableau was being set up in state capitols throughout the country, the Steve Canyon cartoon strip was featuring POW/MIA relatives in its daily sagas, the ABC television network had presented a "POW/MIA Special," President Nixon had changed the official name of Veterans Day to Prisoner of War Day, the *Ladies' Home Journal* had published an article with a tear-out letter for readers to mail, and the U.S. Post Office, amid special fanfare by the president, had issued 135 million POW/MIA postage stamps.[39]

America's vision of the war was being transformed. The actual photographs and TV footage of massacred villagers, napalmed children, Vietnamese prisoners being tortured and murdered, wounded GIs screaming in agony, and body bags being loaded by the dozen for shipment back home were being replaced by simulated images of American POWs in the savage hands of Asian Communists.

Enter VIVA and the Bracelets

It was amid these events that another organization was launching an enterprise that would make the POW/MIA issue the subject of intense passion among millions of Americans for decades. This was the Victory in Vietnam Association, better known by its acronym VIVA.

Back in the spring of 1966, Russell Kirk in the *National Review* had ballyhooed VIVA as a courageous new student-faculty group dedicated to counteracting the rising tide of anti-war feeling on American campuses. Kirk applauded VIVA for counterdemonstrating against the "peaceniks" at the Oakland naval terminal in November 1965 and at UCLA, where the group originated. He also lamented their "penniless" condition, displayed their address prominently, and noted that "as yet they have no financial angels."[40]

Somehow the angels got the message. By October, Gloria Coppin, wife of Los Angeles industrialist Douglas Coppin, whose Hydro-Mill Corporation manufactured airplane parts for major military contractors, was providing a headquarters for the organization and contacts with wealthy and influential members of southern California society. On March 9, 1967, the Victory in Vietnam Association received a state charter from California as an educational institution, and less than two months later the IRS granted it tax-exempt status as a "charitable and educational" organization.[41] VIVA was now able to hold the first of its lucrative annual Salute to the Armed Forces formal dinner dances, organized by its Ladies Auxiliary (made up of wives of wealthy business, military, and political leaders), which allowed the guests—including Barry Goldwater, Alexander Haig, H. Ross Perot, Bob Hope, Los Angeles Mayor Sam Yorty, and California Governor Ronald Reagan—to receive tax deductions for their contributions.[42] With brimming coffers, VIVA expanded rapidly and planned ever more ambitious campaigns to thwart the anti-war movement.

But meanwhile the early 1968 Tet Offensive, as well as ensuing offensives mounted by the Vietnamese insurgents throughout 1968 and 1969, had made talk of U.S. "victory" in Vietnam ring hollow and become politically embarrassing. By the time of the November

1968 elections, "peace," not "victory," had become the catchword, as the nation bet on Nixon's secret peace plan. So in 1969, VIVA ceased to be the Victory in Vietnam Association and became Voices in Vital America.

A few months later, members of VIVA and Robert Dornan, today a Republican representative from California and a leading proselytizer about live POWs, then a right-wing Los Angeles TV talk show host and close friend of Gloria Coppin, contrived the idea of selling bracelets engraved with the names of POWs and MIAs to promote and fund the POW/MIA campaign. In addition to Gloria Coppin, who was chair of VIVA's board of directors from its founding until 1974, one of the prime movers in VIVA's bracelet manufacturing was Carol Bates, who was to take over the directorship of the National League of Families in 1976 and then in 1984 become a principal coordinator of the POW/MIA issue for the Defense Intelligence Agency, a position she still holds.[43] The prototype bracelets were produced just in time for the May 9, 1970, Salute to the Armed Forces Ball, where Governor Ronald Reagan was the keynote speaker, Bob Hope and Martha Raye were made co-chairs of the bracelet campaign, H. Ross Perot was named Man of the Year, and Mrs. Perot ceremoniously accepted the first bracelet.[44]

Later that month, VIVA sold twelve hundred bracelets at the National League of Families convention in Washington and took orders for five thousand more. The bracelet idea quickly mushroomed into a propaganda coup and financial bonanza for the POW/MIA campaign, especially for VIVA, which was soon wholesaling bracelets to the National League, Perot's United We Stand, and Junior Chambers of Commerce across the country. These resellers kept 50 cents for each $2.50 nickel-plated bracelet and a dollar for each $3.00 copper bracelet, with the remaining two dollars going to VIVA, whose costs averaged less than 50 cents per bracelet (further reduced to 30 cents when they ordered five million made of stainless steel in mid-1972). By early 1972, VIVA was distributing more than five thousand bracelets a day; during midsummer the daily average reached almost eleven thousand. VIVA's income soared to $3,698,575 in 1972 and, despite the January 1973 peace accords, to $7,388,088 for 1973. Bracelets were prominently worn by such luminaries as Richard Nixon, General William Westmoreland, Billy Graham, George Wallace, Charlton Heston, Bill Cosby, Pat Boone, Cher and Sonny Bono, Fred Astaire, Johnny Cash, Steve Allen, Princess Grace of Monaco, and of course Bob Hope, who personally distributed more than a thousand. Besides being displayed by stars of entertainment and politics, the bracelet became a kind of fetish for sports stars such as Willie Shoemaker, Don Drysdale, Lee Trevino (who claimed it saved his golf game), and Jack Kramer (who swore it cured his tennis elbow).[45]

By the time of the January 1973 Paris Peace Agreement, between four million and ten million Americans were wearing POW/MIA bracelets.[46] The influence on the national imagination cannot be calculated. Each person who wore a bracelet vowed never to remove it until his or her POW/MIA was either found to be dead or returned home from Vietnamese prison camp. Millions of people thus developed profound emotional bonds with the man whose name was displayed all day on their wrist. Countless American schoolchildren went through some of their most formative years linked to these amulets. How could they not believe in the living existence of their POW/MIAs then—and perhaps today? And the POW/MIA bracelets themselves must still be potent amulets, for even now the National League of Families and other POW/MIA organizations are reportedly selling hundreds daily.[47]

Four More Years of War for the POW/MIAs

In his opening speech at the Paris peace talks on January 25, 1969, newly appointed chief negotiator Henry Cabot Lodge made what at first seemed an innocuous call for "the early release of prisoners of war on both sides."[48] This turned out to be a foot in the door for a demand that was to help stalemate peace negotiations for almost four years: Washington's insistence that Hanoi account for America's missing in action and negotiate the release of American prisoners separately from the question of U.S. withdrawal.

Throughout 1969, the representatives of North Vietnam and the southern insurgents (by midyear the NLF was replaced by its successor, the Provisional Revolutionary Government of South Viet Nam or PRG) insisted that the release of prisoners of war could not be considered separately from a resolution of the war itself. Although this was the customary position of warring powers, it was denounced by the administration and the media as "unprecedented," "inhuman," and "barbaric." What the Vietnamese wanted to talk about was ending the war and the U.S. occupation of half their country. But the more Hanoi and the insurgents refused to negotiate separately about the POW issue, the more Washington made it the central issue of the negotiations. In the unusually long final negotiating session of the year, Philip Habib, acting head of the U.S. delegation, "scarcely mentioned the question of peace, devoting his formal remarks to the prisoner problem."[49] A year later, *The Christian Science Monitor*, in the concluding installment of a five-part series designed to stimulate outrage at the treatment of U.S. POWs, pity for their families, and condemnation of Vietnam for refusing to release them before the United States agreed to end the war, recognized that "at the Paris peace talks, the PW issue has become the most visible of all the current questions."[50]

By this time, the administration had carried out a brilliant propaganda coup. At first, North Vietnam and the PRG simply denounced the POW/MIA issue as a "perfidious maneuver to camouflage the fact that the United States is pursuing the war . . . and misleading public opinion, which demands that the United States end the war and withdraw its troops."[51] When they became more flexible and suggested that they would set a date for the release of all prisoners of war if the United States would set a date for withdrawal from their country, the administration accused them of "ransoming" the POWs and using them as "hostages" and "bargaining chips." The administration's line was parroted by the media. For example, *The Christian Science Monitor* series labeled Hanoi's position "a cruel ploy" and argued: "Never before, in any other war (at least, not so far as State Department officials can ascertain), have prisoners been held as international hostages, ransomed to a political and military settlement of the war."

This dizzying inversion of history conveniently ignored the fact that the United States, like most nations, has never been involved in a war in which either side released all its prisoners prior to an agreement to end the war. But through the strange logic of the administration's negotiating position and its masterful public relations campaign, the American prisoners of war had indeed been successfully transformed—in the public mind—into "bargaining chips" and "hostages" held for "ransom." These metaphors not only would increasingly influence the debates about negotiations to end the war, but also would eventually become central to the postwar POW/MIA myth.

By late 1970, the administration had won an apparent political consensus on the POW/MIA issue in Washington, thanks in part to the efforts of a leading Democrat, House Speaker McCormack. For example, following a suggestion by H. Ross Perot, McCormack set up a joint session of the House and Senate to be addressed by the National League of Families. When some members objected to violating the hallowed tradition against private citizens addressing sessions of Congress, McCormack found a substitute: retired Air Force Colonel Frank Borman, former commander of the Apollo 8 moon orbit, who had resigned from the space program earlier that year to head Perot's American Horizons Foundation, established to publicize "national issues," and who then was immediately selected by President Nixon to be his personal emissary on the POW/MIA issue to twenty-five countries (Borman next became vice president of Perot's Electronic Data Systems corporation). So on September 22, Borman, speaking not as a private citizen but as the president's representative, exhorted the joint session to help mobilize public opinion on behalf of the prisoners so they would not become "political hostages."[52] Soon the House Armed Services Committee, by a vote of 28–2, passed a resolution recommending that the United States not conduct any further negotiations at all until the other side made concessions on the POW issue.[53]

How is it possible to comprehend this truly astonishing position, which seemed ready to trade countless American and Vietnamese lives for several hundred prisoners who would presumably be released anyhow at the conclusion of the war? Looking backward from decades later, we can comprehend such posturing only in the light of the dramatic transformation in consciousness wrought by the POW/MIA campaign for the public mind. Even from the vantage point of 1975, the year Saigon finally fell, this consciousness seemed strangely aberrant. As Jonathan Schell then astutely observed, by 1972 "many people were persuaded that the United States was fighting in Vietnam in order to get its prisoners back," and the nation's main sympathy was no longer for "the men fighting and dying on the front," who "went virtually unnoticed as attention was focussed on the prisoners of war," "the objects of a virtual cult": "Following the President's lead, people began to speak as though the North Vietnamese had kidnapped four hundred Americans and the United States had gone to war to retrieve them."[54]

Peace for the POWs

But by making the POWs central to the entire national debate about the war, and even making it seem that the main purpose of the war was to free them, the administration was digging a potential trap for itself. The logic of its position could easily be reversed. As Frankie Ford, the wife of one of the POWs, said in November 1970: "If it is true that they will not be released until the U.S. gets out, then why don't they set a date and get out now? This war cannot be successful. Why should one more man die on the battlefield or in the prisons."[55]

In the opening months of 1971, while President Nixon was demanding that Hanoi "agree to the immediate and unconditional release of all prisoners of war throughout Indochina" and "to end the barbaric use of our prisoners as negotiating pawns," a number of POW family members began campaigning for a U.S. withdrawal as the means to free their loved ones. Virginia Warner, mother of a downed flier from Ypsilanti and head of the National League of Families in Michigan until she "resigned in disgust," declared, "We've been used to drum up war sentiment"; having previously sponsored billboard messages to Hanoi demanding release of the POWs, she now had these replaced with billboard messages to the president demanding that the United States pull out. The original secretary-treasurer of the National League, Bernard Talley, a conservative Baltimore businessman whose son was a prisoner in North Vietnam, sponsored an ad in *The Washington Post* in which he and other POW relatives asked the president to withdraw U.S. forces in exchange for the prisoners. At the May board meeting of the National League of Families, Louise Mulligan, one of the organization's founders, resigned after the leadership squelched attempts to have the membership polled on whether to pressure the president for withdrawal. Mrs. Louis Jones, whose husband was lost over Laos and whose brother was an MIA who never returned from Korea, POW wife Mrs. James Hughes, MIA wife Barbara Mullen, and a number of others including Delia Alvarez, whose brother had been captured while bombing North Vietnam more than six years earlier in alleged retaliation for the spurious Gulf of Tonkin incidents, in May formed an anti-war organization of POW/MIA family members called POW/MIA Families for Immediate Release; this new group quickly enrolled 350 family members.[56]

On June 10, 1971, North Vietnam and the PRG declared unequivocally that if the United States simply set a date for withdrawal from Vietnam they were prepared to negotiate a full exchange of prisoners even before resolving other questions. "To prove our good-will and flexibility," they were offering to settle the POW issue first even though "normally in all wars, that question is not settled until the settlement of all questions, political, military, economic."[57] The U.S. reply came from Secretary of State William P. Rogers, who asserted that the offer was merely a demand for "ransom," which proved that "the North Vietnamese have decided undoubtedly that they are going to hold these prisoners to try to achieve political objectives, in effect using them for ransom payments."[58]

Rogers's comments themselves had political objectives much closer to home, where publication of the Pentagon Papers was proving to the American people that for many years their govern-ment had been deliberately and systematically lying to them in order to instigate and perpetuate its Indochina war. National revulsion against the war was finally about to be expressed in the U.S. Senate, which on June 22 endorsed Senator Mike Mansfield's amendment to the draft extension bill calling for a reciprocal U.S. withdrawal from Vietnam and release of U.S. POWs. As the administration worked frantically to block House approval of several versions of this proposal, it became increasingly obvious that President Nixon's real goal was not to get the POWs back but to maintain a U.S. proxy regime in South Vietnam. But now tens of millions of Americans were learning from the Pentagon Papers that this was the very policy that had gotten their nation into Vietnam in the first place, a policy covertly designed and implemented back in 1954 by the Eisen-hower-Nixon administration. So the popular groundswell for get-ting American POWs out by pulling out American troops was turning into a tidal wave.

A symptom of the turnabout in the political pull of the POW issue was a new ad placed in newspapers across the country by some of the leading activists from the National League of Families who had made the POW/MIA cause such a prominent political issue and who now pleaded for it not to be a political issue. Headlined HELP KEEP THE POWS-MIAS OUT OF POLITICS, the ad proclaimed:

> There is NOTHING POLITICAL about the Geneva Conventions re-garding treatment of Prisoners of War. . . . The treatment of POWs is a humanitarian question—nothing more!
> But, ambitious politicians both in and out of Congress are trying to *use* the POW issue to support their demand for a withdrawal date for all American troops in Vietnam. They have every right to work for their solutions to the war, but they *must not* be allowed to bring the POWs and MIAs into the political arena.

With a picture of a little boy of one of the "POW/MIA daddies" being victimized by "THE POLITICAL AMBITIONS OF SOME MEN," it called upon all Americans to take this "non-political" stand: "We have only one president at a time. He is Commander-in-Chief. It is his responsibility to get the POWs back . . . support him in his efforts."[59]

In his April 16 news conference, the president declared that U.S. ground and air forces would remain in Vietnam "as long as there is one American prisoner being held prisoner by North Vietnam." Since North Vietnam was making the release of the prisoners con-tingent on a U.S. withdrawal, the logic of Nixon's position could be, as Tom Wicker put it, that "we may keep both troops and prisoners there forever."[60] If that seems absurd, what would follow if it could be made to appear that North Vietnam was concealing some of its prisoners? Then, since it could never be proved that some missing American was *not* "being held prisoner by North Vietnam," the war could literally go on forever.

While the prisoner of war issue could be used by either side in the struggle over the war that was tearing the nation apart, the missing in action issue was much less double-edged and potentially even more ominous. According to that pro-Nixon ad, making "all poli-ticians immediately stop trying to use the POWs-MIAs for political goals" meant insisting "that the Communists in Indo-China account for all MIAs without delay." Implicit in this ultimatum was a means to continue the war indefinitely. Because it would be impossible for any or all powers involved in the war to account for all American MIAs, and because any one of these missing men *might* be a prisoner of the Indochinese Communists, the president's position would justify war without end. (The only solution would be the kind advocated by Sybil Stockdale: "We should land US Marines on North Vietnam and claim it as US territory.")[61] In this corollary of the administration's POW/MIA issue lay a potential nightmare for the future. One wonders whether the president considered the possibility that decades later millions of Americans would still believe that there were American prisoners of war in Indochina and that, following his logic, the Vietnam War therefore still would not be over.

Counting on Discrepancies

The "go public" campaign of the Nixon administration and the publicity activities of VIVA, the National League, Ross Perot, Congress, and the media made many demands, including more regular mail service, inspection of prison camps, better treatment, early or even immediate release of the prisoners, and an accounting for the missing. Over and over again, it was reiterated that each of these questions, as well as the issue as a whole, was "not political" but purely "humanitarian."

Yet even the most innocuous demands had not only a political function but also a hidden military agenda. For example, while demanding more frequent mail privileges for the POWs and international inspection of their camps as strictly "humanitarian" obligations, the United States was clandestinely encoding POW letters to and from family members to provide a flow of military intelligence and was attempting to pinpoint the POW camps in order to clear the way for more intensive bombing of the Hanoi region and to plan rescue missions, such as the November 1970 raid on the Son Tay prison camp, which failed despite half a year of elaborate preparations. Much of Sybil and James Stockdale's *In Love and War* details the codes and physical apparatus used by Naval Intelligence to turn correspondence between a prisoner and his wife into a channel for transmitting intelligence into and out of North Vietnam. What had deterred the Pentagon from wholesale attacks on Hanoi was its imprecise intelligence about the location of the POW camps and corollary political considerations, as indicated by this top-secret analysis:

> Although the North Vietnamese do not mark the camps where American prisoners are kept or reveal their locations, we know from intelligence sources that most of these facilities are in or near Hanoi. . . . Heavy and indiscriminate attacks in the Hanoi area would jeopardize the lives of these prisoners and alarm their wives and parents into vocal opposition. Reprisals could be taken against them and the idea of war crimes trials would find considerable acceptance in countries outside the Communist bloc.[62]

Of course, until the Son Tay raid relatively few Americans suspected any concealed military aims in what seemed the most strictly "humanitarian" aspects of the POW/MIA issue.

In fact, activities addressed to truly humanitarian concerns about the prisoners and their families had begun long before the administration made the plight of the POWs a major public and negotiating issue. During 1968, for example, visiting clergymen and other anti-war activists inspected some of the POW facilities, carried home letters from the prisoners, and even brought back six captured airmen released to them by North Vietnam. These activities expanded throughout 1969, culminating in late December in the founding of a formal organization called the Committee of Liaison with Families of Servicemen Detained in North Vietnam.

The Committee of Liaison was dedicated to taking actual practical steps to alleviate the suffering of the prisoners, their families, and the families of the missing, steps that had already been initiated by its co-chairs, Dave Dellinger and Cora Weiss. As described in its initial letter to POW/MIA family members, the main purpose was to "facilitate communication between American servicemen held in North Vietnam and their families," and the secondary goal was "try to find out if your relative is a prisoner in North Vietnam."[63] The first of these aims soon revealed the phony character of the mail controversy. The second led the committee into playing a major role in the Byzantine drama that would eventually generate the postwar POW/MIA myth.

One of the main charges raised by the administration's "go public" campaign was that American POWs were not being granted the mail privileges specified in the 1949 Geneva Convention Relative to the Treatment of Prisoners of War.[64] Letters had been exchanged, but these were infrequent, often delayed, and limited to only a fraction of the prisoners believed to be held. The Committee of Liaison soon discovered that Washington had acted to exacerbate rather than to solve these problems. Mail from prisoners had been held in U.S. postal facilities for as long as two years. The Defense Department had instructed families to ignore the mailrouting directions provided by North Vietnam and to address mail in ways that Hanoi had explicitly said made delivery difficult or impossible. Beginning in 1969, U.S. officials in Europe had physically interfered with the 1968 U.S.-North Vietnam special arrangement for delivery of POW packages. Hundreds of letters from prisoners being transported by courier were actually seized at an airport by the U.S. Customs Service and released only after loud public outcry.[65]

The Committee of Liaison was soon providing the only effective means of communication between the prisoners and the families, a function it fulfilled throughout the rest of the war. During 1970 alone, it transmitted 3,430 letter to the families including mail from all but six of the prisoners held in North Vietnam. The government responded by repeatedly attempting to interfere with this communication channel. But by warning all family members not to work through the committee and even sending FBI agents to harass some of them, it merely displayed its hypocrisy about this particular "humanitarian" concern and propelled more family members into the anti-war movement.[66]

The committee's efforts to achieve its secondary goal—accounting for the prisoners and the missing—threatened to undermine a strategy central to the POW/MIA issue. Indeed, the administration had been alarmed by the successes achieved by the committee's founders even while the organization was in the process of formation, and the government's response was crucial to the entire subsequent history of the POW/MIA question.

What might be called the battle of the lists had begun in the May 1969 news conference that kicked off the "go public" campaign, when Secretary of Defense Laird demanded that North Vietnam and the NLF immediately provide lists of their prisoners. The Vietnamese stood by their position that they would not discuss the POW issue with the U.S. government at all except as part of an overall settlement of the war but would deal with these matters only with anti-war groups. In the next several months the Vietnamese continued their practice of releasing some POWs to anti-war delegations, and they also began providing to them lists of some of their prisoners. In November, anti-war activists Dave Dellinger and Rennie Davis brought back a list of 59 POWs. On December 23, a delegation from Women Strike for Peace, including Cora Weiss, returned with letters from 132 prisoners, including 36 who had not previously been heard from, an official North Vietnamese list of five airmen who had died in plane crashes, and, in response to status inquiries made on behalf of family members, official notification that North Vietnam had no knowledge of a number of other missing men.[67] In the next several days, Weiss, Dellinger, and others completed arrangements to establish the Committee of Liaison. The

U.S. government immediately responded with a move carefully contrived to guarantee that neither these North Vietnamese initiatives nor these efforts by American citizens—nor any other actions that North Vietnam, the PRG, the Pathet Lao, or the Khmer Rouge might possibly take—could *ever* resolve the POW/MIA issue.

On December 30, the United States presented to the North Vietnam and PRG delegations in Paris a list of what it called "U.S. military personnel missing in Southeast Asia includ[ing] personnel classified internally by the services as either missing or captured." It attached to this list the following bizarre statement: "We are holding the Communist authorities in Southeast Asia responsible for every individual on this list whether or not he is internally classified by the services as captured or missing."[68]

This demand is probably unprecedented in the annals of warfare. It has no basis in international law, which hardly requires belligerent powers to furnish each other with information on the identities of those they have killed. It could never even conceivably be met, for it holds all the opposing forces individually and collectively "responsible for every individual" missing, including those in planes lost at sea or exploding above mountains and jungle. It thoroughly and effectively confuses the question of the missing with that of prisoners. It has been the official policy of the United States government ever since it was issued in 1969. It is the foundation upon which the entire POW/MIA myth has been built.

The list itself consisted merely of the name, rank, and serial number of the 1,406 missing personnel. By providing no information whatsoever on the date, place, or circumstances of loss, the administration scarcely displayed any sincere desire for an actual accounting. The list did not include CIA employees, though any captured would clearly fall under the 1949 Geneva Convention's definition of prisoners of war. Thus Eugene DeBruin, who was captured by the Pathet Lao in 1963 and who is one of the most prominent cases for which the government is still demanding an accounting (see page 30), is not on the list. In presenting the list, the government made no offer to reciprocate by providing the name of each of the hundreds of thousands of Vietnamese, Laotians, and Cambodians whose corpses were tallied for the daily "body count."

The only legitimate aspect of the U.S. position was that the opposing forces should reveal the names of those whom they had captured. This was a demand that could hardly be satisfied by the Pathet Lao or Khmer Rouge guerrillas and would be exceedingly difficult for the NLF, whose handful of American captives was held in scattered jungle camps. North Vietnam, the one opponent that reasonably could be expected to list its prisoners, was already in the process of doing so. After all, it was the lists and notifications brought back by Dave Dellinger and Cora Weiss, and the expressed intentions of the organization they were founding, that evidently had precipitated the government's preemptive strike. And soon Hanoi did release what it certified to be a full list of all American servicemen it held.

As soon as the Committee of Liaison publicly announced itself in mid-January, it began receiving hundreds of requests from family members to determine the status of their missing relatives. As Weiss testified to Congress, the committee's efforts were hindered by the government's duplicity with the families:

> Unfortunately, in too many cases, families were told by the military to report their man missing in North Vietnam when it was known that he was shot down over South Vietnam, Cambodia, Laos or the China Sea.
>
> Since Americans were not supposed to know that we had been bombing Laos for years and losing planes and crews there, their relatives were simply told: "MIA over DRV." This aroused undue anxiety and suffering as the family hopefully waited for some word.

Nevertheless, "132 status inquiries forwarded by COL were acknowledged and dealt with by the Vietnamese."[69]

On April 6, North Vietnam conveyed an official list of the 335

American prisoners it held, including serial numbers and home-towns, to the Committee of Liaison, which first notified the families and then submitted the list to the press. Some newspapers published it.[70] Most, including *The New York Times*, did not. The government pretended that nothing had happened. Later that month, the House and the Senate passed, without a single dissenting vote, Concurrent Resolution 582 declaring that "over 1,500 American servicemen are imprisoned by Communist forces in Southeast Asia."[71]

In late June, after another delegation of anti-war activists returned from Hanoi with confirmation that the tabulation of 335 was indeed North Vietnam's official roster of its captured American servicemen, *The New York Times* at last published the list.[72] At this point, the government finally responded—by trying to discredit and obfuscate the very accounting that it ostensibly sought.

Previously, the government had accused Hanoi of torturing the families by not releasing a list of its prisoners. Now the government accused Hanoi of torturing the families by releasing a list of its prisoners. "The unofficial release of an inaccurate and incomplete list," the Pentagon charged, "can only add to the great anguish of the hundreds of wives, children and parents of the more than 1,500 servicemen who are listed as missing or captured."[73] The only thing "unofficial" about the list was that the Vietnamese had transmitted it through an American organization they felt they could trust rather than through the Nixon administration; few families would be disturbed by this. The real issue was the claim that the list was "inaccurate and incomplete."

Hanoi's previous failure to identify its prisoners was essential to any conceivable logic in the administration's attempt to hold it responsible for each and every missing person (since then any MIA *might* be a POW). Once North Vietnam listed its prisoners, even this tenuous line of reasoning was shattered. Hence it was necessary to discredit its list. The only way to do so was to make a case that North Vietnam was holding more prisoners than it acknowledged.

And so the government proceeded to concoct the issue of concealed prisoners, which would become the core of the postwar POW/MIA myth.

The Pentagon announced that it had its own list of 376 "listed as prisoners of war, or known captured," in North Vietnam and that Hanoi's list "does not include the names of at least 40 men we carry as being captured." Four months earlier administration officials had given a much larger figure when they claimed that "the 500 American prisoners being held in North Vietnam are regarded in Hanoi as hostages to be traded off for some political or military benefit in the future."[74] Although North Vietnam had now listed the names of its 335 captives, the U.S. government refused to divulge the 376 names on its own list because, in the fateful Catch-22 formulation of a Pentagon spokesman: "If we publish our list, then they know whom we know about and whom we don't know about. This could be dangerous. For example, at the end of the war, Hanoi could just keep the men we don't know about."[75]

From that moment to the present, the U.S. government has used secrecy and ingenious numbers games to make it impossible for anyone—including family members, researchers, or the Asian governments accused of not providing a precise accounting—to arrive at a precise accounting. As a high-ranking government official confided to Pulitzer Prize-winning journalist Seymour Hersh: "[O]ne constant American goal was to charge Hanoi with responsibility for as many prisoners as possible. 'I would err on the side of the number of prisoners they have in North Vietnam,' the official, who is a lawyer, explained. He said that technique amounted to 'thinking ahead' about future prisoner negotiations at the end of the war."[76]

At first it seemed that the difference between the two totals was small enough that it might be resolved with a little more information from North Vietnam and simple arithmetic. But Washington soon proved that this was just wishful thinking.

One possible explanation of what the Pentagon called "discrepancies"—another concept that would be basic to the postwar POW/ MIA myth—could be that some airmen had died after being captured. On November 14, the Committee of Liaison reported that it had received from North Vietnam and passed on to the government and the families the names of four prisoners to be added to the April list and six airmen who had died subsequent to capture. Since the Pentagon acknowledged that all six named as dead had been on its list of 376 presumed captured, they should have been subtracted, leaving 370. One of the four newly named prisoners, not being on the old U.S. list, should have been added, making the new U.S. total 371, a difference of merely 32 from the new Vietnamese total of 339. But instead the Defense Department insisted on keeping the six dead men on its list of current prisoners because it claimed to be waiting for information "that corroborates" Hanoi's notification; it also inexplicably added another unnamed person to its total, so that it now "listed 378 men as known prisoners in North Vietnam," thus making a difference of 39.[77]

Citing this alleged lack of corroboration, the Pentagon refused to change the status of the six men who had died from MIA to KIA, thus leaving their families in the same limbo of torture from which the administration was ostensibly trying to free them.[78] Yet at the very same time, the administration used the deaths of these men as its main public justification for the November 20 (November 21 Vietnam time) raid on the empty Son Tay prison camp twenty-three miles from Hanoi.

The administration had intended to conceal this raid, which had been in preparation since May, from the American people, who learned about it only because on November 21 U.S. newspapers published reports broadcast by Radio Hanoi of renewed bombing of North Vietnam, including an attack on the camp. After denying the raid on November 22, Secretary of Defense Laird in a November 23 press conference claimed that it had been carried out because of "new information we received this month that some of our men were dying in prisoner-of-war camps." The following day Laird told the Senate Foreign Relations Committee that President Nixon had made the decision after learning that "Americans are dying in captivity."[79]

The Committee of Liaison, whose list of dead American prisoners furnished by North Vietnam was evidently official enough to justify the Son Tay raid and concomitant massive bombing raids on North Vietnam but not official enough to change the status of these men from missing to dead, now pointed out the government's duplicity in implying that the men had died because of ill treatment. On November 25, while announcing that two days earlier she had notified the families and the government of another 11 American prisoners who had died, Cora Weiss pointed out that there was no evidence whatsoever about the causes of their deaths, which may have included wounds or disease.[80] Running with this new ball, the administration now attributed its refusal to remove all 17 names from its list of current prisoners (which would have reduced the difference between the two lists to 22) to North Vietnam's failure to furnish the causes and dates of death.

The following month North Vietnam attempted to put an end to these atrocious numbers games. It provided what it officially certified as the "full and complete" list of all 339 prisoners it held not to the Committee of Liaison but to representatives in Paris of Senators J. William Fulbright, chairman of the Senate Foreign Relations Committee, and Edward Kennedy. It also gave the two senators an official list of "15 pilots [who] died from grievous wounds when shot down" and "5 pilots [who] died from serious diseases," including their ranks, serial numbers, dates of capture, and dates of death, together with the names of three "pilots killed in plane crash."[81] These lists, which had been requested by the two senators, corroborated all the information previously released by the Committee of Liaison. According to the arithmetic of *The New York Times*, the lists failed to account for a mere "10 airmen carried by the

Defense Department as prisoners in North Vietnam." They also showed that North Vietnam was not unwilling to provide such lists, only to provide them directly to the Nixon administration's representatives in Paris. Thus the Vietnamese also demonstrated that rather than using the prisoners as "hostages," "pawns," or "bargaining chips" in the negotiations, they were attempting to keep them out of the negotiations, making the release of prisoners, as was customary with warring belligerents, contingent on the conclusion of the peace process.

Secretary of State William Rogers immediately responded by denouncing the lists as an "inhumane" and "contemptible maneuver" that merely displayed the "barbarism" of the North Vietnamese. Yet the administration seemed to recognize that it would now have to take the numbers games, and indeed the whole POW/MIA issue, into other dimensions. So ten weeks later President Nixon declared "that as long as there are American POW's—and there are 1,600 Americans in North Vietnam jails under very difficult circumstances at the present time—as long as there are American POW's in North Vietnam we will have to maintain a residual force in South Vietnam."[82]

The POWs in War and Peace

The POW/MIA issue served two crucial functions in allowing Richard Nixon to continue the Vietnam War for four years, even though he had assumed office almost a year after the nation had shown its desperate desire for peace. It was both a booby trap for the anti-war movement and a wrench to be thrown into the works of the Paris peace talks. Perhaps the most startling and penetrating judgment comes from Gloria Coppin, VIVA's chair during almost its entire existence. Although she still fervently believes in the existence of live POWs, she has also come to a painful sense of how she and many others may have been manipulated. As she put it in a 1990 interview: "Nixon and Kissinger just used the POW issue to prolong the war. Sometimes I feel guilty because with all our efforts, we killed more men than we saved."[83]

The Nixon administration's four-year campaign to secure the release of American prisoners of war separate from U.S. withdrawal from Vietnam was doomed, along with its other war goals, by the peace accords signed in Paris on January 27, 1973. The Agreement among the four parties—the United States, the Democratic Republic of Viet-Nam, the Republic of Viet-Nam, and the Provisional Revolutionary Government of South Viet-Nam—called for the withdrawal from Vietnam of all "United States forces and those of the other foreign countries allied with the United States" within sixty days and the return of all prisoners of war to be "carried out simultaneously with and completed not later than the same day" as the U.S. troop withdrawal.[84]

In conformity with the Agreement, North Vietnam had already delivered to the United States and certified as complete a list of its prisoners of war and those who had died in captivity. Within the stipulated two months, the living prisoners on the list, including all those who had been captured in Laos and South Vietnam, were repatriated. Their return was staged as Operation Homecoming, an event transformed by an awesome media blitz into a public relations coup for President Nixon, who boasted at his formal White House dinner party for the ex-POWs that he had achieved "the return of all of our prisoners of war" as part of his successful conclusion of the war in Vietnam.[85]

But the president's claims by no means satisfied many of those who had been agitating about the POW/MIA issue. They argued that there were "discrepancies" between the Vietnamese lists and American information. Some claimed that there were as many as 56 men "known" to have been captured for whom there was now no accounting. The myth of the forsaken POWs, enslaved in captivity by the Asian Communists, was about to emerge from the war to poison the peace.

3 ▪ THE MISSING OF PEACE

War Remains

The terms of the 1973 Paris Peace Agreements were effectively what North Vietnam and the National Liberation Front had offered to the United States in the spring of 1968, a year before American prisoners of war and missing in action were transformed into a major public and negotiating issue. They were the same terms that the United States and the Thieu regime in Saigon had rejected in November 1972, before the "Christmas bombing" dropped more tonnage in twelve days on Hanoi and Haiphong than Germany dropped on Great Britain from 1940 to 1945 and caused more deaths and imprisonments of U.S. airmen than any other air assault in the Indochina wars.[1] In truth, these 1973 agreements essentially returned to the Geneva Agreement between France and the Democratic Republic of Vietnam signed in 1954, the year when the first American servicemen were captured and released. The very first Article is a succinct statement of what the United States had been fighting to prevent for almost two decades: "The United States and all other countries respect the independence, sovereignty, unity, and territorial integrity of Viet-Nam as recognized by the 1954 Geneva Agreements on Viet-Nam."[2] It is staggering to consider what the peoples of Indochina and of the United States would have been spared if those earlier Agreements had been implemented.

And if the 1973 Paris Peace Agreements had been faithfully implemented, undoubtedly Vietnam, Cambodia, and Laos—and the United States as well—would be far better off today. The United States did withdraw its actual combat forces from Vietnam, did cease its direct combat activities in Vietnam, and did get all its prisoners of war back from Vietnam, at least according to such disparate authorities as the returning POWs, the Committee of Liaison, and even President Nixon.[3] But amid endless mutual recrimination, virtually every other part of the agreements was abrogated or nullified. The most flagrant and immediate violations were committed by the United States: contrary to Article 4, it refused to cease its military involvement and active role in the internal affairs of South Vietnam; instead of dismantling all its military bases, as specified in Article 6, it simply transferred them with all their equipment to General Thieu's regime; thousands of U.S. advisers and technical military personnel stayed in South Vietnam in direct violation of Article 5; the administration refused to implement Article 21, which specified that "the United States will contribute to healing the wounds of war and to postwar reconstruction of the Democratic Republic of Viet-Nam and throughout Indochina." About the *only* proviso of the Paris Agreement that was scrupulously carried out by any party was Hanoi's implementation with respect to American POWs of Article 8(a), which called for an exchange of lists of "captured military personnel and foreign civilians" upon signing of the agreements and the repatriation of those prisoners within sixty days.[4] So the use of the POW issue as the main basis for continuing U.S. hostility to Vietnam surely must be one of the most mind-boggling legacies of the Vietnam War.

The United States government has never officially charged Vietnam with failure to implement Article 8(a). What it has continued to allege is that Vietnam has not thoroughly fulfilled its obligations under Article 8(b): "The Parties shall help each other to get information about those military personnel and foreign civilians of the parties missing in action" and shall "facilitate the exhumation and repatriation of the remains" of the dead. The history of the implementation of Article 8(b) is now very long, quite complex, and much in dispute. Vietnam has returned the identifiable remains of more than 300 U.S. servicemen, has helped account for many more, and has participated with the United States in numerous joint searches of crash sites. It is unlikely that the debate about whether Vietnam has provided enough help either in accounting for the missing or in returning the dead will ever be resolved, since one's view of these two issues tends to correlate with one's view of the war. But it is essential to recognize that these are indeed two separate issues, each of which is radically different from the question of whether Vietnam has kept American prisoners of war.

The official U.S. position, reiterated by the Nixon, Ford, Carter, Regan, Bush, and Clinton administrations, is that Article 8(b) is purely "humanitarian" and should therefore be fulfilled in isolation from every other section of the Paris Agreements, even if none of the others is implemented. In the first years after the signing of the agreements, Vietnam's position was that at least two other provisions are just as purely "humanitarian," and should therefore be honored equally. One is Article 21, which, as will be seen, would play a major role in the history of the POW/MIA issue and the ultimate creation of the POW/MIA myth. The other is Article 8(c), whose very existence one would never guess in all the polemics about the "cruelty" and "inhumanity" of those who allegedly are not adequately accounting for American prisoners.

The first prisoners of the Vietnam War were the hundreds of thousands of civilians arrested, tortured, mutilated, and, in many thousands of cases, killed by the Diem dictatorship and its successors; the atrocities committed by the Saigon regime against its civilian prisoners formed one of the main impetuses to the outbreak of armed struggle, the formation of the National Liberation Front, and, long before American POWs became a public issue, the growth of the American anti-war movement (see pages 46-48). Article 8(c) called on "the two South Vietnamese parties" (the Thieu government and the PRG) to resolve within ninety days "the return of Vietnamese civilian personnel captured and detained in South Viet-Nam" in "a spirit of national reconciliation and concord, with a view to ending hatred and enmity, in order to ease suffering and to reunite families." But Saigon released only a few token groups, such as a contingent of 104, described in this news report: "Their bodies, bearing the marks of irons and chains, are like skeletons. Their legs are paralyzed. They are political prisoners who were released by Saigon authorities at the end of last month from the infamous 'tiger cages' on the island of Con Son."[5]

In the meetings of the four-party military team that was supposed to implement Article 8, U.S. demands for faster implementation of 8(b) were often met by demands from Hanoi and the PRG to implement 8(c). As a U.S. commentator noted at the time, "Hanoi and the PRG wish to bargain about the MIAs, a group of great concern to the United States, for the release of Communist civilian prisoners, a group of even greater concern to themselves." But the United States branded as totally "unrelated" any such discussion of what Roger Shields, deputy assistant secretary of defense and the head of POW/MIA affairs at the Pentagon, euphemistically called "Vietnamese civilian detainees." So the Saigon government kept tens of thousands of these civilian prisoners, simply stonewalling until they were finally liberated by the advancing DRV and PRG armies a few days before the fall of Saigon in April 1975.[6]

VIVA and the National League of Families Continue the War

As soon as the text of the Paris Agreement was made public, VIVA initiated a national campaign to prevent implementation of Article 21 by demanding that Congress not authorize the funds for reconstruction promised by the United States. In early February, VIVA, together with thirteen chapters of the National League of Families and forty-two other POW/MIA organizations, ran full-page advertisements in 140 newspapers exhorting: DON'T TAKE OFF YOUR BRACELET—THERE IS MORE YOU MUST DO! Loyal Americans were now supposed to get a "blue star" (available of course from VIVA) to be "placed on your bracelet if your man is still MIA"; to "Ask your radio station to play 'Wake Up America'—100% of the proceeds from this record, which tells the story everyone should hear, go to the POW-MIA cause"; and to obtain from "your local POW-MIA office" bulk materials to be distributed "to schools, churches, clubs, business establishments." But the highest priority action was: "Wire congress. Demand that not one penny of your tax payers [*sic*] money be spent rebuilding North Vietnam unless they return all our Prisoners."[7] In yet another dizzying reversal, before long many of these same organizations would be accusing Vietnam of withholding prisoners *because* the United States had not carried out its promise to help rebuild Vietnam!

VIVA and the League now worked jointly on lobbying, new publicity gimmicks, and public events. While the League received financial support through services provided by the government, VIVA focused on enrolling key political figures onto its own National Advisory Board, which soon contained 35 percent of the members of Congress, thirteen state governors, and more than five hundred other state and local officials. The elected officials on VIVA's board ranged from Senators Barry Goldwater and Robert Dole to Senators Frank Church and Claiborne Pell, Representative Louis Stokes, and Georgia Governor Jimmy Carter.[8]

In July 1973, another front opened when a small group of family members represented by National League of Families attorney Dermot Foley, himself the brother of a missing Air Force colonel, filed suit to halt the normal process of presumptive findings of death, which had already reduced the MIAs from more than 1,300 to 721. The League itself was now torn by the most bitter recriminations and accusations, often pitting wives who wished to get on with their lives against parents who told them that it was "easier to get a new husband than a new son," while some next of kin who joined in the suit were charged with being motivated by a desire to continue the missing man's pay and benefits, which would be terminated if he were declared dead.[9] In any event, the militant minority represented by Foley was soon locked in a struggle for control of the League. In January, the League's executive director, Scott Albright, himself the father of a missing Air Force officer, sent a letter to the membership warning that this "small minority," in flagrant "violation of the Articles of Incorporation and bylaws," was attempting "to override the majority, usurp the authority of the League, and in fact, take over the League."[10]

Then at the June 1974 national convention of the League in Omaha, VIVA, in alliance with this minority faction, staged what some assert was a coup. Navy Captain Douglas Clarke quotes State Department official David Burgess, a leading authority on the history of the League, as claiming that VIVA "essentially bought out the League at the Omaha meeting," a claim based on the "$20,000 contribution made by VIVA to the League at that time, and the acceptance of the non-family member POW/MIA activists from VIVA into the League's staff and leadership hierarchy. The most notable such transplant was Carol Bates . . . who first went to work as an assistant to the League's Executive Director, ultimately rising to the position of Executive Director." To make room for these non-family militants, the bylaws of the League, which had restricted membership to family members, were modified by a new interpretation to include self-proclaimed "adoptive" family members.[11]

In a 1991 interview, Burgess explained that there also had been other factors working to transform the National League into an agency for militant proselytizing of the faith that Americans were still being held captive in Indochina. According to Burgess, the people who took over the League had "packed the hall" at the Omaha meeting. Some had a political agenda and saw the League as a convenient "vehicle"; a few of these were outright "demagogic." Others had "mercenary" motives. "For some people there was a financial motivation to prevent their guy from being declared KIA," that is keeping the pay and benefits. Some were "private opportunists" with even "mercantile" interests: "the bracelets at one point were a fundraiser but later they became a business." Yet "even the most crassly opportunistic had mixed motives," for there was a widespread feeling among those at the convention against "abandoning" any of the missing.

Another view of the metamorphosis of the League at the Omaha meeting might see it as almost inevitable. Most of the families of returned prisoners no longer had any overwhelming reason to remain active. The families who accepted the loss of their missing men would have strong emotional reasons not to attend. So those who flew to Omaha on government-supplied planes were of course the family members with the most fervent faith that some of the missing might still be alive, while the attendees who were not family members were of course people with some other strong stake in the POW/MIA issue.[12]

The group henceforth controlling the League was, until Ronald Reagan assumed the presidency in 1981, profoundly hostile to the administration, first of Nixon, next of Gerald Ford, and then of Jimmy Carter. So the National League of Families, so carefully nurtured and promoted by the White House and the Pentagon, now transformed into a strident critic and even antagonist of the government. Retired Army Colonel Earl Hopper, executive director of the League from mid-1975 to mid-1976, denounced the public statements on MIAs by both President Nixon and Secretary of State Henry Kissinger as nothing but "obviously deceitful lies," while

retired Air Force Colonel Vincent Donahue testified about Kissinger's "Machiavellian" character.[13] George Brooks, the militant
vicechairman of the League, expressed his anger at one symptom of
the new relationship:

> Our office in the American Legion Building had been equipped with
> Watts [sic] lines because we were cooperating with the Government
> and they were using the POW's as an issue, and so forth. Fine. We
> worked with them and they worked with us. When we came back
> from Omaha, we found out that the telephones had been removed
> from our office.[14]

The antigovernment sentiment within the early postwar National
League had been fed by what David Burgess refers to as "three levels
of lies by the DOD." Two of these were well intentioned: "Concealing the most gruesome facts," and "trying to break the news softly,
which gave wives or parents hope when they shouldn't have had
any." But the third level consisted of "outright lies," part of the
cover-up of the so-called secret wars in Laos and Cambodia.[15]

These wars of course were no secret to the people being attacked,
only to the American people or, rather, to those few Americans still
gullible enough to believe their government's increasingly implausible denials. By mid-1973, the Pentagon was having to publicly
acknowledge its own false accounting, or what it called a "double
accounting system," as reported in this AP story:

21 MORE SECRET U.S. WAR DEAD

> The Pentagon added 21 Americans yesterday to the list of those
> killed in secret missions in Laos and Cambodia during the Indochina
> war, and there may be more. That means there were at least 102
> casualties misreported to Congress as having died in South Vietnam.
> On Wednesday, a Pentagon spokesman disclosed that the families of
> 81 men killed on secret missions in Laos and Cambodia were
> originally told the GIs had died in South Vietnam.[16]

The distrust of the government spawned by these lies would eventually reemerge as full-blown conspiracy theories central to the postwar POW/MIA myth.

In one of VIVA's final acts in 1975, as it was essentially folding itself into the League, it attempted to get a majority of Congress to subscribe to this pledge:

> I agree that any economic assistance, trade or technological aid to North Vietnam, Cambodia, South Vietnam, and Laos should be withheld until we get the return of all POWs and the fullest possible accounting of the missing in action and the return of the remains of those who died in the Vietnam conflict. . . . I agree that the resolution of this tragic issue should be one of our nation's top priorities.[17]

Leading the charge for VIVA and the National League of Families in Congress was Mississippi Representative G. V. "Sonny" Montgomery, recognized as their most ardent advocate. It was Montgomery who in 1975 initiated and became the chair of the Select Committee on Missing Persons in Southeast Asia, to which the House granted an exceptionally wide-ranging mandate. Both VIVA and the National League worked closely with the Select Committee throughout its fifteen-month investigation, and the committee gave special thanks to Carol Bates for all her help just before she became the executive director of the National League of Families in the summer of 1976.[18]

The Pentagon's New Math

Was there any basis for the claims that the DRV, PRG, Pathet Lao, and Khmer Rouge were secretly keeping Americans as prisoners? As soon as the Paris Agreements were signed, the Department of Defense started doing its best to make the American people think so. While the administration was basking in glory for bringing home all the American POWs, the Pentagon was issuing a series of conflicting public statements evidently designed to create not only suspicion but also confusion. Readers of these statements—especially the families of the missing—could hardly avoid thinking that some men might be held captive someplace in Indochina. For in drafting its announcements, the Defense Department was using ink as an octopus does, clouding the waters so as to obscure its own activities.

Here, for example, is what readers of *The New York Times* were encountering from day to day in early 1973:

January 26: "The [Defense] department presently lists 587 prisoners—473 in North Vietnam, 108 in South Vietnam and six in Laos—plus 1,335 more men missing in action. In addition, the State Department . . . believes that 51 American civilians have been captured in Indochina, principally in South Vietnam."

January 28: "The list that the North Vietnamese turned over to American officials in Paris today named 27 American civilians as prisoners of the Vietcong, and listed seven other Americans as having died in captivity."

January 29: "As was expected by the Defense Department, the Communists' total of prisoners is somewhat less than that given by the United States. The Defense Department had listed 591 prisoners—476 in North Vietnam, 109 in South Vietnam and 6 in Laos. The North Vietnamese and Vietcong said that they had captured a total of 610 prisoners but that 55 had died in captivity, leaving 555 to be returned. . . . The Defense Department lists 1,334 men missing in action—519 in North Vietnam, 504 in South Vietnam and 311 in Laos."

January 30: "Fifty-six Americans known to have been prisoners of war in Southeast Asia remain unaccounted for by North Vietnam, a Pentagon spokesman said today. . . . There were no clues to the whereabouts of 1,269 men now listed by the Pentagon as missing in Southeast Asia. . . . [T]he total of all American military prisoners and missing had been revised to 1,935 men—including 555 awaiting release from prison camps in North and South Vietnam, 55 prisoners who died, 56 still unaccounted for and 1,269 carried as missing."

February 1: "North Vietnam turned over to the United States in Paris today the names of nine American prisoners—seven servicemen and two civilians—held by Communist forces in Laos. . . . [T]he Defense Department had reported only six American servicemen captured in Laos. . . . The State Department had listed six civilians as captured or missing in Laos. . . . With the Laotian list, the Communist side has now supplied the names of 591 prisoners—562 military and 29 civilian—that it plans to release under the prisoner exchange. In addition, the Defense Department now lists 1,327 men as missing in action in Indochina. Two of the Americans listed earlier by the Defense Department as prisoners in Laos, for unexplained reasons, turned up on Hanoi's list of prisoners being held in North Vietnam."

February 26: "Fifty-four men who were thought by American officials to be prisoners did not appear on the list of 562 confirmed P.O.W.'s held captive in North and South Vietnam and Laos. Nor were they listed as having died in captivity."[19]

Not having access to the elegant mathematics of the Pentagon's computers, American citizens—not to mention the Vietnamese—would have to resort to simple arithmetic to try to understand what was being revealed, or obfuscated, by these shifting numbers.

Begin with the Defense and State departments' original figures, while bearing in mind that the Nixon administration had been trying for more than three years to establish as high a total as possible of Americans believed to be prisoners. The Pentagon listed 587 servicemen it considered likely to be prisoners—473 in North Vietnam, 108 in South Vietnam, and six in Laos. Add to that the 51 American civilians that the State Department thought were captured throughout Indochina. The total is 638. How many did Vietnam and the Pathet Lao release or otherwise account for as having died in captivity? Here is the total:

• Military prisoners from Vietnam released—555

- Military prisoners from Laos released—7
- Civilian prisoners from Vietnam released—27
- Civilian prisoners from Laos released—2
- Military prisoners died in captivity—55
- Civilian prisoners died in captivity—7

- Total prisoners released or died—653

So Vietnam and the Pathet Lao actually released or accounted for 15 *more* prisoners than the Defense and State departments had listed as likely prisoners, even though both agencies had attempted to inflate their figures! (Note also that the State Department's figure included civilians believed to have been captured in Cambodia.) The figures for Laos, which would play a key role in the postwar POW/MIA myth, were especially embarrassing for the Pentagon, which had listed six men thought to be prisoners there. Seven military prisoners were returned from Laos, and in addition two of the six supposed Laotian military prisoners were actually in the hands of the Vietnamese; instead of the six on the Pentagon's list of Laotian POWs, it actually got back nine.

If the Pentagon's accounting could be off by more than a dozen, it is no surprise that the other side, especially the guerrilla movements in South Vietnam and Laos, did not have an accurate and complete record of every single man captured at some time during the many years of this tangled war. There were indeed a few cases—very few—of prisoners they had previously reported for whom no accounting was available. These—particularly David Hrdlicka, Charles Shelton, Eugene DeBruin, who were all captured in Laos between 1963 and 1965 (see pages 29–30), and Ron Dodge, whose body was later returned by Vietnam—would be used over and over again to construct the postwar POW/MIA myth.

But what was truly remarkable about the accounting of American

POWs was how closely each side's list correlated with that of the other. In no previous major war had one belligerent been able to tabulate and identify within a few dozen the total prisoners held by its opponent. This unprecedented accounting offered a shocking contrast to the hundreds of thousands missing from the other side, many of whom had been cremated in huge piles or bulldozed into mass graves.

Roger Shields, the Defense Department's man in charge of POW/ MIA affairs from 1971 through 1976 (including management of Operation Homecoming), is praised by even the most messianic propagators of the POW/MIA myth.[20] Yet Shields himself acknowledged on April 12, 1973, that the Pentagon had absolutely no evidence that there were more prisoners still alive anywhere in Indochina and that none of the missing in action were any longer considered to be prisoners.[21]

Yet at the same time the Defense Department was already charging that the Vietnamese and the Pathet Lao were not adequately accounting for all their American prisoners. In addition to the old political motives, the Pentagon may have had another goal: what is called inside the Pentagon a CYA ("cover your ass") operation. For the Defense Department might have even been attempting to divert attention from the embarrassing fact that 15 more prisoners were being released than it had claimed were being held. Who can tell while the Pentagon continues to cover all its actions and records about the POW/MIA issue under shrouds of secrecy invoked in the name of "national security"?

Certainly the Pentagon's numbers games continued to become more baffling. In 1976, as the House Select Committee on Americans Missing in Southeast Asia tried to penetrate the labyrinth of the government's accounting, Roger Shields summarized the official figures in testimony that seems thoroughly incomprehensible—except as an attempt to cast the most favorable light on the Pentagon while blinding anyone trying to make sense out of what he is saying:

With respect to the other side, their final rosters listed 566 military, 25 U.S. civilians and 9 third country nationals, including 2 military and 1 civilian in China, to be repatriated. The Democratic Republic of Vietnam (DRV) and the Provisional Revolutionary Government (PRG) listed 55 servicemen as having died in captivity. These rosters provided the first specific information regarding 52 servicemen to be repatriated whom the services had previously listed as missing in action. It was interesting to note that 36 of these men were lost in late 1972 and early 1973.

To look at these statistics in another way, at the time of the prisoner repatriations, the services carried 593 servicemen as prisoners of war. The other side listed 513 of these as prisoners and 27 as having died in captivity, for a total of 540. This left 53 for whom there was no accounting by the other side. In other words, the services determined the actual classification with an accuracy of 91 percent.[22]

According to Shields, the Pentagon in late January 1973 had listed 593 servicemen (civilians are not counted in the Defense Department figures) as POWs (as opposed to the 587 it had actually reported on January 26 of that year or the 591 on January 29). If so, and the other side repatriated 566 servicemen and listed 55 as having died in captivity, then they returned or otherwise accounted for 621, which is 28 *more* military prisoners than the Pentagon believed they held. If 53 men listed by the Pentagon as POWs were not accounted for, and if the other side returned 52 men that the Pentagon did not list as POWs, then the net difference in raw totals should have been not +28 but -1 (the 52 not listed but returned minus the 53 listed but not accounted for). With mathematics like these, the Pentagon seems to be in no position to charge the other side with "discrepancies."

Of course the Defense Department's evident inability to add and subtract does not resolve the question of those 53 unaccounted for men that it claimed to list as prisoners. Though slightly lower than the 56 "known" to have been prisoners on January 30, 1973, or the 54 "thought" to have been prisoners on February 26, this figure of

53 "discrepancies" soon became a talisman of the early postwar POW/MIA faith.

The Case of the Disappearing POWs

The House Select Committee, although it carefully reviewed the individual files of two hundred other unresolved MIA cases, scrutinized most intensely precisely such "discrepancies," that is, the cases of unaccounted for men actually listed by the various services as POWs. How many of these were there? It turns out that the number of cases classified as POW was not 56, 54, or even 53, but 36.

Thirty-six was the number presented by the Defense and State Departments. Thirty-six was the number accepted not only by the Select Committee but also by the National League of Families (which by this time was controlled by activists committed to the POW/MIA issue). E. C. "Bus" Mills, then chairman of the League's board of directors (and father of Ann Mills Griffiths, who would play an increasingly prominent role), explicitly stated that the National League of Families considered "each of the 36" to be "a discrepancy that we would hope you would look into" and promised information on each from the League itself.[23]

The committee heard Roger Shields testify that some of these 36 "classifications of prisoner of war were made upon what we know now was erroneous information," and it soon learned from official Pentagon testimony that "at least 12" of the 36 "should not have been classified as POW," that, in fact, there were "less than 20 hard cases in all Southeast Asia."[24] After Shields admitted that for North Vietnam, "we are talking probably about two or three," Chairman Montgomery—who, remember, had been the member of Congress most vociferous in claiming that there were live POWs still in Indochina—grew increasingly agitated, as evident in this revealing exchange:

THE CHAIRMAN. In Laos?

DR. SHIELDS. In Laos, I think we are talking about one man that we know for sure. Another man where the evidence was—two men; one was a civilian, but we heard some negative information on him later. One man, an Air Force officer, who was captured.

THE CHAIRMAN. Less than five in Laos, too?

DR. SHIELDS. Yes.

THE CHAIRMAN. South Vietnam, just a handful again. Just a handful again.*

THE CHAIRMAN. Cambodia?

DR. SHIELDS. Probably some civilians, journalists in Cambodia, and again a handful at most, in which we have not had subsequent information that they died.[25]

The committee conducted an exhaustive study of each of the 36 cases of the men believed to have been captured. This included a thorough analysis of the complete classified case file maintained by each man's own service (Navy, Air Force, Army, Marines) followed by an intensive cross-check with the classified intelligence file maintained by the Defense Intelligence Agency. In addition to this, they heard relevant testimony, some in public and some in executive session, about a number of the cases, including testimony from people who later became prominent figures in promulgating the POW/MIA myth. Their two principal conclusions, which were spelled out with supporting evidence and analysis in the committee's Final Report, are here summarized.

---

* Evidently there is an error in transcription, which leaves the chairman answering his own question about South Vietnam when it was probably Shields who said at least one "Just a handful again."

Nine of the 36 should definitely never have been classified as POW in the first place. One example was an Air Force pilot: "Ejected at high speed at near-ground level and an inert form was reported by eyewitnesses under the parachute on the ground. A rallier since reported a similar incident (believed to correlate) in which the pilot was found dead. This officer was reported by the Vietnamese on September 6, 1976, to have died during his attack on North Vietnam (1965)." The committee was especially critical of the Navy, which "had employed extremely optimistic standards for declaring that a downed aviator was captured. Generally if a pilot parachuted and either waved during his descent or activated his emergency radio 'beeper,' the Navy considered him to be a POW."

More important, however, was the committee's independent evaluation of the then current status of these 36 cases based on all available information. For 15, the committee could find no evidence that the men had been taken alive. Eight of the remaining could have been "possibly" captured alive and 11, 12, or 13 had been at one time "definitely" alive in enemy hands. Of crucial importance were the committee's findings about those 11, 12, or 13 who were indeed known to have been captured:

> In six cases, reports from indigenous sources indicate that the individual died in captivity. Another one was reported in 1973, both by the PRG and by returnees, as having died in captivity in 1967, but for technical reasons his case has not been reviewed. Still another defected to the Viet Cong in 1967, and he could still be alive in Vietnam. There is no evidence in the remaining four cases to suggest whether the individual is now dead or alive, but in no case did any of these four appear in a regular POW camp, and all have been missing for at least 6 years.[26]

This handful of cases is the foundation upon which the whole colossal structure of the POW/MIA myth has been built!

So there were not 56 or 54 or 53 unaccounted for POWs. There were not even 36 or 27 or 20. At the most there were 13 or 12 or 11.

Except for the defector, all but four of these had evidently died in captivity. None of these four had ever appeared in a regular POW camp and there is no evidence that any survived later than 1970.

The Multiplication of the POWs

Of course the POW/MIA faith does not envision a mere four, 11, 12, 13, 20, 27, or 36 American prisoners. Even the old figure of 53 has been subject to hyperinflation. The mathematics of the myth-makers has gone far beyond the strange addition and subtraction of the Pentagon to multiplication constrained only by the limits of imagination.

Parade, the Sunday magazine newspaper insert read by tens of millions of Americans, in 1981 doubled the Defense Department's original number of 56: "When the war ended . . . an additional 113 men, also known to have been held captive in Laos and Vietnam, were not released during 'Operation Homecoming.'" A recent book designed for high school and junior high school readers claims that it is "possible that 644 men are still alive" but, assuming an impartial tone, also cites lower estimates of "around 300" or "at least 100." An influential 1981 article in *National Review* quoted a recently deceased congressional representative: "[O]ver half of these (2,500 MIAs) are men who were either known or strongly suspected to be prisoners of the Vietnamese or Laotians. There are 138 Americans whose names, picture, or even their voices were used by the Vietnamese for propaganda purposes. As many as 750 more were probably in their custody." In 1983, ex-Representative John LeBoutillier initiated a heavily financed national campaign called Skyhook II Project, whose national mailings told how "as many as 253 American prisoners of war yet remain to be rescued. . . . Starved and clad only in filthy rags, American soldiers and airmen are kept chained in tiny bamboo cages . . . made to work like animals pulling heavy plows . . . forced to toil from daybreak to nightfall in steaming tropical heat." (For a sufficient donation, LeBoutillier would send correspondents this message as recorded by Charlton Heston.) By 1990, the authors of the widely circulated book *Kiss the Boys Goodbye* could claim without any evident embarrassment that at least 371 American POWS were withheld by Laos and more than a thousand were kept by Vietnam:

> So where were the 371 and possibly more men known by the U.S. government to have been captured in Laos? . . . Missing from the group of men who were returned by the North Vietnamese were over fifty men known by the U.S. government to have been captured and held prisoner at one time or another. Beyond that there was a large number of men suspected of having been captured by the North Vietnamese. Many returning prisoners had seen such men being taken captive or displayed to Vietnamese villagers, but they had never been seen in the prison system. . . . the U.S. government had a list of over one thousand such men—a list that included detailed knowledge of their capture, physical condition, and whereabouts until 1975, when Saigon fell.[27]

So according to this recent version of the myth, of the 1,335 or 1,334 or 1,327 or 1,325 that the United States listed as still missing in action after Operation Homecoming (the various official figures then publicly released), or of the 1,184 still listed by the Defense Department in 1990 as POW/MIA (though all but one of these had actually been reclassified as presumed dead), at least 1,371 were actually kept as prisoners by Laos and North Vietnam alone.

This new math all depends on another layer of confusion precipitated by the Pentagon in early 1973, which has become steadily thicker and more impenetrable ever since. If the United States listed only 1,335 missing in action in January 1973, when and how did it become customary to speak of "2,500 MIAs," as in the 1981 *National Review* article? In May 1973, the Pentagon nearly doubled its list of unaccounted for men supplied to the DRV and PRG by adding to its previous total of slightly more than 1,300 MIAs another 1,114 names of men who were *known* to have been killed but whose bodies had not been recovered (the KIA/BNR category, discussed on pages 11–13).

This might be considered a perfectly reasonable and legitimate procedure, simply part of the effort to recover the remains of the dead as specified in Article 8(b), except for a revealing fact. Of these 1,114 names of dead men submitted to the DRV and PRG, 781 were cases about which the Vietnamese could not possibly have any useful information: 436 were men whose remains were known to be unrecoverable, mainly because they had been lost at sea or in planes that exploded in midair; 345 were men lost under "non-hostile conditions, generally in areas in which no enemy forces were known to be operating."[28] If the government had been sincerely wanting assistance in recovering the dead, it would have simplified the tasks it was asking of the Vietnamese rather than giving them an obviously impossible job. As the Select Committee concluded:

> Listing cases for which no accounting can be expected erodes the credibility of the United States data base. Surely the Vietnamese must be confused. Worse, it may appear to the Indochinese leaders that the United States has deliberately requested information which they cannot furnish in order to embarrass them or to prevent meaningful talks.[29]

Even worse were the effects on America of the newly inflated figures. After all, these numbers games could hardly confuse or deceive the Vietnamese as successfully as they could the American people. First, expanding the traditional category of MIA into the ambiguous novel concept "POW/MIA" aroused the unfounded belief that any missing person might be a prisoner. Next, when more than a thousand missing bodies were added, the boundaries of this new POW/MIA category were thereby dissolved into a far larger and even more misleading catchall of "unaccounted for." From then on, even 1,114 of the known dead from the Vietnam War could be numbered among those imagined still as captives.

So by the mid 1980s, the numbers of imagined POWs in popular culture had expanded from the original dozens through the hundreds to the thousands. For example, the 1986 Bantam mass-market paperback novel *The M.I.A. Ransom* by Mike McQuay has Vietnam sometime in the future broadcasting this message to the United States:

> The People's Republic of Vietnam is holding a total of 2,045 prisoners of the imperialist war that the American Government waged against the free peoples of Vietnam. These prisoners will be held for a total of seven days, until noon, Sunday, April 19. They will be held until reparations for the damage they have done to our country have been made. The reparations will total one million U.S. dollars in gold per man. If these reparations have not been made by the above-stated date and time, these prisoners of expansionist war will be tried as criminals and executed if they are found guilty. (p. 8)

What *Did* Happen to the Missing Men?

To answer this question, it is necessary to remember the two unique features of the missing in action from the Indochina wars:

1. The number of servicemen missing in action from America's decades of war in Indochina is extraordinarily small in comparison with the missing from any other war in the nation's history.

2. More than 81 percent of the missing were downed airmen.

So the question really boils down to another one: What was the likely fate of an airman lost in flight? That of course depends on the circumstances of loss. For some, there would be no hope of survival. This would include crews of planes that exploded in flight before the crew had an opportunity to escape or even communicate. Those who have never witnessed the fireball that can without any warning envelop a modern airplane may not appreciate how thoroughly and instantaneously the crew and any knowledge of their fate can be annihilated. Obviously, hostile fire or missiles could cause such an explosion, as could even an unsuspected mechanical problem. For example, in April 1958, when I was a navigator in the Strategic Air Command, a B-47 burst into two fireballs right behind my own plane so suddenly that death cut off in mid-sentence its aircraft commander's routine reply to my course correction. The cause of the explosion, which was found only after three more B-47s blew up that week, was metal fatigue in the center-wing section, produced by stress and resulting in immediate rupture and ignition of the fuel lines.[30]

Another kind of hopeless loss occurred in planes that crashed at extremely high speeds before the crew could escape. This included not only planes shot down but also a number that crashed without warning, for example by collision with the gigantic karst outcroppings of Laos, and some that flew directly into the ground because of target fixation.

How such hopeless losses were reported depended on other circumstances. If nobody observed the loss, the men would be reported as missing in action. If the loss was observed, usually—but not always—the crew would be reported as KIA/BNR. Navy Lieutenant Commander George Coker, a fighter pilot released in Operation Homecoming, explained, in a lengthy and illuminating 1973 presentation to the National League of Families, several reasons why some pilots would give a report that would lead to a false MIA classification. Here are just two:

> A guy is flying, he does see his wingman shot down. Two guys go in, and they're deader than a doornail. He's thinking to himself, "If I report that they're dead, the wife's going to be brokenhearted, she'll get death gratuities, and that's it. If I report him MIA, his pay keeps going, and it will cushion the blow for a little while."

> I just saw your son fly into the ground. Do you think I'm going to tell you that? Hell, no, because the way I think, if I tell you your son got target fixation and flew into the ground, to my way of thinking, what

I would be saying to you is, "You know, what you had for a son is a real idiot." That's not true, so what am I going to say? "Well, he flew down, and he probably lost control, he was probably hit by a 57 or something and lost control of the aircraft and went in." But I'm not going to say, "I think he had target fixation." . . . So what are we going to do? We're going to twist the report. But now I've given you a shred of hope. It's not an out-and-out false report. I told you he flew into the ground, but I just twisted "why." So now he has the option of ejecting.[31]

The vast majority of airmen originally categorized as POW/MIA were in fact lost in such hopeless situations. More than three-fourths of the missing airmen actually went down with their aircraft. An exhaustive study prepared by the Joint Casualty Resolution Center revealed that in the entire Indochina war only 179 of the missing airmen were known to have ejected from their planes.[32]

These are the airmen who might have survived the loss of their plane. But then what? To evaluate the likelihood of survival in North Vietnam, South Vietnam, and Laos, one must grasp a crucial fact: any airman surviving a high-speed ejection and parachuting under combat conditions had a very high probability of being injured. An Air Force study of the returning POWs disclosed that a mere 20 percent had escaped injury prior to capture.[33] And these, remember, were the survivors. A number of others who ejected over North Vietnam are known to have died from their injuries before or after capture. In the extremely harsh natural conditions into which downed airmen parachuted, any untreated injury, no matter how minor, was likely to prove fatal. Any open wound, even a relatively slight one, invited deadly infection. Typically the surviving airmen suffered much more serious traumas, including broken bones or internal injuries. So unless medical care was provided quite soon, they would probably be doomed. Hence their only hope for survival was either rescue or capture, which indeed was often a form of rescue—if the captors had adequate medical care available.

With this in mind, one can easily understand why it is so exceedingly unlikely that any of the missing airmen could have survived for very long. In South Vietnam and Laos, where the United States had total control of the air and considerable ability to suppress antiaircraft fire, any airman reported to be downed had an excellent chance of being rescued and of receiving immediate high-quality medical care. In these two regions combined, the extraordinary efficiency of search and rescue operations, together with swift flight to modern medical facilities, in fact resulted in the rescue and survival of 66.2 percent of *all* downed airmen.[34]

Another 14.7 percent of the downed airmen either returned alive from captivity or were known to have died. The remaining 19.1 percent were those originally classified as MIA. These included all those who: disappeared without a trace; went down with their planes; were unconscious or too gravely wounded to activate the radio that directed search and rescue; or fell into the hands of guerrilla units with few or no antibiotics and other medical facilities. Only those in the last group had any chance to survive. But at least 80 percent of them would have been injured before their capture, drastically reducing the possibility that they could have survived for long. And for the hypothetical remaining handful, their life expectancy would be sharply curtailed by malnutrition, dysentery, malaria, intestinal parasites, and a host of deadly endemic tropical diseases such as melioidosis, a bloodstream infection with a fatality rate of 50 percent for untreated cases, not to mention constant threats of U.S. aerial attack by high explosives, rockets, machine guns, cluster bombs, and napalm.

In North Vietnam, where search and rescue operations were hampered by potent antiaircraft defenses, a mere 14.6 percent of downed airmen were rescued by U.S. forces. Amid these fierce defenses, the chances of surviving ejection and parachuting were vastly reduced. And since the population was enraged by the bombing of their country, many of the surviving POWs told of being barely rescued from furious peasants or villagers by soldiers or militia. The systematic targeting of hospitals, as part of the planned destruction of North Vietnam's medical infrastructure, posed still another threat to the downed airmen's survival, for little remained of the medical facilities necessary to treat their injuries.[35] The few intact X-ray machines, which were necessary to treat airmen's shrapnel wounds and broken bones, were already in constant use by surgeons treating wounded civilians, which often involved trying to extract numerous metal fragments from victims of cluster bombs. Antibiotics and intravenous equipment were extremely scarce, medical personnel were working beyond their capacity, and sanitary conditions were so poor that any wound could easily become fatal.

One of the most vicious arguments repeated ad nauseam by proselytizers of the POW/MIA myth alleges that the Vietnamese had a

cruelly bizarre rationale for retaining prisoners . . . [which] becomes less incredible when one considers this fact: of the 591 Americans who were repatriated, *not one* was maimed. Consider it: men ejecting from flaming, exploding aircraft, under missile fire, parachuting into hostile territory: yet not one of these returned to us was missing an eye, an ear, an arm, or a leg—even a finger—and none was disfigured by burns. Common sense tells us that *some* of those captured had to be disfigured. Yet might not Vietnamese paranoia prevent them from repatriating those who had been maimed—whether during combat or torture?[36]

Although this is not quite true—a number of the returning POWs had severe burns, missing digits, and other disfiguring wounds that had been treated by the Vietnamese—the absence of amputees is hardly surprising. A less sinister, but more anguishing, explanation was given by someone drawing not on a sick imagination but on his own experience as a surviving POW:

Why are there no amputees? There's no way in hell an amputee could live. No way. To do it would take an absolute miracle. Not because of loss of blood; not because they didn't get medical attention; they could do everything in the world for him, and nearly everything else in the world being equal, he would live, but infection is going to kill him. I would not even look for an amputee.[37]

Nevertheless, as the POW/MIA myth began to be shaped by propaganda bent on totally demonizing the Vietnamese, the lack of amputees among the surviving POWs became a source for the most grotesque images and implausible explanations of American captives left behind. An influential example is J. C. Pollock's best-selling 1982 novel *Mission M.I.A.*, which comes with an introduction from retired right-wing General John Singlaub and a blurb from Ann Mills Griffiths as executive director of the National League of Families. The hero, an ex-Green Beret who has just returned from fighting as a mercenary for Rhodesia's white supremacist regime, leads a raid by his former buddies to rescue American POWs enduring the vilest tortures of the Vietnamese fiends. After freeing the surviving POWs in a jungle camp and wiping out the whole garrison of a Vietnamese army base, our hero and his superwarriors discover hidden amputees sitting "in puddles of urine and on cement floors smeared with human excrement." Typical is this man: "His face had been badly burned and obviously left to heal without treatment. His right leg had been amputated above the knee, and a long flap of skin trailed the stump as he dragged it behind him." Worse still, the rescuers realize that the seven amputees they have found are the only survivors, for they also discover seven hundred coffins of similar maimed POWs who died after the war was over. Their rage leads to a righteous killing frenzy in which they slaughter hordes of the subhuman Vietnamese, thus inciting the audience of the 1980s to what must be done while any American POWs still survive. Readers of course are not supposed to ask what rational motive the Vietnamese might have for keeping these "mutilated living skeletons" as prisoners for years, because the whole point is that Asian Communists, particularly the Vietnamese variety, are by nature unfathomably vicious.[38]

The miracle is that despite its overwhelming problems, North Vietnam was willing and able to provide enough of its pitiful medical resources to preserve the lives of hundreds of men captured while devastating their country, 80 percent of whom were injured before their apprehension. Most of the returnees received both emergency and routine dental and medical treatment, including immunizations for cholera, typhoid, and polio, and a number had X-ray examinations from the few remaining machines, successful operations, and treatment from North Vietnam's tiny precious inventory of antibiotics. Although primitive compared with U.S. combat medicine, the health care may have been superior to what was available to the general population in Vietnam.[39] While their living conditions were far worse than what they were accustomed to, and though many were tortured during the height of the bombing in the late 1960s, who would choose to exchange their fate with that of Vietnamese captured by U.S. forces, many thousands of whom were tortured to death and tens of thousands of whom are still numbered among the missing? What is surprising is how many, not how few, Americans shot down over North Vietnam were returned, and it is grotesque to use their relatively good health as an argument for Vietnam continuing to hold American captives.

Cambodia

The official United States position that "only the communist governments of Indochina know the answer" to the question "Are Americans still held captive in Indochina?"[40] is patently absurd when applied to Cambodia. During Operation Homecoming, Vietnam released 47 prisoners, all held by Vietnamese forces, who had been either captured or at one time detained in Cambodia. The United States persisted in holding North Vietnam responsible for all other Americans missing in Cambodia,[41] a stance that was either a willful or ignorant refusal to understand that the Khmer Rouge, far from being a puppet of the Vietnamese, were already close to being their enemy.

U.S. "secret" bombing continued to devastate Cambodia for more than half a year after the 1973 Paris Peace Agreements, leading to additional American MIAs. Then in May 1975, President Ford ordered land, sea, and air attacks on Cambodia, ostensibly to rescue the 39 crewmen of the freighter *Mayaguez* (who had already been released), resulting in the loss of 40 U.S. servicemen, including 18 new MIAs.[42] The administration seemed unaware that a major island war was now raging between Vietnam and the Khmer Rouge government of Cambodia.[43]

By the time of the House Select Committee's Final Report in late 1976, 82 Americans (75 servicemen and seven civilians) were listed as either POW/MIA or KIA/BNR in Cambodia. The committee described the total absence of any cooperation by the Cambodian government—during that period, the Khmer Rouge—in efforts to secure an accounting.[44] This stonewalling by the Khmer Rouge continued at least through 1990. In July of that year, the Defense Department listed 83 unaccounted for in Cambodia (37 POW/MIA and 46 KIA/BNR); this included the 18 missing from the *Mayaguez* escapade, 15 of whom were lost at sea, as well as "two Americans who died after being detained by Pol Pot forces in 1975."[45]

If there were any Americans held by the Khmer Rouge in the early and mid-1970s, it is almost inconceivable that any would have survived the wholesale slaughter that ensued. After all, if Pol Pot's Khmer Rouge thought it proper to murder at least hundreds of thousands of their fellow Cambodians, why would they spare any American captives? As the *Final Interagency Report of the Reagan Administration on the POW/MIA Issue in Southeast Asia* was forced to acknowledge in 1989: "It is highly doubtful that the current leadership in Phnom Penh [the government that had replaced and was continuing to fight the Khmer Rouge] can provide significant accountability unless information recovered by others was provided to them. A small number of American civilians who reportedly died at the hands of the Pol Pot regime may appear in records of that era."[46]

Nowhere else, then, does the hypocrisy and cynicism of U.S. government policy on the MIA question stand so nakedly exposed. The United States into the 1990s recognized the Khmer Rouge and its allies as the legitimate government of Cambodia and even lobbied mightily to make sure that they retain Cambodia's seat in the United Nations, despite the refusal of the Khmer Rouge to give any accounting of American MIAs and their likely murder of any American prisoners in their hands. Yet at the same time the United States has refused to normalize relations with Vietnam, which has returned all U.S. prisoners it acknowledged holding and which certainly has cooperated to some extent in attempts to account for the missing. The two ostensible reasons for this policy are Vietnam's alleged failure to give an acceptable accounting and its "invasion" of Cambodia, that is, its war against the Khmer Rouge. And, going a step further in its preposterous logic, the United States demands that the present government of Cambodia—which it refuses to recognize—provide the accounting that only the Khmer Rouge could be expected to give, while the Khmer Rouge, in tacit alliance with the United States, continually attempt to overthrow that government.

Despite all this, the government of Cambodia informed the National League of Families in 1987 that it believed it had located the remains of some missing Americans and in 1990 permitted a U.S. military team to enter the country to try to identify them. After examining 28 sets of remains, the U.S. forensic experts determined that six might be those of American MIAs. In late July 1990 the remains of these six were repatriated to the United States after their coffins were blessed by Buddhist monks at the Phnom Penh airport, but subsequent scientific analysis disclosed that none was an American.[47] If some day any remains of missing Americans are discovered in Cambodia they will form only one grisly detail in the tragedy wrought upon that land by U.S. intervention.

Laos

Operation Homecoming in early 1973 did much to shatter the notion that Vietnam was furtively holding additional American prisoners. Intensive debriefing of the repatriated American POWs, as well as interrogation of tens of thousands of returning South Vietnamese POWs, revealed no evidence whatsoever of any further American captives in Vietnam.

Without ever admitting this, VIVA began shifting the main emphasis of its campaign to Laos. In May, its full-page national advertisements proclaimed *"No prisoners have been released from Laos."* [48] This gross misrepresentation has been used over and over not only to construct the postwar POW/MIA myth but also to provide a scene for dramatic action—first in reality and then in movies.

As noted earlier, although the Pentagon had listed only six servicemen as probable POWs in Laos, seven servicemen and two civilians who had been captured in Laos were released as part of Operation Homecoming along with two others on the Pentagon's list of six probable Laotian prisoners who had actually been captured in Vietnam. VIVA tried to explain this problem away in a devious argument that has been emulated by POW/MIA proselytizers ever since: "The communists pretended to meet the terms of the Peace Treaty by releasing a separate list of 10 prisoners, whom [*sic*] they maintained were from Laos. With the exception of one man who was held in South Vietnam, these so-called Laotian releases were all men who were held in North Vietnam." [49] This argument has two separate, equally treacherous components.

Why would Vietnam pretend to be releasing prisoners from Laos? Because, according to the VIVA ad, "the most heralded aspect of the Peace Treaty was that North Vietnam promised the release of all American prisoners in Southeast Asia." This is another blatant misrepresentation, for the DRV and PRG of course never agreed to release any prisoners except their own. Nevertheless, it has helped to foster the vendetta waged by the U.S. government and encouraged by POW/MIA believers against Vietnam, which is somehow held responsible for the alleged failure of the government of Laos to return or account for supposed prisoners of the Pathet Lao. Consummating this inscrutable logic, the United States recognizes and maintains diplomatic relations with Laos while refusing to normalize relations with Vietnam.

Though it is true that all the prisoners from Laos were "held" in Vietnam, each was in fact captured in Laos, and some were briefly prisoners of the Pathet Lao, who turned them over to the Vietnamese.[50] It is no doubt their good fortune that they were taken to regular prison facilities in Vietnam rather than being kept in Laotian jungle camps. Whether they were captured by Vietnamese or Lao might seem to be of little consequence, except that an increasingly important article of faith in the POW/MIA myth is that no prisoner of the Lao has ever been released. Why this focus on Laos? Because as it became evident how implausible and improbable it was that there were prisoners still in Vietnam, the believers found it necessary—as in three-card monte or the old shell game—to show that they might be somewhere else. Laos was especially convenient because most Americans know so little about that nation and what actually did happen to the majority of airmen downed there.

Here are some representative examples of forms of the Laos myth as formulated since 1983. The first two are from men who risked their lives believing that they were rescuing American POWs from Laos; the third is from a 1987 *Life* cover story; the fourth is from a popular 1990 book:

1. "More than 700 servicemen went down in Laos, and not one of them has been heard from since."

2. "It is a fact that no live U.S. POWs have ever been returned from Laos and Cambodia."

3. "In fact, several hundred servicemen were held in Laos at the war's end—none of whom has returned."

4. "No single prisoner captured by the Pathet Lao was ever released . . . . So where were the 371 and possibly more men known by the U.S. government to have been captured by the Pathet Lao?"[51]

When one first encounters the argument about Laos it seems plausible, even if one knows that actually nine men captured there were released during Operation Homecoming and that Emmett Kay, a CIA pilot captured by the Pathet Lao in May 1973, was released by the Pathet Lao in 1974. After all, what happened to all those other hundreds of airmen shot down over Laos in America's long "secret" war there? Why did none of them survive?

The fact is that many did survive, but not as prisoners. Indeed, airmen shot down over Laos had a *higher*, not a lower, survival rate than those shot down over North Vietnam. According to official Pentagon figures, of the 1,394 airmen downed over North Vietnam, 676 (48.5 percent) returned alive, whereas of the 1,290 downed over Laos, 778 (60.3 percent) returned alive, not even counting those released during and after Operation Homecoming.[52]

What accounts for this survival rate is the extraordinary performance of search and rescue operations. An airman downed in Laos who was not severely injured and who either was observed by other fliers or was able, after ejecting, to activate the small radio he carried had a high probability of being rescued. More than 60 percent of all airmen downed over Laos were in fact rescued. But for those who were not, the chances of survival were exceedingly slim.

Remember that for the entire Indochina war, only 179 missing airmen are believed to have ejected. Of the *surviving* POWs from North Vietnam, only 20 percent had escaped injury prior to their capture. The likelihood of ending up uninjured on the ground after parachuting into Laos was even lower. Anyone landing in the mountains would have to escape its treacherous cliffs and would still likely be battered by the rugged, jagged karst outcroppings. The odds were at least as bad for anyone trying to penetrate the triple canopy of the rain forest, so thick that it sometimes kept high-explosive bombs from reaching the ground. There was little possibility that an injured man could survive in the harsh conditions of Laos, where the average life expectancy then was 33 years and even the most rudimentary medical care was rarely available. Even an uninjured man had little chance of lasting very long alone in the Laotian jungles and mountains, and so unless he were rescued his only hope—contrary to the POW/MIA myth—would be capture. But unfortunately the possibility of capture was quite remote, because most of the terrain where airmen were lost was virtually uninhabited. (The population density of all of Laos was then a mere 34 per square mile, compared with 388 per square mile in North Vietnam.) As Lieutenant Commander George Coker, a former POW, put it while explaining the realities of Laos to the National League of Families, "You're going to say suddenly the likelihood of a POW in Laos is near zero."[53]

Yet there are other reasons why Laos has continued to play an important part in the POW/MIA myth. One, discussed earlier (see page 86), was the elaborate cover-up of the so-called secret war that the United States waged there for well over a decade. The House Select Committee described the effects of this concealment on the POW/MIA issue in these terms:

> Under constraints from the executive branch of the government, the Department of Defense was prohibited from admitting that American armed services were engaged in military operations in Laos. Whatever the other consequences for the American public, the so-called "secret war" in Laos had a profound impact on the POW/MIA issue and the next of kin of missing Americans. The Defense Department was put in a position where, deliberately and intentionally, it

had to falsify reports and information conveyed to the next of kin. Coordinates of loss had to be fabricated to show that pilots were lost in different locations over North or South Vietnam.

Inevitably there were inconsistencies. Continued falsification could not withstand the pressure of close scrutiny. Pressed by family members to explain discrepancies in reports of their missing relatives, service spokesmen could only retreat into vagueness and obscurantism.

When the secret war in Laos became public knowledge, some next of kin discovered, to their utter dismay, that the services they had trusted for accurate information had been misleading them, in some cases for years. The disillusionment was profound.[54]

Even this analysis understates both the absurdity and the consequences of the government's falsifications.

Anyone who read a major daily newspaper was aware of the intense air war on Laos, and many of the missing men's wives already knew that Laos was their husbands' principal assignment.[55] As early as 1967, media around the world were carrying this UPI dispatch: "The U.S. Air Force officially confirmed yesterday that it is bombing Communist targets in neutral Laos on a daily basis and has been doing so for more than three years." By 1968, a typical daily newspaper story, headlined THE AIR FORCE'S WAR OVER LAOS—OPEN "SECRET," noted that the intense bombing of Laos "is a 'secret' only to American diplomats," who have perpetrated "one of the most outrageous fibs of the war" that among the airmen in Thailand has become "the source of much comedy at squadron bars."[56] So having lost faith in the honesty of the Pentagon and unable to fathom the apparent senselessness of its deceptions, many family members and others wondered after the war not only whether there was still some cover-up about the missing men but also why.

One answer was indirectly suggested by a book that appeared just before the end of the war, Alfred W. McCoy's 1972 *The Politics of Heroin in Southeast Asia.* McCoy revealed that U.S. involvement in Indochina had from the beginning been intertwined with opium and heroin and that Laos in particular was the scene of a vast, intricate involvement of U.S. agencies in the international drug trade. When some of the most dedicated advocates of the POW/ MIA myth rediscovered *The Politics of Heroin* in the late 1980s and when they learned that the CIA had conducted a successful campaign to discredit McCoy's book, Laos suddenly became crucial to a view of MIAs that would have horrified the originators of the POW/MIA issue.[57]

Vietnam: Or What the Garwood Case Really Shows

By 1976, it had become clear that there was simply no credible evidence that Vietnam was holding any American prisoners of war. Extensive data did indicate, however, that one particular former POW might quite likely still be living in the country.

When the House Select Committee scrutinized all 36 cases of men missing throughout the Indochina war and still carried as POWs by the Pentagon, they discovered that there had been evidence of capture for only 11. Of these, six were known to have died, and there was no evidence that four of the others had survived later than 1969. The committee concluded that the remaining one "could still be alive in Vietnam." Although the committee never named this man, he is clearly identified in their Final Report:

> One American, captured in 1965, was known to have collaborated with the enemy from 1967 to 1969, and perhaps until as late as August 1973. (p. 26)
> . . . a Marine enlisted man was captured by enemy forces in 1965. Evidence shows that in 1967, when he was offered his release, he elected to remain with the Viet Cong. The defector was observed by American captives and was seen to bear arms with the enemy, and to participate in interrogation of other American prisoners of war. The records show that he was promoted to lieutenant in the Viet Cong forces. (p. 193)

Perhaps there is no greater testimonial to the work of the House Select Committee than the fact that this very man, the only POW they thought might still be alive, is the only POW or MIA who has turned out to be alive.

This is also a testimonial to the highly regarded "memory bank" of the POWs, their systematic record of all known prisoners. Indeed, a major problem for the thesis that American POWs remained in Indochina came directly from the men returned in Operation Homecoming, including the nine from Laos, as well as Thai and Lao nationals released by the Pathet Lao in the prisoner exchange of 1974 and various captured citizens of other countries. Extensive intelligence debriefing clearly established that not one former prisoner was aware of any living American captive who had not been repatriated.[58] Many POWs, however, were aware of one—and only one—former prisoner still evidently living in Vietnam, the same one believed by the House Select Committee to be alive.

This was also the verdict of the CIA, as reported in 1976 by its deputy director, Lieutenant General Vernon Walters:

> Although there were several reports alleging Americans were being held in captivity after Operations [sic] Homecoming, none could be equated to Americans who had not been accounted for. There is, however, one exception. An American was captured in Quang Nam Province, South Vietnam in 1965, but later "crossed over" to the enemy and possibly is still alive in South Vietnam. According to U.S. returnees who had contact with this individual, he was a legitimate prisoner from 1965 to 1967, before joining the ranks of the enemy. As a collaborator with the enemy, this individual performed escort and guard duties and other camp chores associated with the confinement of the U.S. PWs. As both a PW and later a collaborator/deserter, he had contact with U.S. PWs until 1969. Intelligence reports confirm the activities of this individual as reported by the U.S. returnees.[59]

This one man, by every indication the only living POW or former

POW in Vietnam, was Robert Garwood, who finally arranged for his return to the United States in 1979. Did this suggest to the believers in dozens of live POWs that they might have been wrong? Quite the opposite. Robert Dornan, originator of VIVA's bracelets and by then a Republican congressional representative, declared that Garwood's reappearance showed that "the past three Administrations had carried out a charade to cover up the fact that American servicemen remained alive in Vietnam."[60] Dermot Foley, the former National League of Families attorney who had filed suit to block the government from presumptive findings of death for MIAs, now scurried to Garwood's father and got himself retained as Garwood's lawyer; in this role he issued public statements that the case proved that the U.S. government was trying to "sweep" all the POWs "under the rug."[61] Donna Long, an exceptionally militant POW/MIA crusader, took Garwood into her home, became his lover, and began using his case to propagandize about other Americans whom she—not he at the time—claimed were still held as prisoners in Vietnam.[62]

After hearing abundant testimony from his former fellow captives about Garwood's bearing arms with their captors and about his own tales of military exploits against U.S. troops, Garwood's court-martial in 1980 found him guilty of collaborating with the enemy. Although Garwood claimed that Vietnam had held him for years against his will, he never offered as part of this defense any assertion that there were any other American captives held in Vietnam after the war, which surely would have been his most effective supporting argument. Nor did he make any such claim in his 1983 biography, which did give his very detailed and self-justifying account of his years in Vietnam during and after the war. In fact, there he acknowledged that he had been lying when he had once told a foreign visitor to Vietnam there were other Americans being held, that he had simply made this up just to get attention and make his own story more believable.[63]

But in 1984, Bill Paul, a *Wall Street Journal* staff reporter who has played a major role in promulgating the POW/MIA myth, published a lengthy article alleging that Garwood told him "that there were at least 70 Americans held prisoner in Vietnam as of the late 1970s" and recounting several detailed stories about these prisoners.[64] Garwood's ever more embellished tales soon became a mainstay of the POW/MIA faith. For example, they constitute the most important direct "evidence" in the Stevensons' 1990 *Kiss the Boys Goodbye*, which devotes numerous lengthy sections to Garwood's stories.

Garwood's allegations are obviously suspect simply because they are so self-serving: if there were dozens of other Americans held against their will, then perhaps he was too; if he was held against his will, then maybe he wasn't really a collaborator; if he wasn't the only one, then maybe he shouldn't be blamed so much; and so on. There are other problems. Why didn't he tell his stories to Dermot Foley in 1979, or, if he did, why didn't Foley, one of the most ardent of all POW/MIA proselytizers, make them public? Why didn't Garwood mention these other prisoners to his biographers two years after his court-martial? Why did he state on television in 1979 that he had not talked to another American for "about ten, eleven years"[65] (a time frame that precisely fits the date of the last contact he was known to have had with Americans)?

But perhaps the most damning refutation comes from the men who were with him in NLF jungle prison camps. Not only did their testimony at his court-martial prove that he was an armed guard rather than a fellow prisoner but, back in 1975 when Garwood's fate was still a mystery, they had declared that "he was such a liar that we could never decide" if anything he said was true. He told people whatever they wanted to hear and frequently invented detailed narratives about himself, including "a half-dozen tales of how he was captured."[66]

Those who offer Robert Garwood's stories as proof that Vietnam has been keeping American POWs actually demonstrate the opposite. It is especially revealing that Garwood, a fine specimen of POW/MIA mythmaking, began telling his tales of live POWs in Vietnam only after the first POW rescue movies had begun their transformation of American culture.

"Live Sightings"

As soon as the last American POWs were repatriated by Vietnam, rumors arose that other live Americans had been seen in captivity. These reports of "live sightings" continued to swell until now there have been almost as many sightings of live POWs as of live Elvis Presleys.

Such reports were the major impetus to the formation of the House Select Committee, as stated most frankly in its final report: "Because of the multiplicity of the reports of Americans still held captive . . . the select committee began its investigation on the assumption that many of those classified as MIA might also still be alive and held captive." But after its fifteen-month investigation, the committee became convinced that all these reports were at best erroneous and that "MIA families and the American public had been misled too long and too often by charlatans, opportunists, intelligence fabricators, and publicity mongers, who preyed on the hopes and sorrows of patriotic citizens."[67]

Financed by the desperate hopes of distraught families and the fury of revanchists unreconciled to the U.S. defeat in Indochina, a new industry sprang up in Thailand, manufacturing "sightings" and even phony physical evidence on demand. As Ernest Brace, a CIA pilot captured in Laos in 1965 and held as a prisoner for eight years in Laos and North Vietnam, testified to the committee:

> If you want information about POW's, I have been back in Bangkok several times since I got out, and if you take a wallet full of money over there, you can buy all the information you want on POW's on the streets. They will give you pictures and everything else, introduce

you to contacts, but when you try to run them down, they fizzle out somewhere down the line.[68]

As the flow of refugees swelled from the ravaged nations of Indochina, reports of live sightings increased with them. Many came in response to advertisements in Vietnamese and Lao language newspapers offering large cash sums to those who told of seeing American prisoners and intimating that any such witnesses would be granted entry to the United States as an additional reward. In some cases, such solicited "live sightings" led military officials to inform wives of missing men that their husbands might still be alive, only to discover later that the reports were complete fabrications.[69] By the mid-1980s, leaflets in several languages offering a $2.4 million reward for the return of any live American POW were being circulated in Thailand and even within Laos. Despite this immense inducement, no prisoner has been produced, though in 1984 Donna Long and a companion briefly became new prisoners when they were apprehended distributing these leaflets inside Laos.[70]

As the publicity campaign about "live sightings" continued to surge, congressional hearings about these reports were held in 1988. At the hearings, the Defense Intelligence Agency testified that it had received altogether 1,053 reports of live sightings of people believed to be Americans "under some degree of incarceration" throughout Indochina. The DIA had by then resolved 911 of these reports. Of these, "688 pertained to known, identified, accounted for people," including "approximately 250" that turned out to be "eyewitness sightings of former United States Marine Corps private Robert Garwood." The DIA noted: "Many of those 900 reports are wartime sightings of individuals who spent their time in the prisons of North and South Vietnam and have returned. Others of those are sightings of individuals who were incarcerated at the fall of Saigon and since released. Then there are the various sightings of missionaries, of aid workers, of an Australian citizen who, on a dare from his buddies, swam the Mekong River onto the banks of the Lao border and spent about a year in jail for his troubles." Another 223 sightings were simply "false," including many from "sources" who "admitted they had not told the truth." Of the 142 reports still under active investigation, "66 pertain to individuals sighted in a non-PW environment (i.e. working as a truck driver, married with a Vietnamese family)." When sifted out, "the number of live sighting reports that deal with unaccounted for individuals is extremely small; it is not as large as a dozen."[71]

One astonishing revelation in the DIA's presentation to the committee was the testimony of Joseph Schlatter, chief of its Special Office of Prisoners and Missing in Action, about "a large body of reports that we know are absolutely false" because they are "part of a managed misinformation effort by a foreign intelligence agency." Colonel Schlatter maintained that the DIA knew that these reports were "sourced through a hostile intelligence service," and "we've proved it over and over again."[72] Although Schlatter did not name the nation that was planting phony evidence of live POWs, the obvious candidate is the one that is determined to keep the United States from normalizing relations with Vietnam, that armed and instigated the 1975 and 1978 Cambodian incursions into Vietnam, that conducted a massive invasion of Vietnam in 1979, and that Americans fostering the POW myth might be embarrassed to be serving. And the DIA is well aware that Vietnam has for many years been insisting that various stories and "evidence" of live POWs have been manufactured in China.[73] One participant in a failed POW rescue incursion into Laos claimed that an intelligence agent of the People's Republic of China actually met with the raiders in Representative Robert Dornan's office to help plan the mission in order to "slap the hand of Vietnam."[74]

Among all the raiders and scouts and would-be rescuers, this man—Scott Barnes—is also the only one who has claimed to have actually seen a live American prisoner anywhere in postwar Indochina. But his published statements, including several interviews he gave in the early 1980s and his own 1987 book, offer yet another explanation of live sightings, one that actually undermines the belief in POWs left over from the Vietnam War.

Barnes insists that his 1981 incursion into Laos, sponsored by a supersecret Pentagon agency, did discover two American captives, whom he and another team member photographed from afar while hearing them speak English through a long-distance spy microphone. But Barnes believes that these were recent captives, probably CIA operatives engaged in planting phony evidence of "Yellow Rain." According to his story, the CIA ordered the team to kill the two prisoners and later destroyed all the photographic evidence furnished by Barnes and the other team member, Jerry Daniels. Daniels, a known CIA operative who had voiced public doubts about Yellow Rain, in fact was found dead in Bangkok under very mysterious circumstances a few weeks after the alleged cross-border foray.[75]

If Barnes's story has any credibility, it suggests that any American observed in captivity in Indochina might be not a POW from the war but some clandestine operative engaged in postwar secret hostilities. To various conspiracy theorists of the late 1980s and 1990s, Barnes has also suggested a motive for what they believe are conspiracies by the CIA and other covert agencies to interfere with a resolution of the POW/MIA issue.

Why?

The most bothersome problem for the postwar POW/MIA advocates has always been the question of motive. During the war, the POW/MIA campaign had focused on two issues: the DRV's mistreatment of American POWs and its refusal to provide a "complete accounting" of the captured men to the U.S. government. *Why* the Vietnamese would not give this account did not seem a terribly vexing question. Indeed, several more or less plausible reasons were put forth: the uncertainty arising from the absence of a definitive list, as part of the "inhuman" and "cruel" torture of the prisoners and their families, was intended to create even more pressure to end the war and bring the men home; by providing lists directly to delegations of anti-war activists, the DRV was trying to demonstrate that it considered the anti-war movement, rather than the U.S. government, to be the legitimate representative of the American people; a complete list of POWs might be used as a "bargaining chip" in the negotiations.

But once the DRV and PRG, in conformity with the Paris Agreement, listed and released all the prisoners that they claimed to hold, there would seem to be no reason for them to secretly retain a few dozen. Torturing the men and their families would serve no political purpose whatsoever. Releasing their names to the anti-war movement would merely be a declaration of outright lying to the U.S. government. And so the postwar POW/MIA campaign has always had to contend with this simple and troubling question: What conceivable motive could the Vietnamese have for keeping American prisoners for years and years while denying their existence?

One contention is that Vietnam has been using them as slave laborers. But to make any sense at all of this absurd proposition its advocates have had to multiply the possible numbers of prisoners from a handful to hundreds, to forget that Vietnam already has millions of underemployed peasants and workers who are far more accustomed to the harsh conditions of labor in that devastated tropical land, and to ignore both the uselessness and the likely life expectancy of aging prisoners in those visions conjured up by Hollywood or narrated by Charlton Heston for Skyhook II: "Starved and clad only in filthy rags, American soldiers and airmen are kept chained in tiny bamboo cages . . . made to work like animals pulling heavy plows . . . forced to toil from daybreak to nightfall in steaming tropical heat."

The imagined prisoners have been referred to as hostages or

bargaining chips. But what good are hostages to a nation that denies holding any? How can you bargain with a chip that you swear doesn't exist?

The crudest answers rely on the supposed inscrutable cruelty of Asians and the perfidy of Communists. While these familiar themes from the Yellow Peril and Red Menace traditions underlie almost all of the explanations, they can often be heard only as background strains in more superficially reasonable and plausible arguments. The most sophisticated—in fact downright Byzantine—of these arguments would eventually turn into a potential Frankenstein's monster for the government that had vivified the POW/MIA creature to prolong the war and would then unleash it to abrogate the terms of the peace.

Reparations and POWs

Article 21 of the 1973 Paris Peace Agreement stipulated that the United States "will contribute to healing the wounds of war and to postwar reconstruction of the Democratic Republic of Viet-Nam and throughout Indochina." The precise terms of this pledge had been secretly negotiated between Henry Kissinger and Le Duc Tho, and were spelled out five days after the signing of the agreement in a secret letter from President Nixon to Prime Minister Pham Van Dong of the DRV that promised: "The Government of the United States of America will contribute to postwar reconstruction in North Vietnam without any political conditions." The president's letter pledged that "the United States contribution to postwar reconstruction will fall in the range of $3.25 billion of grant aid over five years" plus additional aid "in the range of $1 billion to $1.5 billion, depending on food and other commodity needs of the Democratic Republic of Vietnam."[76] Although this letter was in fact a codicil to the Paris Agreement, which Hanoi had insisted upon as an adjunct to Article 21, President Nixon evidently never had any intention of carrying out the promises he was making on behalf of the United States.[77]

The Nixon administration used three tactics to renege on this commitment. First, it claimed that Article 21 was not binding because of alleged DRV military violations of the agreements. Second, it categorically denied the existence of the president's pledge, despite Hanoi's insistence that it had such a commitment in writing. For example, on February 8, 1973, Secretary of State William Rogers testified to the House International Relations Committee: "We have not made any commitment for any reconstruction or rehabilitation effort" to the DRV. The third stratagem was to use the POW/MIA issue, which had been so successful in prolonging the war, to make sure that conflict with Vietnam would now be virtually endless.

Yet just as the POW/MIA issue began to turn against the administration in 1971 and 1972, when more and more POW/MIA family members came to realize how the issue was being manipulated, so in the postwar years the issue would assume a potent life of its own contrary to the designs of the government. Without an understanding of the administration's arcane strategy, it is impossible to make any sense of the issue's strange postwar evolution.

For example, how is it possible to explain the growing hostility between the government and the militant wing of the POW/MIA movement? After all, VIVA and the National League of Families were specifically targeting Article 21, arguing that the DRV was not entitled to the pledged reparations because, in violation of the agreement and of the most fundamental principles of humanity, it was still holding American prisoners of war. This would seem to be just what the president needed in order to wriggle out of his promise, and it is tempting to speculate that the administration was secretly encouraging this new public campaign, which was neatly insulated from the White House itself. But the president was claiming that he had brought all the POWs home, and he was doing everything he possibly could to associate himself with the freed prisoners as a shield against the exploding Watergate charges. So clearly he did not want the American people to believe that he had left Americans as prisoners in Vietnam. But then why did the Pentagon and the State Department play all those numbers games so carefully calculated to make it seem that there might still be some POWs? And why did Gerald Ford, who took over the presidency after Nixon was forced to resign in 1974, keep up the ambiguity while intensifying the contradictions with the POW/MIA militants? And why have all subsequent administrations—Carter, Reagan, Bush, Clinton—also maintained an ambiguous and troublesome position on the POW/MIA issue?

The answer is that each of these administrations has attempted to perpetuate the belief that live POWs *might* exist while avoiding the position that they *do* exist. This explains those baffling numbers games played not just in January 1973 but all the way through to the latest edition of the Defense Department's *POW-MIA Fact Book.* By asserting the *possibility* of living American captives, each administration has been able to justify and rationalize policies that it wishes, for entirely unrelated reasons, to conduct in relation to Vietnam. So it has been necessary to keep the belief in this *possibility* of live POWs active and potent in the consciousness and imagination of millions of American citizens. But at the same time, obviously no administration can afford to take the position that live Americans *are* being held captive in Indochina, because then it would have to do something about them. Hence the hostility between each administration and the most militant believers, with all its puzzling contradictions.

Of course, the ground between demanding an accounting for MIAs and a return of POWs is slippery indeed. A revealing episode occurred when Ronald Reagan, challenging President Gerald Ford for the Republican nomination in 1976, accused the incumbent of having made overtures to Hanoi aimed at normalizing relations. Secretary of State Henry Kissinger immediately replied that "a complete accounting for the M.I.A.'s" is "the absolute precondition" for normalizing relations with Vietnam. But the very next day President Ford contradicted this while engaging in the customary confusion between MIAs and POWs: "I never said we were going to normalize relations or recognize the North Vietnamese. . . . [T]here is no prospect of it, and there is nothing that would convince me otherwise. We are interested and will do, below that level, anything to get our MIA's back."[78]

This episode itself was part of the unfolding, shocking revelation of Nixon's secret codicil to Article 21. Before going to Hanoi in December 1975 to discuss the POW/MIA question directly with the Vietnamese government, the House Select Committee asked Secretary of State Kissinger and other high administration officials whether there was any secret correspondence or understanding of which they should be aware. They were assured repeatedly that no such letter, note, codicil, or agreement existed. But when Representative Montgomery and other members of the committee arrived in Hanoi, they were immediately confronted with impassioned statements to the contrary by high government leaders, and portions of the secret letter from President Nixon to Prime Minister Pham Van Dong were actually printed in an official Hanoi newspaper. Had the members of Congress been lied to by their own government and were they now being told the truth by America's long-term enemy? On their return, angry and humiliated, they demanded an explanation from the State Department. So Philip Habib, undersecretary for political affairs, appeared before the committee on July 21, 1976—and in his testimony proceeded to repeat the same lies they had already heard. Habib continued to swear to the committee that "there is no agreement or secret memorandum" and "there is no agreement with respect to the question of aid" involved in any letter from Nixon to Hanoi.[79] The State Department then refused to comply with the committee's request to see Nixon's letter, which both the Ford and Carter administrations continued to conceal until

May 19, 1977, when, in response to a congressional threat to subpoena the disgraced former president, the document was finally declassified and made public.[80]

In a grotesquely ironic twist, Nixon's duplicity and broken promise, together with the successful public and lobbying campaign by VIVA and the National League of Families to prohibit aid to Vietnam until it returned POWs it denied holding, now provided the only ostensibly logical argument to explain why the Vietnamese would have any motive for holding American POWs in the first place. As Special Forces Colonel Trautman shouts at Murdock, the quintessential government "stinking bureaucrat" in *Rambo: First Blood Part II*: "In '72 we were supposed to pay the Cong four and a half billion dollars in war reparations! We reneged! They kept the POWs!"

4 ◼ MYTHMAKING IN AMERICA

Crucifixion and Resurrection

The militant faction that took over the National League of Families in 1974 had an ambivalent relationship with the Ford administration, which by 1976 was being attacked by both Ronald Reagan and Jimmy Carter for being too gentle with Vietnam on the MIA issue. In what had become a presidential ritual, President Ford addressed that summer's annual convention of the League and, after praising Carol Bates, vowed "to obtain a full accounting of those missing in action or still listed as prisoners of war." Though everybody greeted this pledge by standing to sing "God Bless America," many in attendance expressed considerable suspicion to the media.[1]

In September, the administration announced that it would veto Vietnam's application for membership in the United Nations because of its failure, in the president's words, "to provide a full accounting of all Americans missing in action." Such "brutal and inhumane treatment of the families" of hundreds of Americans still unaccounted for in Indochina, according to U.S. Ambassador to the UN William Scranton, proved that Vietnam "lacked the commitments to peace and humanitarianism necessary for membership in the United Nations." The following month, in the debate between

President Ford and challenger Jimmy Carter, each tried to upstage the other on the MIA issue. The president declared, "As long as Vietnam, North Vietnam, does not give us a full and complete accounting of our missing in action, I will never go along with admission of Vietnam to the United Nations," adding that he meant both a "complete accounting" and a "full accounting." Carter replied by accusing Ford of not being sufficiently "aggressive" with Vietnam and thus being responsible for leaving "the M.I.A. families in despair and doubt," while he himself promised that until the MIAs were accounted for he "would never formalize relationships with Vietnam, nor permit them to join the United Nations."[2]

In November, the United States carried through on its threat, casting its eighteenth veto to block Vietnam's UN membership, ostensibly because of that nation's failure to account for all the American combatants missing in Indochina. While echoing the administration's condemnation of Vietnam for attempting "to play upon the anguish and uncertainties of the families of these men in order to obtain economic and political advantages," *The New York Times* editorialized that "the M.I.A. issue still cannot justify the American veto, which violates the principle of universal membership by all legitimate governments."[3]

Then in December came the great betrayal. Sonny Montgomery—VIVA and the National League's champion in Congress—released the report of his House Select Committee, with its conclusions that "no Americans are still being held alive as prisoners in Indochina, or elsewhere, as a result of the war in Indochina," and that "a total accounting by the Indochinese Governments is not possible and should not be expected." The committee even had the audacity to point out that "there are no examples in world history to compare with the accounting now being requested."[4]

Ann Mills Griffiths immediately denounced the committee report, and Carol Bates, in her new position as executive director of the National League of Families, penned a scathing reply. Montgomery himself was now vilified as a new Judas or, even worse, another Jane Fonda, by the POW/MIA crusaders, who began referring to him as "V. C. Mont-GOMER-y" ("V. C." stood for Viet Cong; "gomer" was one of the racist epithets GIs applied to Vietnamese).[5]

By this time Jimmy Carter had won the presidency. One of his first acts after assuming office was appointing a special presidential commission to go directly to Vietnam to seek a resolution of the MIA issue. Chaired by Leonard Woodcock (soon to be the chief U.S. representative to China) and accompanied by Roger Shields of the Defense Department and Frank Sieverts of the State Department, the commission visited Vietnam and Laos in March 1977. The commission's final report turned out to be another betrayal: it reached the same unholy conclusions as the House Select Committee. More ominous still, in presenting the Commission's report to the media, President Carter spoke of the "great friendship" the Vietnamese had shown to the commission and suggested that he was prepared to accept their proposal to "reinitiate diplomatic discussions in Paris without delay, to resolve other issues that might be an obstacle to peace between our two countries, and friendship between our two countries, and normalization of relationships within our two countries."[6]

In August and September came two more blows to the cause. The United States, faced with an unprecedented array of 150 nations sponsoring Vietnam's bid for UN membership, abstained instead of vetoing. And President Carter announced that he would let each military service resume making presumptive findings of death whenever the evidence seemed appropriate for each case of the 712 men still carried as missing. The POW/MIA faithful had been denouncing every movement toward resolution of the MIA issue, whether through presumptive findings of death or improving relations with Vietnam, as an attempt to "wipe out" or "kill off" the missing men. Carol Bates condemned the administration as "deceitful and disgraceful" and fumed that the "decision to administratively 'kill-off' the remaining POW/MIA's by declaring them all legally dead is the final blow in what has become a long list of broken promises."[7]

But all hope was not lost. For President Carter did not, as he had indicated in early 1977, move toward opening diplomatic relations with Vietnam or ending the U.S. trade embargo, even though the only outstanding issue was the alleged failure to account for the MIAs.[8] Soon the Carter administration had another pretext for continuing its economic and political warfare against Vietnam.

As the United States and China moved into a strategic alliance, China followed up its 1974 seizure of the Paracel Islands from Vietnam by initiating incursions on Vietnam's northern border while arming and instigating a Khmer Rouge invasion of Vietnam's Tay Ninh province. At the end of 1978, Vietnam finally responded to the Khmer Rouge's warfare by allying with insurgent Cambodian forces to sweep Pol Pot's forces out of both countries by early January 1979. Ensconced across the border in Thailand, the Khmer Rouge soon received direct political and indirect military support from the United States, while in February hundreds of thousands of Chinese troops, spearheaded by armored columns and backed by air attacks, invaded northern Vietnam.

For well over a decade the United States would now offer *two* reasons for refusing to recognize Vietnam and maintaining its crippling trade embargo on that devastated nation: Vietnam's invasion of Cambodia and its failure to provide an acceptable accounting of all Americans missing in Indochina. New life for the POW/MIA issue came from a helpful source, China's intelligence services, which began planting rumors and phony evidence about Vietnam and Laos holding American prisoners.[9]

In 1978 President Carter openly began to reverse course not just on possible relations with Vietnam but also on détente in general, leading, in the final two years of his administration, to restoring draft registration, removing SALT II from consideration by the

Senate, embargoing grain sales to the Soviet Union, boycotting the Olympics in Moscow, and initiating the biggest arms buildup in U.S. history. At the same time, the Committee on the Present Danger—whose directors included Ronald Reagan, George Shultz, William Casey, Jeane Kirkpatrick, Richard Allen, Colin Gray, Paul Nitze, Max Kampleman, Kenneth Adelman, and Edward Teller— was conducting its massive propaganda blitz designed to wreck détente, dismantle arms control agreements, and launch an uncontrolled arms race.[10]

Essential to this process of remilitarization was a rewriting and reimaging of the history of the Vietnam War, which would restore the discredited vision of idealistic, courageous Americans heroically battling hordes of sadistic Oriental Communists. On the academic front, the charge was led by a brigade of revisionist historians who attempted to obscure the causes of the war and whitewash America's conduct of it. Their task was formidable because the evidence, like some kind of treacherous mine field, kept getting in their way.[11] Those who fought on the popular culture front had a much easier job, for they could simply ignore the history and rely entirely on manipulative images. And no image had proven more powerful during the war than that of American prisoners.

By far the most influential work in this campaign was the lavishly financed movie *The Deer Hunter*, which the New York Film Critics' Circle designated the best English-language film of 1978 and which received four Academy Awards, including Best Picture of 1978. *The Deer Hunter* succeeded not only in radically reimaging the war but in transforming POWs into crucial symbols of American manhood.

The reimaging was quite conscious, though most critics at the time seemed oblivious to it. The basic technique was to take images of the war that had become deeply embedded in America's consciousness and transform them into their opposite. For example, in the first scene in Vietnam, a uniformed soldier throws a grenade into an underground village shelter harboring women and children, and then with his automatic assault rifle mows down a woman and her baby. Although the scene resembles *Life's* pictures of the My Lai massacre, he is not an American soldier but a North Vietnamese. He is then killed by a lone guerrilla, who is not a Viet Cong but our Special Forces hero, Robert DeNiro.

When two men plummet from a helicopter, the images replicate a familiar telephotographic sequence showing a Viet Cong prisoner being pushed from a helicopter to make other prisoners talk;[12] but the falling men in the movie are American POWs attempting to escape from their murderous Viet Cong captors. The central structuring metaphor of the film is the Russian roulette the sadistic Asian Communists force their prisoners to play. POW after POW is shown with a revolver at his right temple, framed to match with precision the sequence seen by tens of millions of Americans in which the chief of the Saigon secret police placed a revolver to the right temple of an NLF prisoner and killed him with a single shot; even the blood spurting out of the temple is exactly replicated. There is absolutely no evidence that any such atrocity was ever committed against a single prisoner of the NLF or North Vietnam.

Those who doubt that this reversal of crucial images is intentional, purposeful, and political might wish to look at subsequent works that built with less subtlety on *The Deer Hunter's* message and methodology. For example, take *P.O.W.: The Escape*, a 1986 POW rescue movie starring David Carradine as superhero Colonel Jim Cooper. Set during the last days of the war, the movie opens with a televised newscast: "The Paris Peace talks go on. The North Vietnamese continue to refuse to agree to the release of our POWs, even if we set a date for the withdrawal of U.S. forces. President Nixon stated today this is of course very cruel on their part." Carradine, whose motto is "Everybody goes home," has been selected to lead an attack on a secret POW camp, "one of those places where the Communists won't admit that they're still holding American prisoners," because President Nixon "wants the message to be loud and clear: we want *all* of our men back." In ominous tones, his commanding officer informs him that a cease fire is scheduled to go into effect in five days: "Any POWs who aren't accounted for by then will be reclassified as missing in action. They'll disappear! Forever!" What this means is displayed when the evil North Vietnamese camp commander executes an American prisoner with a revolver shot to the right temple in a tableau modeled even more precisely than *The Deer Hunter's* on the sequence of the Saigon secret police chief executing the NLF prisoner. Then, just in case viewers missed it, this scene is replayed later as the movie's only flashback sequence.

The continuing influence of the original image is demonstrated by an even later attempt to invert it, the cover story of the November 1988 issue of *The 'Nam*, an immensely popular comic book dedicated to reimaging the Vietnam War. The 1968 execution sequence is literally redrawn so as to center on what are portrayed as the real villains of the story, the photojournalists who put the original image on the "front page of every newspaper in the states!"[13]

The Deer Hunter's subliminal manipulation of images culminates in the long sequence when DeNiro is convincing Christopher Walken that their only hope of escape is to use the Russian roulette revolver to kill their captors. The fiendish Orientals have placed them in a half-submerged tiger cage, behind which we see a single vertical and a single horizontal strand of barbed wire, which somehow frequently replace the bars of the tiger cage in the camera's field of vision. Whatever inscrutable reason their captors may have had for this arrangement, it allows the camera to show only the heads and torsos of the two men, and the lighting is arranged—by the director, not the Communists—so that throughout much of this sequence the heads and torsos are seen only as silhouettes in profile. In frame after frame, each conveniently silhouetted profiled head and torso forms the logo, including the single strand of barbed wire, of the POW/MIA flag.

Intercut with this sequence are images of the POWs as crucified

Christs, bloody headbands replacing the crown of thorns, with the hands of soldiers hauling them up to their torture and death. The patriotic and religious messages of *The Deer Hunter* are unified from the beginning, when a banner proclaiming *Serving God and Country* hangs over the wedding celebration, to the very end, when, just as at a National League of Families convention, everybody joins to sing "God Bless America." And the unifying images are those of American white working class men as crucified prisoners of the Vietnamese.[14]

But for the POWs and MIAs to become an authentic myth gripping the heart of America, less subtle visions had to be shaped by the men from Hollywood. Who could resurrect those missing American fighting men who had been crucified by the Asian Communists and their domestic accomplices? This was a job for true heroes, led by one of VIVA's original sponsors, Ronald Reagan.

Hollywood Heroes I: Bo Gritz and Ronald Reagan

The story of the heroic American prisoners abandoned in Southeast Asia could not become a major American myth until the Hollywood dream factory geared up its assembly line for mass production of the essential images. But Hollywood was actually involved in creating the historical raw materials that the POW rescue movies were later to fantasize.

The character central to the POW/MIA story as it attained its full mythic status in the 1980s was retired Special Forces Colonel James "Bo" Gritz, who organized raids into Laos to rescue men he already envisioned in images that would later be projected on movie and TV screens around the world. With devout faith in the existence of living POWs abandoned by their government to cruel Asian Communist slavery, Gritz conceived of their rescue as a mission forced upon him by destiny. Why was he the chosen one? Because the only two other men capable of such intense "action," as he put it, were no longer around to do the job: "both Teddy Roosevelt and John Wayne are dead."[15]

But two other men of action were at least available to help finance the mission: Captain Kirk of the starship *Enterprise* and Dirty Harry. William Shatner put up $10,000 and received movie rights to the Gritz story. Clint Eastwood, who contributed $30,000, was assigned a far more crucial role in the adventure.[16]

Ever since the Paris Agreement of 1973, POW activists had been elaborating the theme of a conspiracy high in the government to deny the existence of American prisoners. The villains were government "bureaucrats," devious operators in the CIA, and liberal politicians, personified by President Carter himself. With the inauguration of Ronald Reagan in early 1981, the myth evolved a new twist: the good president amid the evil officials. Ronald Reagan's heart yearned to save the POWs, but the president was surrounded and kept in ignorance by that claque of scheming bureaucrats and liberals now known collectively as the "doorkeepers" or "gatekeepers." Who could possibly get by the all-powerful evil gatekeepers and bring the truth to the good president?

The one man in America that Colonel Gritz knew he could rely on for the job was Clint Eastwood. The entire plan hinged on two tête-à-têtes between Eastwood and the president. On the night of November 27, 1982, after receiving definite word that Gritz's team had crossed the Mekong River from Thailand into Laos, Eastwood was to fly from his California ranch to a prearranged meeting at Reagan's California ranch and inform the president about the raid. When the raiders had actually released live American POWs, they were to send a message via "nuclear fire plan boxes" ("state-of-the-art . . . Indirect Transmission Devices" furnished by Litton Industries) to their base in Thailand, which would relay the message to their "Angels West" base in Los Angeles, which would in turn relay the message to Eastwood, who would then once again fly to see his old friend Ronald Reagan, who would then have to do what he wanted to do all along: send U.S. aircraft and military forces to rescue the POWs.[17] So crucial was Eastwood's first meeting with the president that Gritz led his men across the Mekong before most of their weapons arrived so that they would be in Laos by the night of the 27th, California time. Eastwood reportedly carried out his assignment, either flying from his Shasta ranch to Reagan's Santa Barbara ranch to meet with the president at the appointed time or, in a less theatrical version, at least informing the president about the raid by telephone. When the raiders returned from Laos to Thailand on December 3, they found this message from a team member in California waiting for them:

CLINT AND I MET WITH PRESIDENT ON 27TH. PRESIDENT SAID: QUOTE, IF YOU BRING OUT ONE U.S. POW, I WILL START WORLD WAR III TO GET THE REST OUT. UNQUOTE.[18]

Whether the president indeed said these words we will never know. But they would certainly be in character. After all, Ronald Reagan had been active with POW issues ever since he himself had actually been a POW of Asian Communists during the Korean War—as the star of the 1954 movie *Prisoner of War.*

Gritz's raid, however, was not entirely a Hollywood production. So unlike all those scenes in the subsequent movies inspired by their adventure, the American heroes did not ambush and wipe out hordes of Asian Communists. In fact, almost as soon as they arrived in Laos they were ambushed, routed, and forced to flee as fast as they could back to Thailand. The ambushers, contrary to their initial assumptions, were not even treacherous Communists but a rival anti-Communist Laotian group whom Gritz's men had offended in Thailand and to whom Gritz, ironically enough, reportedly had to pay $17,500 ransom to recover a captured American teammate.[19] The raiders of course encountered no POWs.

In fact, neither this raid nor ones that Gritz claimed to have carried out deeper into Laos in the ensuing months yielded any tangible evidence of American POWs. Thirty rolls of photographs taken with high-tech cameras, which Gritz promised to give to a congressional committee investigating his raids, never materialized.[20] Alleged remains of two American POWs that Gritz brought back with him turned out to be bones from two Asians mixed with animal bones.[21]

Yet Gritz was actually overmodest in claiming how effectively he had achieved one of his principal goals: "We have heightened public awareness of the POW question."[22] For his escapades were to be vital to what the Reagan administration was privately calling, in the same words used by Gritz, its "public awareness" campaign, initiated just as Gritz was preparing his raiders. As the *Final Interagency Report of the Reagan Administration on the POW/MIA Issue* phrased it, "From its inception in 1982, the public awareness campaign steadily gained momentum."[23]

As it left office in 1989, the Reagan administration could truthfully exult that this "aggressive public awareness campaign," waged "in coordination with the National League of POW/MIA Families," had "raised domestic consciousness of this issue to the highest level since the end of the war" while causing "media coverage" to increase "dramatically." With the full "integration of the National League of Families into our efforts," the League became even more thoroughly intertwined with the government than it had been with its creator, the Nixon administration. The 1990 edition of the *POW-MIA Fact Book* published by the Department of Defense states outright: "United States Government policy regarding the POW/MIA issue is coordinated through the POW/MIA Interagency Group (IAG). Membership in the IAG includes the Defense Department, the White House National Security Council (NSC) staff, the State Department, the Joint Chiefs of Staff (JCS), the Defense Intelligence Agency (DIA) and the National League of POW/MIA Families."[24]

President Reagan vastly expanded the POW/MIA section of the Defense Intelligence Agency (DIA), more than tripling its staff and adding "a special team deployed in Southeast Asia" to solicit "refugee information."[25] A key addition to the DIA staff was Carol Bates, cofounder of VIVA and its bracelet campaign and executive director of the National League of Families during the period when it transformed into the leading public booster of the belief in live POWs.

Three days before the news of Gritz's first raid burst upon the public and while he was conducting his second raid, President Reagan, who had been kept closely informed, declared to a special meeting of the National League of Families that from now on "the government bureaucracy" would have to understand that the POW/MIA issue had assumed "the highest national priority" (a phrase echoing VIVA's "one of our nation's top priorities").[26]

In the next few months, Colonel Gritz became a star of magazines, newspapers, radio, and TV. But he was a fast-fading luminary, for the story of his raids was hardly a tale of spectacularly successful heroism. Hollywood would now have to show how the story was supposed to look.

Hollywood Heroes II: Gene Hackman and Chuck Norris

Amid the media hoopla about the Gritz raids, the first fantasized movie version began shooting. Starring Gene Hackman as a retired Marine colonel, *Uncommon Valor* made it to the screen in time for the Christmas season of 1983. The following year came *Missing in Action*, with Chuck Norris as retired Special Forces Colonel James Braddock, an even less thinly disguised impersonation of retired Special Forces Colonel Bo Gritz. And in 1985 the POW/MIA story attained its apotheosis in *Rambo: First Blood Part II*, with Sylvester Stallone now incarnate as the true American superhero of our epoch.

The ideological agenda of *Uncommon Valor* is suggested by the identity of its coproducers: John Milius, whose neofascist vision is expressed most clearly in two films he directed during this period, *Conan the Barbarian* (1982) and *Red Dawn* (1984), and Buzz Feitshans, Milius's frequent collaborator whose other productions include *First Blood, Conan the Barbarian, Red Dawn, Rambo: First Blood Part II, Rambo III,* and *Total Recall.* The movie also draws heavily on J. C. Pollock's best-selling 1982 novel *Mission M.I.A.,* a rabidly racist and militarist tract explicitly designed to incite popular demand for mercenary raids to rescue American POWs allegedly still being brutalized by demonic Asian Communists.

In fact, this first POW rescue movie, *Uncommon Valor,* cannot be disentangled from either the Pollock novel or the actual raids, for Pollock's fiction and Gritz's adventures are intertwined. Gritz was organizing—and publicizing—his raids in 1981 while Pollock was writing *Mission M.I.A.,* and an extended excerpt from the novel appeared in the same March 1982 issue of *Penthouse* that printed a long interview with Gritz about his plans. So evidently Gritz and Pollock gave ideas to each other as well as to *Uncommon Valor.*

The film was labeled a mere "Okay grind actioner" by *Variety* and dismissed at first by most reviewers, whose reactions were summed up in this headline: COMIC-STRIP-LEVEL HEROISM MAKES "UNCOMMON VALOR" A COMMON BORE.[27] But within a few weeks, critics were trying to comprehend the startling audience response to what was turning out to be the "biggest movie surprise" of the 1983–84 season. The best explanation seemed to come from "an ordinary moviegoer who said with satisfaction of the bloody ending in which dozens of the enemy are mowed down by the Americans, 'We get to win the Vietnam War.'"[28]

Uncommon Valor's formula for such revision of history was identified by one critic in terms that would soon also apply to its spectacular successors:

> The Vietnam war is not really over . . . and we—America—can still
> pass for a touchdown at Ho Chi Minh Stadium and eke out a last

second victory in the Rice Paddy Bowl. Just send a few good boys back there, kick some Asian ass, liberate a few MIAs. The Laotians—or Cambodians, or Vietnamese, for they are really all alike—will fall like Indians in a John Wayne movie, and America will be proud and regain its honor.[29]

This message would become explicit later in 1984 as full-page shoot-'em-up ads for *Missing in Action* proclaimed: THE WAR'S NOT OVER UNTIL THE LAST MAN COMES HOME!

Yet the revised history offered by *Uncommon Valor* was not quite as "mindless" as many critics labeled it. For they were ignoring a subtext based on the POW/MIA pseudohistory already widely diffused throughout sections of American society and accepted by many viewers as a true, even essential, version of the Vietnam War.

The experience of Colonel Jason Rhodes (Hackman), whose son has been missing in action for more than a decade since the end of the war, helps to transform details of this pseudohistory into mythology that became part of the shared cultural inheritance for the America of the 1980s and 1990s. Like Colonel Gritz, Colonel Rhodes learns that there have been "over four hundred live sightings of men held against their will" and "there are compounds all over northern Laos." Why Laos? The case for live POWs in Vietnam was so untenable that true believers had been forced to shift the burden of their argument onto Laos. Colonel Gritz had testified to Congress: "[N]early 700 airmen were shot down over Laos during the Vietnam War. Not one has been returned."[30] In fact, as previously discussed, during and shortly after Operation Homecoming, more prisoners were returned from Laos than the Defense and State Departments had listed as probable prisoners there; subsequent investigation had demonstrated no more than five others had ever been captives in Laos, and each of these almost certainly had died in the mid or late 1960s (see pages 108–113). Yet by the time *Uncommon Valor* was screened, millions of Americans believed the Gritz version.

In a scene charged with a shock of recognition for viewers familiar with the widely accepted pseudohistory, Colonel Rhodes becomes convinced that his son is a prisoner in one of these Laotian camps. After ten years of being brushed off by government bureaucrats and victimized by con men in Thailand, Rhodes finally learns the truth from an active-duty Air Force colonel. Noting with a sigh, "I suppose someone could call this treason," the officer pulls from his briefcase a photograph taken from an SR-71 Blackbird high-altitude reconnaissance plane. "There's your proof," he declares, "it's a prison camp in Laos." While this picture might not emotionally resonate for most of the movie's reviewers, countless members of the audience recognized it as a counterpart of the famous "Fort Apache" photograph that had inspired Colonel Gritz's raids, and they were thrilled that the film anticipated their recognition.

The scene thus enshrines the Fort Apache photograph while wiping away its tarnished history. Word of such a photograph or photographs, taken either from an SR-71 flying at 80,000 feet and 2,000 miles per hour or from a spy satellite, began leaking out soon after Ronald Reagan assumed the presidency in January 1981. The exegesis that revealed a POW camp was through this photo interpretation: thirty men, who were in some kind of formation, cast shadows that were too long for Asians; they seemed "posed in a secret body-language code taught to selected airmen facing a risk of capture"; tools were evident that were too big for Asians; one structure might be a guard tower; on one side of the camp there appeared to be a 5 and on the other side a 2, no doubt meant as either a call for help or a coded signal from the prisoners or both, referring to the number of men held in the camp or the crew of a B-52 or the number of hostages being held in Iran.[31]

The ostensible chronology of subsequent events is central to the POW/MIA myth. Colonel Gritz, with considerable assistance from the Pentagon, immediately began training a team to rescue the prisoners from Fort Apache, a mission he dubbed Operation Velvet

Hammer.[32] But according to his account: "In mid-March 1981, at almost the precise moment that the 'VELVET HAMMER' team was preparing for overseas movement, I was informed that the new Reagan administration had become fully persuaded of the existence of American POWs in Southeast Asia and had decided on an official rescue mission. . . . I was asked, therefore, to abandon the VELVET HAMMER Operation." The official raid was to be carried out by Delta Force commandos. "In May 1981, the official rescue mission—the DELTA OPERATION—was also cancelled," Gritz testified, proof to him and to later true believers of government cowardice and betrayal.[33]

One would never guess from the POW/MIA movies and writings and folklore that the U.S. government did in fact stage a raid into Laos, a raid that penetrated to the site of the alleged Fort Apache, only to discover that it was not a POW camp after all. This mission, by Laotian mercenaries trained, equipped, and paid by the CIA, was carried out in May 1981; the failure of its on-site photographs to disclose any evidence whatsoever of POWs was the real reason that the Delta Force raid was called off. And that Delta raid, involving more than a hundred helicopters and transport planes, had been primed to go.[34]

Nevertheless, U.S. government cowardice and betrayal could now be built into the mythological structure of *Uncommon Valor* and the other POW rescue movies. Hackman's efforts to recruit and train a team to rescue his MIA son, which take up more than half the film, are constantly menaced by "the politicians" and omnipresent government agents equipped with high-tech spy mikes and phone taps. These sinister figures also try to intimidate the Texas oil tycoon who finances the raiders' training camp (he too has an MIA son) by threatening an IRS audit of his corporation. Just as Hackman and his team of all-American heroes are about to launch their mission from Thailand into Laos, U.S. intelligence agents have them apprehended by Thai authorities, who confiscate their weapons, forcing them to rely on a Bangkok gun dealer and an aged Laotian drug runner.

The images of a nation run by "bureaucrats," "politicians," and shadowy secret agents in business suits who revile and betray its true warrior heroes form part of the tableau that gives the POW/MIA myth such potency. For the myth rejects and repudiates not only the history of the Vietnam War but also what it portrays as the quintessence of everyday life in post-Vietnam America. The idealism, virility, warlike powers, and heroism of men who dedicate their lives to rescuing their abandoned comrades, sons, and fathers are presented as the alternative to a weak, decadent America subjugated by materialism, hedonism, and feminism. The picture can be recognized by those familiar with the culture of fascism and nazism.[35]

Colonel Rhodes reestablishes patriarchal order by recruiting a team composed of his son's former buddies and the son of another MIA. The Vietnam veterans incarnate the manifest ways in which American society supposedly deforms, perverts, and castrates military and manly virtue, and their rescue mission also rescues them from the corrupting and degrading bonds of civilian life. A blond hulk reduced to telling war stories to youngsters on a California beach is allowed to restore his old identity as Blaster, an almost legendary explosives expert. The beefy bruiser known as Sailor, who has become a mere drunken street brawler in urban America, can once again be a fearless warrior in the jungles of Southeast Asia. A Black helicopter pilot is released from a humdrum life as a hospital administrator. But the most revealing salvations are for two team members liberated from women.[36]

Wilkes, an expert on conducting ambushes, has been kept from his true identity by a wife who now convinces him to hide from Colonel Rhodes, whom she tries to block physically and with her angry plea: "It's taken me ten years to get that goddamn war out of his head." Shoving her aside, Hackman successfully rends these enfeebling domestic fetters by shouting to Wilkes: "What did you send your wife out here for? Don't you have the guts to come out here and talk to me yourself?"

Helicopter pilot Charts has become an even more miserable prisoner of peace, permanently shut in from the world behind sunglasses and headset, and married to a blond floozy whom we see about to traipse out to a happy hour at a local club. Embodying the fusion of American women with hedonism and materialism, she finally asks Hackman, "If he did go, how much would he be paid?"

Colonel Rhodes himself is called to his mission by the memory of his son as a young boy, who comes to his parents' bedroom seeking help. While his wife lies oblivious in sleep, Rhodes reaches out to clutch his son's hand, a bond that becomes the pivotal symbol of the movie. His sleeping wife (who never does get to speak a word in the film) personifies women's irrelevance to the bonds between warriors and between fathers and sons.[37] Colonel Rhodes explicitly articulates the central message: "There's no bond as strong as that shared by men who have faced death in battle."

The bonding among the men is first consummated, however, in their training camp, a world without women where one's skill at killing is the pinnacle of the entire moral structure. The pleasures of this buddy-buddy society are ritualized as the men dance with each other, some holding their assault rifles at upright angles from the groin as they bump bottoms. Thus primed, these muscular heroes are ready to slaughter hordes of puny little Asians, rescue their enslaved comrades, give the Vietnam War a noble ending, and redeem America.

Though flashing images of strong men in action, *Uncommon Valor* presents no figure of an individual superhero; indeed, it stresses the importance of arduous training and dedicated teamwork. The cult of the superhero, incarnate in a fetishized male body, would become manifest in the next two POW rescue movies, each one of exponentially greater cultural influence. The emblem of things to come was the figure of Chuck Norris in that full-page ad for *Missing in Action*, headband half-restraining his savage locks, sleeves rolled up to reveal bulging biceps, and a huge machine gun seeming to rise from his crotch, which is blackened by its great shadow. Like Sylvester Stallone as Rambo, Norris as Colonel Braddock alone combines all the powers and martial skills of Colonel Rhodes's entire team and thus has the potency to vanquish singlehandedly any number of Asians and Communists.[38]

There is another crucial difference between these superheroes and Gene Hackman's Colonel Jason Rhodes: Rambo and Braddock are themselves former prisoners of war in Vietnam, and their superhuman power comes partly from the torture to which they were subjected by the cruel Asian Communists. Rambo's torture and scarred body are vivid emblems of his identity in *First Blood* (1982); the character of Chuck Norris as Colonel Braddock had already been created as a prisoner horribly tortured during the war in *Missing in Action II—The Beginning*, which was actually shot before *Missing in Action* though not released until 1985 as its "prequel." These two figures thus draw much of their inspiration and emotional appeal from another key icon of the POW/MIA myth, the images of actual American prisoners of war promulgated in the celebration of Operation Homecoming.

Whereas during the war the most influential POW narrative had been that of an enlisted man who had come to identify with the cause of the insurgents (George E. Smith's 1971 memoir *P.O.W.: Two Years with the Viet Cong*), after the war the nation was deluged with dozens of narratives by officers who described their own harrowing torture, indomitable courage, and unbounded patriotism. This wave crested in 1976 with two volumes published and widely promoted by Reader's Digest Press, John G. Hubbell's *P.O.W.: A Definitive History of the American Prisoner-of-War Experience in Vietnam, 1964–1973* and Jeremiah Denton's *When Hell Was in Session*.[39] Hubbell, who had blank-check financing from *Reader's Digest* and unlimited military cooperation,[40] constructed a collage of interviews stressing the fiendishness of the Vietnamese Communists and the heroism of their American captives, which of course would become raw materials for the POW rescue movies. Denton's *When Hell Was in Session* was turned into a sensationalist TV movie in 1979, which, together with his widely distributed book, helped Denton become elected as senator from Alabama during the Reagan landslide of 1980. In such works lie roots of the supersexualized male bodies of Chuck Norris and Sylvester Stallone, restrained by their heroic asexual purity and sharply contrasted to hordes of ratlike, scrawny, rutty, envious Asian Communists. Denton even attributes some of his torture to guards' sexual jealousy incited by the response of Vietnamese women to the naked bodies of American men:

> Interestingly, Nursie and the female guard were hanging around, watching as I walked into the bath area. Vietnamese women seemed to enjoy looking at the American prisoners. Because of poor diet, most of the North Vietnamese were underdeveloped, and the women obviously admired our muscular bodies and hairy chests.[41]

In *Missing in Action*, Vietnamese government soldiers and officials ogle Norris with hatred and envy after they break down a hotel door and find him and a beautiful young American woman naked in bed. But what they are staring at is merely a deception, a clever military stratagem, for Colonel Braddock wants to make war, not love.

A liberal senator, accompanied by Ann Fitzgerald from the State Department, has gone to Ho Chi Minh City (formerly Saigon) to capitulate and sell out on the MIA issue. Braddock, whose own sadistic torture by one of the high-ranking Vietnamese officials we witness in a flashback, has gone along with this delegation to accomplish his own mission. But he finds himself the focus of Vietnamese Communist propaganda. Into the elegant meeting room of the diplomats is marched a line of miserable-looking peasants, who have all made sworn statements that Braddock was a notorious war criminal. Echoing wartime claims that many of their prisoners were in fact war criminals who had intentionally slaughtered civilians and used chemical defoliants to poison forests and croplands, the principal Vietnamese official declares that Braddock "was not a prisoner of war but a common criminal" whose victims included "innocent women, children, and old men." But when Braddock confronts his miserable accusers, they all lower their heads in shame; an old man even murmurs to him, "I'm sorry."

Thus the movie consciously reverses history and wipes out the bitterest lessons Americans had to learn about their war in Indochina. Just as the POW issue was consciously created in 1969 amid shocking revelations about U.S. conduct—including massacres such as My Lai, torture as in the tiger cages of Con Son, the systematic bombing throughout the north of schools and hospitals, and the widespread use in the south of chemical weapons such as CS gas, Agent Orange, Agent Blue, Agent White, and Agent Purple (nicknamed the Purple People Eater)—*Missing in Action* uses the POW issue to indoctrinate the audience of the 1980s with the notion that Americans were not the victimizers but the victims.[42] Those who have forgotten, or are too young to remember, learn that all accusations of U.S. war crimes are merely insidious Asian Communist propaganda designed to hide the crimes the Vietnamese are still perpetrating against innocent Americans.

This vicious trick merely fans the flames of righteous and explosive anger burning in Braddock's manly chest, which we get to behold in the next scene. Ann, whose job is to keep him from carrying out his mission, invites him to her room the night of the peasant accusations for a "nightcap." As soon as he steps through the door, Norris begins stripping, peeling down to nothing but his tight black underpants. Fascinated, Ann responds coquettishly, not realizing that Braddock is merely doffing his civilian clothes, which represent the enfeebling bonds of civil society, so that he can swiftly don his black commando outfit for a night of murder and mayhem in Saigon. He climbs out her window and down the wall of the hotel—like a Spiderman episode he had earlier watched on American TV—tortures and murders a high Vietnamese official, kills a few soldiers, and rescales the walls while troops are combing the city for him. Without a second to spare, he once again strips, then rips off Ann's black negligee, tosses her into bed, and fakes a passionate embrace just as the enemy smashes through the door. Later, in Bangkok, he doesn't even seem to notice the nude nightclub dancers gyrating next to his table and of course he scornfully rejects an old buddy's invitation to frolic with a couple of naked lovelies. Sex is just an alibi or distraction for this pure warrior.

When the real action that the audience has been waiting for explodes, Vietnamese bodies pile up faster and faster as Braddock's exploits become ever more implausible. The Vietnamese have conveniently situated the POW camp eight kilometers from the coast, easily accessible from Braddock's bulletproof assault boat; after vowing to complete the entire mission in fourteen hours, he single-handedly wipes out an entire POW camp; a helicopter he had chartered in Bangkok arrives with seconds to spare so that he can escape with his freed POWs and fly them back to Saigon; thus just as the U.S. delegation is nodding to the evil Vietnamese official's declaration "In conclusion, we categorically deny that there are any living MIAs in the People's Republic of Vietnam," Braddock bursts into their splendiferous meeting room, with ragged and emaciated POWs in tow. While these escapades may all seem ludicrous to those who do not share the movie's creed and are therefore stunned by its smashing returns at the box office, such incredulity itself is a revealing sign. For myths often seem absurd to nonbelievers—indeed myths must defy commonplace plausibility and transcend everyday logic—and the POW/MIA story was by this time transforming into genuine myth.

Hollywood Heroes III: Rambo

The transformation into myth was consummated in a fantasy whose hero's name would soon become a term in the political discourse and everyday vocabulary not only of the nation but of the world. Without this movie (or some equally sensational dramatization), the POW/MIA issue could not have assumed its mythic role in the lives of tens of millions of Americans, for essential to their faith was personally witnessing some powerful visual display of the key elements of the myth.

Six weeks after the opening of *Rambo: First Blood Part II*, President Reagan projected himself in its star role—while symbiotically hyping the film with a presidential plug—as he declared (ostensibly as a microphone test before his national address on the release of U.S. hostages in Beirut): "Boy, I saw *Rambo* last night. Now I know what to do the next time this happens."[43] Later that month, members of Congress "signaled a new tough-minded attitude" on foreign relations by invoking the image of Rambo a dozen times in debating a foreign aid bill.[44] Rambo's political repercussions have continued to ricochet around the world. In late 1990, for example, President Saddam Hussein of Iraq defiantly responded to the U.S. threat of war with his own bluster in the guise of cultural criticism: "The Americans are still influenced by Rambo movies, but this is not a Rambo movie."[45]

As *Rambo* packed theaters with audiences who howled with pleasure and wildly cheered every slaying of a Vietnamese or Russian by its invulnerable hero, the nation was flooded with Rambo "action dolls," watches, walkie-talkies, water guns, bubble gum, pinball machines, sportswear for all ages, TV cartoons, and even "Rambo-Grams," messages delivered by headbanded musclemen sporting bandoleers across their bare chests. A *Rambo* TV cartoon serial transformed Rambo into "liberty's champion," a Superman-like figure engaged in global struggles against evil; designed by Family Home Entertainment "for ages 5–12," it began its extended run in 1986. And for "adult" audiences there were the pornographic video spinoffs such as *Ramb-Ohh!* (1986) and *Bimbo: Hot Blood Part I!* (1985) and *Bimbo 2: The Homecoming!* (1986).

When Coleco Industries began mass-producing its Rambo "action figure, action figure accessories, and other play items," Michael Felker, who had served as a hospital corpsman with the Marines in Vietnam, wrote to suggest: "The Rambo doll should have removable hands, feet, legs and arms, to be interchangeable with miniature prostheses—tiny mechanical hooks and limbs; as a 'play item' Coleco should also manufacture a little electric wheelchair to move the Rambo doll from one room to another after he's been paralyzed from the waist down by a piece of 'play' shrapnel from 'friendly fire.'" Coleco replied that its Rambo products were designed to "encourage imaginative and constructive play," for "Coleco believes that the character RAMBO has the potential to become a new American hero."[46]

This new American hero was constructed in Hollywood through highly sophisticated manipulation of recycled cultural materials. Rambo's roots tap into the very foundation of American self-identity: the myth of the frontier, whose corollary "myth of regeneration through violence became the structuring metaphor of the American experience."[47]

Originally designed to express the divine purposes of the conquest and slaughter of the "Indians" by Europeans who considered themselves the first Americans, the myth of the frontier has continually metamorphosed to meet the changing cultural needs of the nation. The hordes of devilish savages from the earliest version of the myth, brought by Hollywood into the living imagination of several generations of twentieth-century Americans, are reincarnated in the swarms of fiendish Vietnamese mowed down by John Rambo.[48] Here *Rambo* perpetuates the wartime vision of Vietnam as "Injun country." However Rambo is not just the Indian fighter, recognized as the first national hero of the American state, but also the Indian. For as the myth of the frontier continued to evolve, its hero metamorphosed from being just the captive and destroyer of Indians into a figure coalescing with the Indian and the wilderness.[49]

The quintessential version of this icon is the lone frontiersman who, rejecting the conventions of civilized society, wanders deep into the country of wild Indians, who capture and torture him until he becomes more Indian than they are.[50] Contemptuous of danger, rebellious, almost superhumanly resourceful and deadly in warfare, he merges with the wilderness in body and spirit. John Rambo, we are told, is of "Indian-German descent," "a hell of a combination": "what you choose to call hell, he calls home." His long dark hair restrained by a headband, a necklace dangling above his bare chest, armed with a gigantic caricature of a bowie knife and a bow that shoots not just flaming but exploding arrows, Rambo appears almost magically from behind trees and waterfalls and literally rises out of the mud and water of the land to ambush his savage enemies.

But Rambo's powers exceed those of the mythic frontiersman, for he introduces into the POW/MIA myth the figure of the super-human savior. Rambo the mythic warrior was carefully designed, as Gregory Waller has shown, to fit the ancient formula of the semi-divine quest hero:

> *Rambo* begins quite unmistakably as the story of a quest . . . . He is called forth by Trautman; freed from prison; . . . and armed . . . with "the most advanced weapons in the world." The familiar conventions of the romance quest are explicitly evoked: Rambo is dubbed the "chosen one"; his task is a "mission" of national importance . . . his personal preparations assume through close-ups the status of the ritualized arming of the questing warrior; and his dangerous journey will take him on a perilous harrowing of "Hell" (as Vietnam is called in the film).[51]

But the main models for Rambo come much more directly out of American popular culture, a genesis that helps account for his tremendous impact on audiences. Perhaps the most popular author in America, Edgar Rice Burroughs, created two of Rambo's forebears: a martial arts expert and veteran of a defeated American army who fights for good causes in alien lands against seemingly insurmountable odds (John Carter); and a bare-chested muscular he-man who merges completely with the tropical jungle to carry out spectacular deeds of heroism (Tarzan). And Rambo draws much of his psychological power from one of America's most distinctive cultural products, the comic-book hero who may seem to be an ordinary human being but really possesses superhuman powers that allow him to fight, like Superman, for "truth, justice, and the American way" and to personify national fantasies, like Captain America. No wonder Rambo can stand invulnerable against the thousands of bullets fired at him, many from point-blank range, by America's enemies.

Rambo, who is crucified by the atheist Russian Communists, remains as pure as he is purely male. Indeed, the only women in the movie are a Vietnamese prostitute whom we glimpse servicing the lecherous Vietnamese guards, and Co Boa, a beautiful Vietnamese (played by model Julia Nickson, whose elaborate makeup stays unsmeared through jungle chases and shoot-outs) totally dedicated and subservient to Rambo and his goal. Co Boa even assumes the role of the prostitute to rescue Rambo, and is rewarded with a chaste kiss just before she is killed off in time for him to complete his mission all by himself. The erotic center of the movie, and the immediate source of its most potent audience appeal, is Stallone's glistening, fetishized, hypermuscular male body, ardently ogled by the camera. When this embodiment of the American male dream unleashes himself upon them, the hideous Yellow Peril and Red Menace intrinsic to the creed of live POWs finally meet their nemesis.

Yet for Rambo, the real enemy is neither the treacherous little Vietnamese nor their sadistic Russian masters, who are merely the perils that a hero must overcome, something like ferocious hordes of rats or schools of man-eating sharks. The real enemy is the "bureaucrats" and "politicians" who run "the system" with marvelous technology and utter cynicism. It is the "they" conjured up in full-page ads that summarize the entire plot: "They sent him on a mission and set him up to fail. But they made one mistake. They forgot they were dealing with Rambo."

In *Uncommon Valor* and *Missing in Action*, the imprisonment to which American society subjects its Vietnam veterans is mostly domestic and metaphoric. But when we first see Rambo in *First Blood Part II*, he is performing slave labor, breaking rocks in a desolate prison as punishment for his rebellion against the brutal lawmen of *First Blood*, so he suffers the same fate in America as his buddies, abandoned by America, suffer in Vietnam. When his former commanding officer, Green Beret Lieutenant Colonel Trautman, offers him freedom in exchange for his mission in Vietnam, Rambo makes his famous reply: "Do we get to win this time?" Resonating in the question are years of rewritten and reimaged history that have taught the 1985 audience that we could have won the war if only the politicians, the media, the liberal establishment, bureaucrats, draft-dodging college students and their pinko professors, hippies, wimps, bleeding-heart housewives, and Jane Fonda hadn't tied our boys' hands and stabbed them in the back.

The real enemy is personified by the archetypal bureaucrat, the perfidious, gutless, but seemingly omnipotent Marshall Murdock. Accused of being "a stinking bureaucrat that's trying to cover his ass," Murdock, who explicitly represents "Washington," replies, "Not just mine . . . a nation's." Trautman advises Rambo, "Let technology do most of the work," referring to Murdock's wondrous computer complex and high-tech weaponry. But Murdock uses his machines and underlings to sabotage the mission. The climax of the movie comes after Rambo returns with the POWs he has rescued, when he proceeds to blast Murdock's computers with automatic weapon fire and uses his gigantic knife to subjugate the whining, quivering, wimpy traitor.

So *Rambo* projects a fantasy in which the audience gets to beat the enemies of everyday life, the boss and his computerized control over work life, the bureaucrats and politicians who conspire to emasculate America's virility and betray the American dream. The audience finds its surrogates both in the POWs who embody humiliated American manhood and who are betrayed to remain enslaved to Vietnam, and in the warrior hero who can rescue them when he escapes the imprisonment of post-Vietnam America.

The Plots Thicken

The advent of *Rambo* helped make the MIA religion not only a distinctive feature of American culture but also a lucrative market. Rescuing POWs from the evil Vietnamese Communists now became almost a rite of passage for Hollywood heroes, as the formula degenerated through *P.O.W.: The Escape*, the 1986 Israeli production starring David Carradine, to *Operation Nam*, a 1987 Italian production starring John Wayne's son Ethan Wayne, which might be called the first spaghetti rescue movie. In 1987 appeared the first issue of *Vietnam Journal*, a comic book prominently displaying on every cover the POW/MIA logo next to a lead about an MIA feature. In 1985, Jack Buchanan published *M.I.A. Hunter*, a mass-market paperback novel featuring a POW rescue mission by Mark Stone, a former Green Beret who "has only one activity that gives meaning to his life—finding America's forgotten fighting men, the P.O.W.'s the government has conveniently labeled M.I.A.'s, and bringing them back from their hell on earth"; by 1987, Buchanan had published six more volumes in what had become the immensely popular *M.I.A. Hunter* series, each promising more blood than the last: *M.I.A. Hunter: Cambodian Hellhole* (1985); *M.I.A. Hunter: Hanoi Deathgrip* (1985); *M.I.A. Hunter: Mountain Massacre* (1985); *M.I.A. Hunter: Exodus from Hell* (1986); *M.I.A. Hunter: Blood Storm* (1986); and *M.I.A. Hunter: Saigon Slaughter* (1987).[52]

These cultural products that disseminate the MIA mythology and help to give it potent forms in the popular imagination have tended increasingly to project a vast government cover-up and conspiracy. *Vietnam Journal*, for example, in 1990 ran a three-part series entitled

"Is the U.S. Hiding the Truth About Missing Soldiers?" (numbers 11, 12, 13; the answer of course was yes). In the 1989 TV movie *The Forgotten*, starring Keith Carradine and Stacy Keach, high government officials actually conspire to torture and assassinate POWs held by Vietnam until 1987 so they won't reveal that these officials had colluded with North Vietnam to sabotage a POW rescue mission. Jack Buchanan's M.I.A. Hunter constantly battles against "Washington" and its sinister operatives, and in *M.I.A. Hunter: Cambodian Hellhole* he can pursue his quest only "after demolishing a C.I.A hit team sent to arrest him."

Meanwhile, however, Rambo was also having his influence in the government itself. No postwar U.S. White House spokesperson actually claimed that American prisoners were still being held in Vietnam until October 1985, while *Rambo*, which had been released in May, was still packing the theaters. The assertion, that "there have to be live Americans there," was made by none other than Robert C. McFarlane, President Reagan's national security adviser, to a forum for business executives and political consultants sponsored by syndicated columnists Rowland Evans and Robert Novak.[53]

But just as in the movie, Rambo was already proving to be difficult to control by the government once he was unleashed and empowered. Within weeks of the release of the film, its messages were being taken too literally by a grouping of POW/MIA activists known as the "Rambo faction." At the July convention of the National League of Families, a speech declaring that the government had "attempted to track down every lead, and respond to every allegation, and we will continue to do so" was interrupted by chants of "Rambo! Rambo!"[54]

In December, CBS TV's influential program *60 Minutes* aired a segment on the POW issue entitled "Dead or Alive." Its producer, Monika Jensen-Stevenson, claimed that the show was designed to present the "two sides" of the issue. One side was the official position of the Reagan administration: there might be live POWs in Southeast Asia; when and if their existence were proved, the government would use all necessary means to recover them. And what was the other side? That live POWs were merely a myth that had now become a distinctive feature of American culture? No, the other side was the position of the "Rambo faction": the government itself was engaged in a vast conspiracy to conceal its own certain evidence of the existence of dozens if not hundreds of live POWs.[55]

Jensen-Stevenson, soon aided by her husband, William Stevenson, British author of *A Man Called Intrepid* and *Ninety Minutes at Entebbe*, spent the next five years building a case for this enormous conspiracy inside the State Department, Defense Department, Central Intelligence Agency, and other branches of government under the Reagan administration. But before the Stevensons published *Kiss the Boys Goodbye: How the United States Betrayed Its Own POWs in Vietnam* in the fall of 1990, an even more radical attack on the government appeared as a volume entitled *A Nation Betrayed* by none other than Colonel Bo Gritz.

With belief in live POWs now an article of faith in American culture, there was no longer a pressing need to explain why the Vietnamese would wish to retain hostages whose existence they denied. Once the Vietnamese were transformed into the sadistic little monsters imaged in *The Deer Hunter, Uncommon Valor, Missing in Action*, and *Rambo*, Asian cruelty and Communist perfidy had once again become good enough explanations. So the question had shifted from why in the world the Vietnamese government would hold these men to why in the world the U.S. government would abandon these heroes and even cover up their fate. *Uncommon Valor* and *Missing in Action I* and *II* had dramatized an answer in the form of "bureaucrats" and "politicians" cynically pandering to a feminized, opportunist, materialist society. But the specific motives of these bureaucrats and politicians remained rather vague until the explanation given in *Rambo: First Blood Part II*, that the government was covering up a broken secret promise: "In '72 we were supposed to pay the Cong four and a half billion dollars in war reparations! We reneged! They kept the POWs!" Yet this could hardly explain a conspiracy within the government that keeps mushrooming years after it was revealed that the Nixon administration had reneged on this obligation and long after Vietnam had given up any hope that it would be honored by subsequent administrations.

Colonel Gritz presents an argument with more plausibility, at least to those aware of some of the Byzantine relations among the CIA, various White House officials, covert military operations, and the international drug trade. In 1987, Gritz made his second trip to a remote region in Burma that forms part of the Golden Triangle, one of the world's major sources of heroin, to interview the drug lord and warlord General Khun Sa about American POWs in Laos. But the interview, which Gritz videotaped, evidently consisted mainly of detailed allegations by Khun Sa about his dealings with U.S. government agents, including officials high in the Reagan and Bush administrations, who were using the Joint Casualty Resolution Center in Bangkok not to resolve the POW/MIA question but mainly as a cover for their own illicit activities. The following year, Gritz published *A Nation Betrayed*, an astonishing document whose thesis is: "a parallel government has existed for decades, which led us into a war that cost more than 58,000 lives and infused our nation with drugs"; this "shadow government has used drug and arms trafficking to fund illegal covert operations"; and the agents of this "cancerous bureaucracy," realizing that the discovery of American POWs would lead to the unmasking of their own sinister activities in Indochina, have systematically sabotaged every effort to find and rescue the prisoners.[56]

Kiss the Boys Goodbye elaborates Gritz's argument with considerably more detail and documentation, incorporating it into a wider thesis: "America's wars in Southeast Asia had not ended with the fall of Saigon"; the "rogue secret wars in Asia," conducted by "a really deep-cover privatized CIA" and other covert agencies, were financed by a "trillion-dollar drug trade."[57] The Stevensons thus explain not only why Vietnam, Laos, and Cambodia would continue to hold American POWs, but also why officials and agencies of the U.S. government would conspire to conceal the existence of the POWs, even resorting to assassinations of those who knew too much: the Indochinese governments keep prisoners because wars are still being waged on them, and the U.S. war makers are afraid that discovery of the POWs would expose the connections between their covert wars and their own complicity in the global drug trade.

Ironically, the Stevensons build much of their case from materials that Gritz had revealed about a government conspiracy not to block but to facilitate his POW rescue attempts. In 1981, Gritz had supplied *Boston Globe* reporter Ben Bradlee, Jr., with extensive documentation of Pentagon support for his planned forays, and in early 1982 Bradlee received Defense Department confirmation that the supersecret Pentagon agency Gritz claimed to work with did indeed exist.[58] But it was not until his congressional testimony of March 1983 that the most interesting cat Gritz was letting out of his bag began to attract significant public attention. In both his oral testimony and his prepared written statement, he kept referring to a supersecret Pentagon outfit known as The Activity, which he insisted had been working with him on planning a POW rescue raid.[59] One of the very few people who noticed these references, much less took them seriously, was *New York Times* reporter Raymond Bonner, whose investigation led to his exposure several weeks later of the Intelligence Support Activity (ISA), a clandestine Army unit whose covert operations were subject to virtually no scrutiny or oversight and whose existence led to further disclosures of a Byzantine labyrinth of similar organizations.[60] The Stevensons use these revelations, especially as synthesized in Steven Emerson's *Secret Warriors: Inside the Covert Military Operations of the Reagan Era*, to argue their case for a vast government conspiracy involving American prisoners in Indochina, conveniently ignoring the fact that the Pentagon conspirators were plotting not to conceal but to reveal and rescue the alleged POWs.

Kiss the Boys Goodbye has certainly reinforced the faith of believers in live POWs and has won hosts of new converts. But it will hardly convince any skeptical or careful readers, for the Stevensons' book consists largely of accounts of interviews with shadowy pseudonymous figures from the world of covert operations, and its argument is riddled with inconsistencies and permeated by exaggeration. Yet its underlying case about secret wars, government deceit, drug connections, and other illegal government activities rests on a solid foundation, built by its principal written sources. Like *A Nation Betrayed*, *Kiss the Boys Goodbye*—to the surprise of those who would regard both books as right-wing tracts—relies heavily on written sources generally perceived as coming from the left, such as Jonathan Kwitny's *The Crimes of Patriots: A True Tale of Dope, Dirty Money, and the CIA*, legal papers from the Christic Institute, and, most fundamentally, that classic work of scholarship, Alfred McCoy's *The Politics of Heroin in Southeast Asia* (whose discrediting by the CIA is also documented by the Stevensons).[61] Though it fails to demonstrate how the existence of covert, illegal government activities proves the existence of live POWs, the Stevensons' book does succeed in suggesting why those engaged in these activities might desperately want to keep unrestrained POW/MIA investigators from mucking around in Southeast Asia. And the main effect of the Stevensons' volume may be to introduce believers in live POWs to the scholarship demonstrating that the Vietnam War itself was one of those "murky foreign wars" conducted for interests shrouded by U.S. government duplicity and waged by "disposable soldiers."[62]

As it moves into opposition to that government, *Kiss the Boys Goodbye* also turns to attack the main organization sponsoring the POW/MIA issue for two decades, the National League of Families. Repeating charges that the League is merely "an arm of government to discourage questions about administration policy on prisoners in Vietnam," the Stevensons deride Ann Mills Griffiths, "the salaried Executive Director of the National League," as "a mournful figure who appeared in official photographs that were taken whenever the U.S. president displayed a periodic concern for missing Americans by attending a League meeting." "Usually dressed in black for these occasions," they go on, her main function seems to be to dismiss those who truly labored on behalf of live prisoners as "'profiteers and charlatans.'"[63] To clinch the argument, *Kiss the Boys Goodbye* includes as an appendix a letter from President Reagan described as follows: "In this letter the National League of Families is identified as a member of the Government Interagency Group." Thus the official status of the National League, which had been publicly acknowledged by the Defense Department's own annual *POW-MIA Fact Book* since the early 1980s, is here offered as shocking evidence of a high-level conspiracy not to concoct but to conceal the existence of live American POWs in Southeast Asia.

In the 1970s, the Pentagon Papers and Watergate had shocked a generation of Americans with revelations about government and presidential lies and conspiracies. Ironically, all this had helped prepare the ground for the seeds of the postwar POW/MIA myth, with its vision of the Nixon, Ford, and Carter administrations conniving out of sheer cowardice to cover up their betrayal of the POWs. Then under the sponsorship of the Reagan administration, with the enthusiastic cooperation of Hollywood, and nourished by a flood of jingoism, the myth was boosted into something tantamount to a national religion by the mid-1980s. But the contorted history of the POW/MIA issue was about to receive still another ironic twist. The Iran-Contra exposés of 1986 and 1987 offered glimpses into depths of government intrigue, venality, and duplicity that made the crimes of the Watergate burglars and their commander-in-chief seem like normal and customary Washington behavior. Tens of millions of TV viewers learned that any government scheme, no matter how outrageous, might be masked by "plausible deniability," which the Pentagon Papers had earlier exposed as the official locution for lying to the people. No government conspiracy to betray the POWs now seemed too farfetched, too vicious, or too rapacious, not even the machinations presented in books like *A Nation Betrayed* and *Kiss the Boys Goodbye*. Who could have imagined that the revelations about the government which had once fueled the movement to stop the war would now be used to make the war virtually endless?

By 1991, national debate about the POW/MIA issue had devolved into a contest between two positions. One maintained that there were certainly Americans still being held prisoner in Vietnam and that the government was covering up its own failure to get them back. This was the view of the majority of Americans.[64] The minority position held that the government was doing a responsible job of investigating the evidence that there might be American prisoners still in Indochina. Almost entirely absent from public consciousness was the truth: the government of the United States had concocted the POW/MIA issue in the first place, had perpetuated it for decades, and since 1982 had actively collaborated in turning it into a national myth.

So as the final decade of the twentieth century dawned, the POW/MIA myth, which had already assumed a life of its own, was becoming a Frankenstein's monster for the forces that had fabricated it out of spare parts of older myths. Whether it can be disposed of, once it has fulfilled the varying purposes that it has been serving since 1969, remains to be seen.

5 ■ STILL MISSING

Recovery

Sooner or later the myth that there are still live American POWs in Southeast Asia must fade away. Since not a shred of verifiable evidence of a single living prisoner has ever surfaced, it seems safe to predict that no such being will ever be discovered. As it becomes less biologically likely, or even possible, that anyone who might have been a prisoner could still be alive, the rescue fantasies will certainly become obsolete, unless they take the form of time-travel fiction.

And sooner or later the political motives for creating the myth in the first place should die out. The United States has been waging military or economic warfare against Vietnam directly or indirectly ever since the end of World War II. For close to half this period, this warfare has been rationalized first by the POW issue and then by the POW/MIA myth. As we have seen, the POW issue was originally fabricated in early 1969 to protract the Vietnam War, which it helped to do for four years. Conceived as a means to foment pro-war moral passion, obscure the atrocities the United States was perpetrating, deadlock negotiations, and dehistoricize Americans' understanding of the war, it proved to be a roaring success, and a far more powerful and long-lived creature than even its makers might have imagined, thus helping to legitimize the ensuing political and economic warfare. But at some point the United States will probably finally recognize and establish normal relations with Vietnam. When U.S. corporations begin major investments and enterprises in Vietnam, it will then no longer be in the interest of the dominant U.S. economic and political institutions to have millions of citizens believing that secretly imprisoned someplace in that land are live American POWs from a war that ended in the 1970s.

What may very well survive, however, is a lingering belief that once upon a time there were American prisoners who were betrayed and abandoned. So even in that form, the myth may retain considerable potency. For its power springs from sources much deeper than the Vietnam War itself, though intimately related both to the motives that led America to wage that war and to the war's aftermath in America.

In the final analysis, the POW/MIA myth must be understood not just as a convenient political gimmick for rationalizing various kinds of warfare and jingoism but also as a symptom of a profound psychological sickness in American culture. One path back toward mental health would be through an honest self-examination of how and why a society could have been so possessed by such a grotesque myth.

But the disease can never be cured so long as we fail to confront the true tragedy of the missing in Vietnam. We certainly need a "full accounting," but one far more painful than the kind demanded by our government.

A Story of the Missing and the Missing Story

It seemed to me that an appropriate ending for this book would be the story of the first joint American-Vietnamese excavation of a crash site, a story that reveals the simple, painful truth about the people still missing from the Vietnam War and encourages us to face this truth honestly and bravely. Many of the details of the story, reported by American correspondents on the site where a B-52 had crashed into a small village north of Hanoi, had appeared in the U.S. press, from which I had an extensive file of clippings. From one of the clippings—but only one—it was possible to identify the B-52 and the two surviving crew members, who had been captured and released in Operation Homecoming.

This particular UPI dispatch, which had appeared in the Newark, New Jersey, *Star-Ledger* of December 1, 1985, under the curiously misleading headline BOMBER ADDS LITTLE TO MIA HUNT, indicated that the team of "U.S. experts and Vietnamese laborers" had recovered "two of the B52 bomber's engines, flight manuals, landing struts and a life raft." It seemed odd that the U.S. officers maintained that they were nevertheless "unable to identify the plane," especially since Colonel Joe Harvey, head of the search team and also chief of the Joint Casualty Resolution Center in Thailand, seemed to contradict this when he stated in the report that "U.S. records show the bomber was one of three that took off from Utapao Airbase in Thailand" and that it had exploded at "30,000 feet" after being hit by "two Soviet-made SAM missiles." In fact, Vietnamese officials actually revealed to the UPI reporter and other American journalists the identity of the two surviving crewmen, "the copilot and navigator of the excavated bomber, Lt. Paul Granger and Capt. Thomas Klomann," who "parachuted to safety, were taken prisoner and released in 1973."

Searching through all the other clippings, I discovered no further reference to Utapao, to the shoot-down, or to the two survivors by name, although many articles did state that two crewmen from the bomber were taken prisoner and later released. Following research methods used elsewhere in this book, I moved from the clipping file to a systematic search of electronic data bases of major U.S. news-papers, magazines, news services, and scholarly bibliographies. I found several AP stories, a few magazine articles, and a number of newspaper stories, almost all based on a series of UPI dispatches from Yen Thuong, the village where the B-52 had crashed. Not one of these stories mentioned Utapao, the shoot-down, or the names of the two surviving crewmen. This in itself seemed rather curious, simply because of the human interest in these details and even more because these facts could be used to establish a precise identification of the four men missing from the crew of six, thus allowing us to account for four MIAs.

But the real shock came when I searched the UPI data base itself. There were seventeen stories about Yen Thuong, the crash site, and the missing bomber, all dispatched between November 1985 and November 1986. But missing without a trace from the UPI data base was the one and only story that contained the names of the surviving crewmen, mentioned the recovery of major components of the B-52, and told of its flight and shoot-down. Since none of these facts appear in any other press report that I have been able to locate, evidently they have been completely wiped out of all press records. So unless you happen to have an actual physical newspaper or clipping from December 1, 1985, you may be unable to verify crucial parts of the story that I will soon tell.

Perhaps there are innocent explanations for all this. Maybe this erasure of history was done by accident, not by conscious conspiracy. But certainly consciousness was involved in not pursuing the most interesting and revealing aspects of the story. Clearly the Vietnamese officials who told the American reporters the names of the surviving crewmen meant to be telling the whole story to the American people, including the details that would identify the four MIAs. It is our own officials who in private know full well that the four missing crewmen died in the crash of that B-52 while they tacitly encourage the American people to imagine that they might still be suffering untold horrors in a Vietnamese prison camp. And whether by design or not, it is our own media that allow the fate of those four men to remain part of an ambiguous story about MIAs instead of becoming part of the true story of what is still missing from our confrontation with the reality of the Vietnam War.

Goaded by the mystery of the disappearing facts, I continued my investigation along other paths and was able to reconstruct crucial missing elements from the story of the B-52 that had crashed into Yen Thuong village. This true story offers a powerful antidote to the poisons of the POW/MIA myth.[1]

In November 1985, while American audiences were still packing movie theaters to cheer Rambo, the first joint Vietnamese-American search of a crash site in Vietnam began. The American team included four experts from the U.S. Army's Central Identification Laboratory, two explosives experts, a medic, and two Army engineers to operate the technological equipment they brought with them, including metal detectors, metal cutting tools, water pumps, and a 21,000-pound excavator. The site was in the small farming village of Yen Thuong, nine miles north of Hanoi, where a B-52 had crashed during the Christmas bombing thirteen years earlier.

On the night of December 20, 1972, that B-52 was preparing to drop its forty tons of bombs on Hanoi. But as it approached the city, it was hit, first by fire from a MiG fighter and then by a volley of two or three surface-to-air missiles. With an internal fire, its right wing in flames, without electrical power, unable to communicate, and lacking even its intercom system, the plane spun out of control. All six crewmen were reported as missing in action.

Two of the men, however, did manage to bail out, copilot Paul L. Granger and bombardier-navigator Thomas J. Klomann. Both were immediately captured. Granger was sent to Hoa Lo Prison (the Hanoi Hilton), where he says he spent the majority of his time "playing cards and chess" until he was released three months later in the last plane from Hanoi. Klomann gives this account of his captivity:

> Apparently, I was unconscious when I landed and was taken to a North Vietnamese hospital. I didn't regain consciousness for about a

week and remained semi-conscious for another two weeks. The other POWs had asked the Vietnamese to feed me intravenously, which they did, and also take care of a large bed sore which had developed on my tailbone. They also gave me leg splints to keep my feet from dropping. I spent a little less than two months in Hanoi and was among the first to be returned.[2]

The other four crewmen have remained part of the total of MIAs reported in the media ever since.

That is the story of the lost bomber and its crew from the American point of view. For the villagers on the ground in Yen Thuong, it was a different story.

Nguyen Duc Tru, who was then forty-three, vividly remembers that night, when suddenly "there was a great explosion and a big fire." "Dust and smoke covered the whole village," and the people, believing they were being bombed, took refuge in their air raid shelters. But eight villagers did not escape, for they were killed by the crashing bomber. Two of these were the husband and twelve-year-old son of Nguyen Thi Teo, who were in their little house, which was totally demolished as the wreckage of the giant plane with its forty-ton bomb load exploded deep into the earth itself.

In the morning, all that remained were scattered pieces of metal and a deep crater filled with water. A few days later, another part of Yen Thuong village was more than half destroyed by B-52 bombs, and many more villagers were killed. None of the survivors could have been more grief-stricken than Nguyen Thi Teo, who for two weeks wept and could eat nothing but rice soup. Perhaps the members of the National League of Families who lost either a husband or a son could understand, for she had lost both a husband and a son.

When the American-Vietnamese team arrived in Yen Thuong in November 1985, hundreds of peasants flocked to gaze at the nine-ton excavator as it drove down the narrow dirt country road and came to the site of the 1972 crash, which was now Nguyen Thi Teo's vegetable garden. But to gain access to the dig, the team first had to demolish two houses that stood in the way. One of them was the new home of Nguyen Thi Teo, now sixty years old. "It is difficult to have this memory come again," she replied when American reporters asked her how she felt about all this. "I don't hate the Americans," she said. "I don't have any feelings but sadness for the loss of my son and husband." She, who had her own missing in action, went on to say, "If they find something of my loved ones, then that is good."

Indeed, on the first day and in the first few feet of digging, the excavators discovered eighteen or twenty small human bone fragments embedded in the wet, dark earth. When the excavation ended two weeks later, it had spread over five hundred square feet and had bored to a depth of thirty-six feet. No further human remains were found. As for the bone fragments recovered the first day, they were taken away by the Americans and sent to the U.S. identification laboratory in Honolulu to determine whether they were remains "of American MIAs." There is no hint in any U.S. press report that anyone considered the possibility that they might be remains of Vietnamese MIAs, such as the husband and son of Nguyen Thi Teo, though they were unearthed days before the diggers reached major components of the B-52, in the earth just beneath their demolished home.

In reality, as opposed to the POW/MIA myth, the missing Americans cannot be separated from the missing Vietnamese. The bones of many Americans have mingled not just with the earth of Vietnam but also with the bones of many Vietnamese. Those who are still missing are just as dead as the husband and son of Nguyen Thi Teo, and the Vietnamese dead are just as missing as those dead Americans. When we recognize and confront all that we—and the peoples of Indochina—have truly lost and that will remain forever missing in Vietnam, Laos, and Cambodia, perhaps we can at least recover some of our lost moral and psychological health.

When Colonel Harvey met with Yen Thuong village chief Nguyen Van Thanh to thank him for the commune's cooperation and to apologize for the two-week disruption, the Vietnamese responded, "We hope what is left from the past will be resolved and U.S.-Vietnamese relations will improve day by day. Let bygones be bygones." If the villagers of Yen Thuong, with all their losses, can feel this way, perhaps someday we will learn to share their wisdom.

6 ■ "THE LAST CHAPTER"?

Flush with what seemed America's glorious victory in the Persian Gulf War, President George Bush on March 1, 1991, bragged to a nation festooned in jingoist yellow ribbons, "By God, we've kicked the Vietnam syndrome once and for all!"[1] Kicked? Syndrome? Had Vietnam become America's addiction? Its pathology? In his strange choice of language, the president may have revealed more than he intended.

The president's diagnosis proved far more accurate than his prognosis. A year and a half after claiming to have cured us of our Vietnam disease, George Bush was on national TV shouting "Shut up and sit down!" at MIA family members heckling him at the July 1992 annual convention of the National League of Families.

Between these two exclamations by the president, the POW/MIA issue had metamorphosed into outlandish new forms contorting American politics and psychology. One victim was a new Vietnam policy adopted by the White House; another may have been the president himself, defeated in an election skewed by the candidacy of Ross Perot, that original POW/MIA huckster.

On April 9, 1991, a month after declaring that the "Vietnam syndrome" had been "kicked," President Bush, perhaps emboldened by his popularity as leader of "Operation Desert Storm," handed

Vietnam a "Road Map" toward normalizing relations within two years. This timetable outlined four phases, each contingent upon Vietnam's making what Washington considered satisfactory progress in resolving "all remaining POW/MIA cases." As part of the process, an office for ongoing joint investigation of American MIAs was opened in Hanoi. Evidently under some corporate pressure to lift the trade embargo, the administration hinted that the normalization process might even include limited trade before the end of 1991.[2]

Instantly the smoldering POW/MIA issue was fanned into a firestorm. In Congress the incendiary crew was led by Republican Senators Jesse Helms, Charles Grassley, Hank Brown, and Bob Smith. In May, Helms released, in the name of all Republicans on the Senate Foreign Relations Committee, *An Examination of U.S. Policy Toward POW/MIAs*, a hundred-page pseudohistory alleging that Communist regimes have been retaining U.S. POWs since 1917, that *thousands* of U.S. POWs were abandoned in Indochina, and that some are still alive, concealed and betrayed by a vast Washington conspiracy.

Helms's *Examination of U.S. Policy Toward POW/MIAs* claimed that the U.S. POWs "repatriated by the North Vietnamese during Operation HOMECOMING" were merely "12% of the figure of 5,000 held by the North Vietnamese reported by *The New York Times*."[3] Where did Helms and his cohorts get the figure 5,000? From a March 1973 *New York Times* story as cited in an AP dispatch: "'While the North Vietnamese did not list a number of prisoners they wanted freed, *The New York Times* reported from Saigon today that American sources set the demand at 5,000.'" After it was pointed out that the figure 5,000 in both the AP dispatch and *Times* story referred not to U.S. POWs but to the number of prisoners North Vietnam was demanding from Saigon, Helms's staff removed the quotation from later printings but kept the 5,000 count, now documented by unnamed "sources interviewed by the Committee staff."[4] As Deputy Assistant Secretary of Defense Carl Ford was later to testify, the report is so permeated by falsehoods that "to catalogue the inaccuracies would require a document of equal length."[5]

The report's principal author, Helms staffer Tracy Usry, was publicly exposed in November 1991 as having falsified much of its evidence about abandoned POWs.[6] Finally in January 1992 several increasingly embarrassed Republican members of the Senate Foreign Relations Committee, who had not even been consulted before the report was issued in their name, forced Helms to fire most of his top staff members, including Usry.[7]

Nevertheless, *An Examination of U.S. Policy Toward POW/MIAs* continued to be mailed out daily by the Senate Foreign Relations Committee. By mid 1992, well over a hundred thousand copies were in circulation, all printed and distributed at taxpayer expense and bearing the seal of the U.S. Senate.[8] POW/MIA activists, who refer to it as "The Senate Report on POW/MIAs," cite it by chapter and verse. More ominously, the report helped the men behind its creation—including Helms, Grassley, Brown, and Smith—create the Senate Select Committee on POW/MIA Affairs and secure positions that would shape the committee's assumptions and procedures.

Senator Smith's staff had helped engineer the Helms document, and he then tried to set up a Senate committee designed to give this thesis respectability and keep it before the public. But by mid July 1991, he was making little progress and the Senate was due to recess on August 2.

Suddenly on July 17 began one of the most spectacular media coups in U.S. history, orchestrated largely by Smith and his associates. A photograph allegedly showing U.S. POWs from the Vietnam War still held captive in Indochina exploded as the lead story on national TV and radio networks. Newspapers across the country front-paged the picture under banner headlines. The three men were identified as John Robertson, Albro Lundy, Jr., and Larry

Stevens, three pilots shot down over Vietnam and Laos between 1966 and 1970. Within a week photographs ostensibly showing two more POWs in Indochina—identified as Navy pilot Daniel Borah, Jr., and Special Forces Captain Donald Carr—hit the media. According to a *Wall Street Journal*/NBC News poll, 69 percent of the American people now believed that American POWs were being held in Indochina and 52 percent were convinced that the government was derelict in not getting them back.[9] A headline in the August 2 *Wall Street Journal* read "Bring on Rambo."

The same day a stampeded Senate unanimously passed Bob Smith's resolution to create a Senate Select Committee on POW/MIA Affairs—along with a resolution to fly the POW/MIA flag over federal buildings. Breaching the custom of majority control, Republicans got as many seats on the committee as Democrats, who included Harry Reid, sponsor of the POW/MIA flag-flying resolution, and John Kerry, named chairman. The six Republicans included Helms; Grassley (who had helped craft the Helms document); former POW John McCain; Hank Brown, who had authored resolutions reiterating President Reagan's 1983 pledge that the POW/MIA issue must be "the highest national priority"; and Smith, named vice chairman. Brown and Smith had been working together with dubious POW/MIA fundraisers Captain Eugene "Red" McDaniel and Billy Hendon since at least 1987, when they and nineteen other Republican members of Congress had each pledged $100,000 toward McDaniel and Hendon's $2.4 million-dollar reward for the return of a live POW, an offer which generated a tidal wave of phony live sightings, dog tags, and photographs.[10]

The photos that launched the Senate Select Committee later proved as bogus as all the other "evidence" of live POWs in the last two decades. "Daniel Borah" turned out to be a Lao highlander who had happily posed because he never had his photograph taken before.[11] "Donald Carr" was a German bird smuggler photographed in a Bangkok rare bird sanctuary.[12] The picture of "Robertson,

Lundy, and Stevens" was a doctored version of a 1923 photograph reproduced in a 1989 Soviet magazine discovered in the Phnom Penh national library; the three men were actually holding a poster proclaiming the glories of collective farming (mustaches had been added and a picture of Stalin subtracted).[13]

All the photographs were the handiwork of notorious scam artists. Each was used by POW/MIA crusaders to blitz the media and manipulate the public—and thus help create the Senate Select Committee. Senator Smith provided the "Daniel Borah" pictures to the Pentagon and then went on the *Today* show to display them to a national TV audience.[14] The "Robertson, Lundy, Stevens" picture had been released by Red McDaniel, head of the right-wing American Defense Institute, who has been promising the faithful since 1986 that as soon as they contribute enough money he will produce live POWs. McDaniel got it from Jack Bailey, head of a crooked POW/MIA fundraising operation known as Operation Rescue. Bailey, who had conspired to fake the "Donald Carr" photos, assaulted two ABC reporters on camera when they confronted him in the rare bird sanctuary where the pictures had actually been taken.[15]

As vice chairman, Smith was able to place fanatical POW/MIA crusaders from his staff in key posts on the committee's staff. Smith staffer Dino Carluccio, a major designer of the Helms report, was given the powerful office of deputy staff director. Carluccio worked closely with another Smith staffer, former Republican Representative Billy Hendon, whose shady solicitations of hundreds of thousands of dollars for McDaniel's American Defense Institute had prompted numerous calls for investigating and possibly prosecuting him. *Time* reported that Hendon's presence was one reason the Select Committee "made little progress in its inquiry into those who prey on families of missing service personnel." As one insider said, "How can we investigate Hendon when Hendon's on the staff?"[16]

A flagrant example of how these committee staff members conducted their investigation occurred in October 1991, when Vietnamese defector Colonel Bui Tin arrived from Paris to testify. Before he could be met by his host, he was intercepted by Carluccio and Hendon, who tried to strong-arm him into testifying, despite his repeated denials, that American POWs are being held in Vietnam.[17] Eventually the behavior of Carluccio and Hendon became so outrageous that Chairman Kerry in July 1992 fired both from the committee's staff. Co-chairman Smith immediately put the duo back in his own office.

John Kerry's own staff unanimously argued against his trying to steer a committee with the Helms-Grassley-Brown-Smith crew on board through the treacherous POW/MIA swamp, but he overruled them.[18] Kerry himself may have been unaware of how the POW/MIA issue had been used back in April 1971, when he joined hundreds of other antiwar Vietnam veterans to throw their medals at the Capitol. Panic-stricken by these actions and the growing antiwar movement among the POW/MIA wives, top Nixon aide H. R. Haldeman had dashed off a memo to fellow White House staffer General James Hughes, arguing that "after the Veterans' effort last week, we've got to be doubly sure we are keeping the POW wives in line." General Hughes responded: "According to Al Haig, the next eight weeks are critical and the efforts of the Ad Hoc Coordinating Groups on POW/MIA matters will be devoted to keeping the families on the reservation in order to buy this time."[19]

Ironically, Kerry now accepted the spurious history of the POW/MIA issue promulgated by those bent on continuing the conflict, including the ludicrous notion that the government during the war and ever since had been minimizing and perhaps concealing the possibility of prisoners being kept after the U.S. withdrawal. POW/MIA crusaders were thus allowed to define the committee's assumptions, goals, agenda, and procedures.

Although the committee's final report asserts "every single individual or group that has claimed to have information on the issue has been invited," the committee adamantly refused to allow testimony from anyone prepared to expose how and why the POW/MIA issue was concocted and used by the government itself to prolong the war and legitimize continuing hostilities against Vietnam ever since. The only witnesses allowed to testify were, in fact, either defenders of the government or its attackers from the POW/MIA movement.[20] So the investigation turned out to be an expanded version of Monika Jensen-Stevenson's 1985 *60 Minutes* show, an arena where government spokespersons were pitted against partisans of the Rambo faction (see page 157).

Watching the Select Committee's parade of Pentagon and State Department witnesses was a strange experience for anyone familiar with their actual roles. The very characters who had concocted the belief in live postwar POWs solemnly testified that now they believe there might have been live postwar POWs. This led to such curious episodes as Senator Kerry berating former Nixon officials Roger Shields, Frank Sieverts, and Henry Kissinger for pretending after Operation Homecoming that there were no POWs left in Indochina. In fact, all three men had been key players in the Nixon administration's fabrication of the postwar POW/MIA issue as a pretext for the United States to break its pledge of reconstruction aid to Hanoi, made in Article 21 of the Paris Peace Agreement and spelled out in the president's February 1, 1973, secret letter to Hanoi Prime Minister Pham Van Dong (see pages 122–26 and Appendix A).

When Henry Kissinger went to North Vietnam in early February 1973, before the completion of Operation Homecoming, he confronted the Hanoi government with "some 80 files of individuals who we had reason to believe had been captured," as he testified during the September 1973 Senate hearings to confirm him as secretary of state. Because "we are extremely dissatisfied" with Hanoi's accounting for these MIAs, Kissinger had concluded, "we cannot proceed in certain other areas such as economic aid negotiations."[21]

In other words, Kissinger and Nixon used the MIA issue to renege on Nixon's secret pledge, whose very existence was denied by the White House until 1976.

Why did Kissinger's list contain eighty names when the highest number of such cases then publicly claimed or secretly listed by the U.S. was fifty-six? The truth came almost two decades later from Roger Shields, the Pentagon's main POW/MIA man in 1973, who finally admitted in late 1992 that Washington had deliberately included on Kissinger's list a number of cases that the Vietnamese could not possibly account for, supposedly as a "control group."[22] Thus the Nixon administration created an issue that could never be resolved.

The Select Committee acted as though official U.S. policy in early 1973 was fully articulated by Nixon's boasts that he had liberated all the POWs. But Nixon spelled out the core of his actual policy in his 1973 report to Congress, which bragged about pressuring "the Communist side" to adhere to the "unprecedentedly specific" commitment "to secure the fullest possible accounting for each of our men."[23]

Indeed the demand for such an accounting of the missing was unprecedented. It is also a demand that can never be satisfied. Having no intention of honoring their pledge of aid, Nixon and Kissinger therefore made *accounting* for the *MIAs* the issue. But accounting is a meaningless issue unless there is some belief in the possibility of live *POWs*. Hence the Nixon, Ford, Carter, Reagan, Bush, and Clinton administrations have each tried to exaggerate—not minimize—this *possibility* of live POWs. But there is a contradiction between the government's efforts to keep the belief in the existence of POWs alive and to keep it comatose, ready to be either disconnected from its life-support machine or resuscitated as the circumstances of *Realpolitik* dictate. Seeking to maintain this ambiguous status, the government has fed the paranoia of true believers, thus turning a sleeping giant into the Frankenstein's monster of the POW/MIA myth. Hence such grotesque spectacles as 1992 Senate hearings where POW/MIA fanatics wrestled with Pentagon apologists for the mind of the nation.

Although POW/MIA crusaders created the Select Committee and constituted much of its membership, investigative staff, and witnesses, the committee was unable to produce a shred of verifiable or even credible evidence of the existence of live postwar POWs. So it is no surprise that the Select Committee concluded with a 1,285-page final report that merely restated the ambiguity created by the senators' own Republican and Democratic administrations, while also asserting that the POW/MIA issue should continue to be treated as the " 'highest national priority' by our diplomats . . . and by the nation, as a whole."[24]

While unearthing no evidence that U.S. POWs were in fact held after the war in Indochina, the committee did stumble upon potentially explosive evidence of how the Reagan administration and its right-wing allies had connived to inflate and then exploit the POW myth. But "due to time constraints, the Committee was unable to pursue these reports" of how the government, operating through the National Security Council (NSC), used the POW issue and private POW organizations "as a cover for providing . . . non-appropriated funds" to anti-government mercenaries in Indochina.[25] Before being halted by the pretext of "time constraints," the investigation produced something the media failed even to notice, much less recognize as the committee's only major discovery: a byzantine and illegal government scheme for Indochina strikingly similar to what came to be known as the Iran-Contra scandal.

Remember that in laying the groundwork for transforming the POW/MIA issue into what he designated "the highest national priority," Ronald Reagan had placed Carol Bates, original coordinator of VIVA's bracelet campaign and later executive director of the National League of Families, into his expanded POW/MIA section of the Defense Intelligence Agency, and positioned Ann Mills Griffiths as the central figure in the IAG (POW/MIA Interagency

Group). Meanwhile, as the committee confirmed, "the Government sanctioned, encouraged, funded, approved, and provided logistical support" to Bo Gritz for "some of his overseas reconnaissance and rescue operations."[26] In early 1981, while Gritz was beginning to organize for raids into Laos, the administration sent Congressmen Billy Hendon and John LeBoutillier to Laos, ostensibly to "establish a dialogue on POW/MIA issues."[27] LeBoutillier's conception of "dialogue" was revealed when he was caught purchasing weapons for Laotian mercenaries. The Bureau of Alcohol, Tobacco, and Firearms' recommendation that he be prosecuted for firearms violations was overruled by a Justice Department official who affirmed that "LeBoutillier's activities had been sanctioned by the U.S. Government."[28]

LeBoutillier, working closely with Ann Mills Griffiths and Colonel Richard Childress, NSC director of Asian affairs and political military affairs from 1981 to 1989, set up "Skyhook II," an organization that raised large sums of money, ostensibly to free POWs. Griffiths got Betty Bartels, an official of Support Our POW/MIAs, Inc., a moribund California organization with tax-exempt status, to set up several bank accounts in Bangkok and elsewhere to receive the funds. According to Bartels's sworn deposition, Carol Bates and Griffiths insisted that the "entire matter be kept in strictest confidence; that the National League of Families Boards were not aware of this. Only a U.S. Senator, to remain unnamed, and the White House, Ann, Carol and myself were aware." The funds were moved through a Bangkok bank account to mercenary forces in Laos known as the "Lao resistance."[29]

This unauthorized roundabout funding of covert operations outdid Iran-Contra in ingenuity, for it included a mechanism to sustain itself indefinitely. The "Lao resistance" produced a stream of phony evidence of live POWs for LeBoutillier to use in his Skyhook II propaganda to raise more funds for the "Lao resistance," which was then able to supply still more phony evidence of live POWs to raise still more funds and so on.[30]

Skyhook II has been raking in millions of dollars, allowing it to employ two sophisticated telemarketing companies. One had LeBoutillier's outfit claiming in October 1992 that "our effort to have the government admit to live POW/MIAs in Southeast Asia has been so relentless" that the Senate Committee "subpoenaed our records," proving "we are now closer than ever to bringing these war heroes home."[31]

The media circus invoked by the Select Committee and other assorted POW/MIA crusaders in 1992 soon featured two spectacular novel acts, one by a newcomer to the big top—Russian President Boris Yeltsin—the other by its original ringmaster, now would-be U.S. president, Ross Perot.

On Monday, June 15, Yeltsin told NBC-TV that "our archives" show that some U.S. POWs from Vietnam "were transferred to the territory of the former USSR and were kept in labor camps. We don't have complete data and can only surmise that some of them may still be alive." He must have forgotten that on Friday, June 12, he personally reported to the committee that Soviet archives had disclosed absolutely "no data" about any "US citizens listed as missing in action in Vietnam and other countries of South-East Asia."[32] Or maybe the Russian president thus showed how much he had learned from U.S. presidents about how to manipulate the POW/MIA issue to implement his own political agenda.

Yeltsin had three goals. First, he wanted to turn the issue into a weapon to use against those forces in Russia hostile to his rule, particularly the remnants of the Communist Party. Second, by presenting himself as the champion of the American people seeking to liberate their POWs from the clutches of these evil Communists, he hoped to gain billions of U.S. dollars to support his rule. And third, recognizing that normal political and economic relations between the United States and Vietnam would wipe out what remained of Russian economic interests in Vietnam, he was firing a well-aimed salvo at the process of normalization.

While President Yeltsin was fighting for his political life, so was

President Bush. And so now the very man who boasted about healing America's Vietnam wounds tried to win reelection by reopening them, eventually turning what Bill Clinton had or hadn't done during the Vietnam War into the Republicans' main campaign issue. The Democrats responded by juxtaposing what Dan Quayle had or hadn't done against Al Gore's army service in Vietnam. But meanwhile Ross Perot launched his own campaign as the wartime champion of the POWs and a Rambo-like hero who would rescue not only the dozens allegedly still alive in Indochina but also the nation itself. John LeBoutillier called the POW issue "the metaphor" for Perot's campaign.[33] As one astute commentator put it: "The country is the prisoner, held hostage by lobbyists and professional politicians, and he and the American people together will create a commando team to rescue it."[34]

Unlike the Republican and Democratic candidates, Perot had no national party apparatus. What he used as a remarkably effective substitute was a ready-made national infrastructure, a network of activists motivated by near religious fervor and coordinated by grassroots organizations: the POW/MIA movement. A master of potent symbolism, Perot chose ex-POW James Stockdale as his running mate and ex-POW Orson Swindle as his campaign manager. Homecoming II, an organization leading the Rambo faction of the POW/MIA movement, directly challenged the federal government by turning the Vietnam Veterans Memorial into a perpetual campaign prop for Perot.[35] John LeBoutillier described the typical Perot rally:

> The POWs are all over the place. It's incredible. He has POW flags all over the stage. He has former POWs and their families up on the stage with him and he introduces them, and he always works into his speech how it's horrible to leave guys behind.[36]

POW activists and their organizations were central to the phenomenally successful petition campaigns that got Perot on the ballot in

every state.[37] Dolores Apodaca Alfond, national chairperson of the
National Alliance of Families for the Return of Missing Servicemen,
asserted that "most of the volunteers heading up his candidacy"
were POW/MIA activists. MIA family member, longtime movement leader, and Perot associate Jeffrey Donahue contended that
"99.8% of the POW activist element out there are *aggressively* pro
Ross Perot," and acknowledged that "obviously to me Ross Perot is
the great white hope." In June, Donahue predicted that the only
way that Bush could "save his skin" would be by preempting the
POW/MIA issue.[38] A few weeks later, Donahue was the man to
whom George Bush futilely turned for help while being heckled at
the July National League of Families convention.

Without the Perot candidacy, Bush might very well have beaten
Bill Clinton in a one-on-one race. Certainly in the televised debates,
Perot's ferocious attacks on the administration—ranging from his
remorseless exposure of the national debt to his shrewd debunking
of the glorious Gulf War—inflicted major damage while allowing
Clinton to keep the blood off both his hands and his face. The
demographics of the Perot vote—by race, class, and region—also
suggest that he drew disproportionately from traditional Republican voters. If indeed Perot was responsible for Bush's defeat, then
certainly the POW/MIA issue was central to the election's outcome,
for without it Perot would certainly not have been a national political figure, much less a presidential candidate. In fact he would not
have even made his first billion dollars, which largely came from
favors accorded to him by the Nixon administration for selling the
POW/MIA issue to the American people in the first place.

During the war, Perot claimed that his POW campaign (described in Chapter 2) was entirely his own idea and had no connec-
tion with the Nixon White House.[39] Later he claimed that he was
merely recruited into the campaign by Nixon and Kissinger.[40] The
historical record shows that neither claim is true.

Ross Perot began telephoning Richard Nixon daily two weeks

before the presidential inauguration on January 20, 1969.[41] By April, the Nixon staff was leaning on the army and other government agencies to award contracts to Perot's EDS corporation because "H. R. Perot of Dallas, Texas, was most substantial Nixon backer in 1968."[42] When the president in May created the Richard M. Nixon Foundation, Perot was named as one of its trustees along with John Ehrlichman, H. R. Haldeman, Nixon's brothers, Herbert Kalmbach, and John Mitchell.[43] The main item on the agenda for the president's meeting with Perot a few days later was "the best use" of Perot's offer of "$50 million in the purchase of television time."[44] Ehrlichman pressured the IRS to overrule the tax examiner who disallowed Perot's deduction for the services of EDS employees to the 1968 Nixon campaign.[45] Thanks to the intervention of the White House with government agencies and sweetheart contracts that allowed EDS to get 90 percent of the computer work on Medicare claims, by 1971 Perot had become what one writer accurately dubbed "the first welfare billionaire."[46]

In June 1969, Perot was proposed to head the pro-war committee that would coordinate Nixon's newly announced POW campaign.[47] Henry Kissinger advised the president that while "both the State and Defense Departments" are doing everything possible "to keep the heat on" in "the propaganda offensive in the POW issue with North Vietnam," they needed what seemed an independent citizens' movement, and he stressed the need to make it appear that "there is no U.S. Government involvement with the ladies," that is, the organization of POW/MIA wives being set up with help from the Pentagon.[48] Perot then presented to Nixon his plan to create a public uproar demanding that Hanoi immediately release the POWs. This would include "full-page ads in the nation's 100 largest newspapers" and all major national magazines, "credit card billing enclosures," "service station handouts (with the cooperation of oil companies)," and even "arranging for the Boy Scouts to deliver handouts door-to-door."[49]

The November national advertisement demanding that North Vietnam immediately release all the POWs, run in the name of Perot's United We Stand, was planned jointly by Perot and the White House. A week later, TV stations in fifty-nine cities broadcast *United We Stand*, a heart-wrenching program about POWs and MIAs. It ended with narrator Frank Borman calling upon every American to send a check pledging "100% support" for the president's Vietnam policies to UNITED WE STAND, BOX 100,000, DALLAS, TEXAS. Perot had previously submitted Borman's entire script for approval by the White House, where Alexander Butterfield forwarded it to his boss Bob Haldeman with the hope that it would help sustain "at least a moderate level of Flag waving and other visible rallying of the masses to the support of the President."[50] The president followed up by having Perot and Borman meet with him in the Oval Office on December 4 to plan more of what Charles Colson referred to, without a trace of irony, as "the outside efforts we are trying to organize."[51]

The meeting focused on "Perot's ideas for various outside activities in support of the Administration," including tax-exempt status for various pro-war and right-wing organizations, as well as "continuation of United We Stand and other Perot efforts to mobilize massive popular support." According to Haldeman's notes: "It was agreed that Borman should stay in the general television area under Perot's sponsorship."[52] Several days later, Butterfield submitted to Nixon a report on the POW campaign, including Perot's "plan of action for future months." The plan laid out in detail actions that Perot would indeed perform right on schedule, including "Christmas Plane to Hanoi (To Hold for Final Release at Bangkok or Vientiane)" to generate "worldwide publicity"; "Charter plane to transport to Paris approx. 100 wives and children of American POWs"; a Christmas vigil by the wives in Paris "with heavy press and television coverage" to embarrass Hanoi's delegation; a variety of other transcontinental and worldwide media events; scheduled appearances by Perot on *Meet the Press*, the *Today* show, *Here's Barbara*, *Mike Douglas*, et al.; and a "National Conference of Wives and Parents of Captured and Missing U.S. Servicemen" to launch the National League of Families.[53] Perot soon was off to Vientiane with two chartered jets filled with Christmas presents for the POWs and, according to Butterfield's report to the president, "Reporters from *Time*, *Life*, *Newsweek*, AP, UPI, *Los Angeles Times*, *Reader's Digest*, *Look*, *New York Times*, *Washington Post*, *Dallas Morning News*, and some five-six other publications." Butterfield explained how "we were able to give Ross a good bit of behind-the-scenes assistance."[54]

Perot's use of the POW/MIA issue in 1992 was even more wily and adroit. Despite making the POW/MIA issue his crucial symbol and subtext, Perot kept it out of the debates and his own national TV commercials. In fact, he chose to make his national presentation on the POW/MIA issue as a witness before the Senate Select Committee precisely during the summer interlude when he was supposedly not a candidate. Why? Interviewed two months earlier, Perot associate Jeffrey Donahue was sure that eventually Perot would produce major evidence of live POWs while fellow POW/MIA crusader John LeBoutillier, who referred to Perot as "a snake, a clever snake" and "a pathological liar," thought he was accepting Billy Hendon's advice not to "be typed as a one-issue candidate."[55] But the real reason came out during that Select Committee appearance, when Perot, masterfully playing the role of the lone outsider from Texas ready to ride into Washington to save us from its sleazy bureaucrats and politicians who had betrayed the POWs and the American people, failed to produce a shred of evidence. Perot, who had taught some of these bureaucrats and politicians how to create and manipulate the POW/MIA issue, showed his awareness that its profound power comes from American culture, not Vietnamese reality.

The most revealing symptom of the Vietnam syndrome in election year 1992 was that no national candidate ever made an issue of

America's ongoing economic and political warfare against Vietnam. Yet in the closing days of the campaign, the Pentagon and White House claimed that they were on the verge of ending hostilities by forcing Vietnam into resolving the POW/MIA issue. So George Bush now presented himself as the man who was about to lead the nation to "begin writing the last chapter of the Vietnam War."[56]

The president was responding to two events. One was Vietnam's all-out efforts to resolve the POW/MIA issue, including actions utterly unprecedented between belligerent states, such as opening their military archives and museums to U.S. inspection, conducting joint searches and interviews of witnesses throughout their country, and allowing short-notice U.S. inspection of suspected or former prison sites. The other was intense pressure from various U.S. corporations anxious not to lose potentially lucrative business opportunities to foreign competitors already swarming into Vietnam.[57]

But neither corporate anxiety nor Vietnamese cooperation could overcome the powerful forces wielding the POW/MIA issue, forces still including its original engineer, Richard Nixon. On December 30, 1992, Nixon sent a judiciously leaked memo to the Select Committee, insisting the "it would be a diplomatic travesty and human tragedy to go forward with normalization" until Hanoi "fully accounts for the MIAs." As the *Los Angeles Times* observed, "Nixon's written statement provides the strongest evidence so far that he and officials of his former Administration constitute a powerful and determined, though largely hidden, lobby against normalization."[58]

So instead of following his own Road Map, Bush merely allowed U.S. enterprises to begin negotiating for future business, which "only made matters worse," according to the *Wall Street Journal*, for "Mr. Bush's action sent a wake-up call to the Asian and European businesses," causing them to "accelerate their efforts before the Americans come in full force."[59] This left a curious situation in the early months of the Clinton administration: U.S. corporate interests, which had supported and profited from the Vietnam War, furtively leaning on the former anti-war demonstrator to end the war. Even the *Wall Street Journal*, for decades one of the master builders of the POW/MIA myth, ran a major story headlined "President Clinton, Normalize Ties with Vietnam" and arguing that "by any account, the Vietnamese have more than met" all the conditions of the Road Map, including the requested "help in resolving the fate of American MIAs."[60]

The ending of the embargo and eventual normalization now seemed inevitable. Indeed, the embargo was already so leaky that it was possible to buy U.S. products from Coca-Cola to Caterpillar tractors in Hanoi.[61] Why, then, such a slow and secretive process?

A few of the corporations involved have frankly acknowledged the roadblock: their own fear of the POW/MIA movement. Some companies scheduled for a trade mission to Vietnam dropped out after receiving a faxxed message from the National P.O.W. Strike Force summed up by its leader: "We will go out of our way to destroy your company because you want to do business with filthy Communists who are holding American prisoners."[62] The government also seemed frightened. When French President François Mitterrand condemned the U.S. embargo, Clinton White House spokesman George Stephanopoulos replied, "We want to make sure that we have a full accounting of all MIAs, and that's the policy we'll continue."[63] All this suggests the profound effects of the POW/MIA myth on American society.

Just as it once covertly slid into the Vietnam War, the government is now covertly sliding out of it. The secrecy comes from the same motive: fear of the American people. But in the 1960s, the government feared the people's opposition to war with Vietnam. Now, with the history of the war thoroughly rewritten by the POW/MIA myth, which has thus helped radically militarize American culture, the government fears the people's opposition to peace with Vietnam.

In early April 1993, the Clinton administration was exploring some quiet, timid steps toward normalization, such as allowing the IMF meeting scheduled later that month to release funds to Vietnam. "Bill Clinton may be on the verge of finally ending the Vietnam War," declared the April 12 *Wall Street Journal*, which went on to warn, however, of "an orchestrated campaign" to stop him.[64]

Right on cue, in the same day's *New York Times* came a sensational front-page story: "Files Said to Show Hanoi Lied in '72 on Prisoner Totals": a "top secret" document "discovered" in Moscow by "Harvard researcher" Stephen J. Morris "has been authenticated by leading experts" (all unnamed) as a Russian translation of a September 15, 1972, report to Hanoi's Politburo. This so-called "smoking gun" supposedly "proves" Vietnam withheld "hundreds" of U.S. POWs. For an "expert" opinion, the *Times* turned to Zbigniew Brzezinski, the main man responsible for persuading Jimmy Carter not to normalize relations with Vietnam in 1978. Since, as Brzezinski well knows, there are no live U.S. POWs in Vietnam, he offered an explanation which was sooner or later destined to become part of the POW/MIA mythology: "the great likelihood is that the Vietnamese took hundreds of American officers out and shot them in cold blood, in a massacre like the one in the Katyn woods."[65]

In a replay of the phony photos of July 1991, the "smoking gun" now exploded as the lead story on every TV network, including PBS, whose balanced coverage showcased a MacNeil/Lehrer panel consisting of three disinterested "experts"—Zbigniew Brzezinski, Henry Kissinger, and Morris himself.[66] Brzezinski's Katyn massacre scenario was repeated in newspaper editorials across the country. Headlines blared "North Vietnam Kept 700 POWs after War: 'Smoking Gun' File Exposes '20 Years of Duplicity'"; "Viets May Have Lied about POWs in 1972"; "POWs: The Awful Truth?"; "We Can't Set Up Ties with Killers of Our POWs."[67]

In the bizarre history of the POW/MIA myth, this document is one of the grossest frauds. Its purported author, identified in the document as "General Lieutenant Tran Van Quang," "the Deputy

Chief of the General Staff of the VPA," did not hold this position until 1974. More important, not a single one of its "facts" about POWs conforms to the historical record.[68]

This alleged report to the Hanoi Politburo claims that as of September 15, 1972, North Vietnam was holding 1,205 "American prisoners of war" in "11 prisons": "Earlier there were 4 main prisons, but, after the attempt of the Americans to liberate their prisoners of war in Son Tay, we increased the number of prisons to 11. In each of these is held approximately 100 American prisoners of war." The historical record shows just the opposite. As a result of the November 1970 raid on Son Tay, the Vietnamese *reduced* the number of POW camps, moving all U.S. POWs from the thirteen facilities where they had been housed into six prisons, with almost all concentrated in three (nicknamed by the POWs "Hanoi Hilton," "Zoo," and "Plantation").[69] No high Vietnamese official would be ignorant of this fact, which alone proves the "report" is spurious.

According to the document, officers were segregated by rank: 16 colonels "we are holding together," "we are also holding 104 American lieutenant colonels in one place," and "235 majors are concentrated in two places." Since no released POW ever experienced such segregation by rank and since such numbers of officers of these ranks are not missing, this is logically impossible.

The "report" states "until now we published a list of only 368 prisoners of war, the remainder we have not revealed." However, in August 1972 North Vietnam had disclosed that it was holding not 368 Americans but 383.[70]

The constant use of the term "prisoners of war" is another interesting slip. Hanoi tenaciously refused to designate its captives as prisoners of war. This was a major issue from 1969 right through the signing of the January 1973 Paris Peace Accord, which refers to "captured American military personnel," never "prisoners of war." An even more revealing failure to take a Vietnamese point of view appears in the list of demands related to U.S. POWs. Not even mentioned is the one demand Hanoi kept insisting must be linked to the release of U.S. POWs: the release of thousands of political prisoners held by the Saigon regime.[71]

There are many other absurdities, such as asserting that all Americans captured in South Vietnam, Laos, and Cambodia were being held in North Vietnam and claiming that the POWs included "three cosmonauts" and "368 . . . holding progressive views" who would be released before the 372 "holding a neutralist position" and the 465 "holding reactionary views." Indeed, the astonishing aspect of this latest scam is that such a blatantly bogus document could be taken seriously.

Those determined to keep the Vietnam War going apparently believe that America's faith in the POW/MIA myth is so zealous that phony POW "evidence" no longer needs even a veneer of plausibility. Perhaps they are right. This clumsy hoax stalled the normalization process, and a *Wall Street Journal*/NBC News poll conducted between April 17 and 20, 1993, indicated that once again two-thirds of Americans believe that U.S. POWs "are still being held in Southeast Asia."[72]

The poll did not measure how many of the other third believe in Brzezinski's fable of hundreds of American officers being massacred in "cold blood." Though conveniently disposing of the chimera of live POWs—which eventually would be biologically impossible anyhow—this scenario may become the primary fantasy preventing true closure of the Vietnam War.

Some day the embargo will be over and possibly for the first time ever there will be normal diplomatic relations between the United States and Vietnam. But the last chapter of the Vietnam War cannot be written so long as millions of Americans remain possessed by the POW/MIA myth.

"POW/MIA"

I.   In the jungle of years,
lost voices are calling. Long
are the memories,
bitterly long the waiting,
and the names of the missing and dead
wander
disembodied
through a green tangle
of rumors and lies,
gliding like shadows among vines.

II.   Somewhere, so the rumors go,
men still live in jungle prisons.
Somewhere in Hanoi, the true believers
know,
the bodies of four hundred servicemen
lie on slabs of cold
communist hate.

III.   Mothers, fathers,
        wives and lovers,
        sons and daughters,
        touch your empty fingers to your lips
        and rejoice
        in your sacrifice and pain:
        your loved ones' cause
        was noble,
        says the state.

IV.   In March of 1985, the wreckage
        of a plane was found in Laos.
        Little remained of the dead:
        rings, bone chips, burned
        bits of leather and cloth;
        for thirteen families,
        twenty years of hope
        and rumors
        turned acid on the soul
        by a single chance discovery.

V.   Our enemies are legion,
        says the state;
        let bugles blare
        and bang the drum slowly,
        bang the drum.

VI.   God forgive me, but I've seen
that triple-canopied green
nightmare of a jungle
where a man in a plane could go down
unseen, and never be found
by anyone.
Not ever.
There are facts,
and there are facts:
when the first missing man
walks alive out of that green tangle
of rumors and lies,
I shall lie
down silent as a jungle shadow,
and dream the sound of insects
gnawing bones.

                                      —W. D. Ehrhart

W. D. Ehrhart served in Vietnam as a U.S. Marine, where he received numerous decorations including the Purple Heart. He is now recognized as one of the finest poets and nonfiction writers to emerge from the Vietnam War. "POW/MIA" appears in *Just for Laughs*, the most recent of his four volumes of poetry. Ehrhart's seven other books include *Going Back: An Ex-Marine Returns to Vietnam*, *In the Shadow of Vietnam: Essays 1977–1991*, the influential collection *Carrying the Darkness: The Poetry of the Vietnam War*, and his acclaimed autobiography *Passing Time*.

Appendix A: Selected Articles from the Agreement on Ending the War and Restoring Peace in Viet-Nam, Signed in Paris, January 27, 1973*

Article 4

The United States will not continue its military involvement or intervene in the internal affairs of South Viet-Nam.

Article 5

Within sixty days of the signing of this Agreement, there will be a total withdrawal from South Viet-Nam of troops, military advisers, and military personnel, including technical military personnel and military personnel associated with the pacification program, armaments, munitions, and war material of the United States and those of the other foreign countries mentioned in Article 3 (a) ["foreign countries allied with the United States"]. Advisers from the above-mentioned countries to all paramilitary organizations and the police force will also be withdrawn within the same period of time.

Article 6

The dismantlement of all military bases in South Viet-Nam of the United States and of the other foreign countries mentioned in Article 3 (a) shall be completed within sixty days of the signing of this Agreement.

Article 8

(a) The return of captured military personnel and foreign civilians of the parties shall be carried out simultaneously with and completed not later than the same day as the troop withdrawal mentioned in Article 5. The parties shall exchange complete lists of the above-mentioned captured military personnel and foreign civilians on the day of the signing of this Agreement.

(b) The parties shall help each other to get information about those military personnel and foreign civilians of the parties missing in action, to determine the location and take care of the graves of the dead so as to facilitate the exhumation and repatriation of the remains, and to take any

---

*Source: *U. S. Treaties and Other International Agreements* (TIAS 7542).

such other measures as may be required to get information about those still considered missing in action.

(c) The question of the return of Vietnamese civilian personnel captured and detained in South Viet-Nam will be resolved by the two South Vietnamese parties [the Republic of Viet-Nam and the Provisional Revolutionary Government of South Viet-Nam] on the basis of the principles of Article 21 (b) of the Agreement on the Cessation of Hostilities in Viet-Nam of July 20, 1954. The two South Vietnamese parties will do so in a spirit of national reconciliation and concord, with a view to ending hatred and enmity, in order to ease suffering and to reunite families. The two South Vietnamese parties will do their utmost to resolve this question within ninety days after the cease-fire comes into effect.

Article 21

The United States anticipates that this Agreement will usher in an era of reconciliation with the Democratic Republic of Viet-Nam as with all the peoples of Indochina. In pursuance of its traditional policy, the United States will contribute to healing the wounds of war and to postwar reconstruction of the Democratic Republic of Viet-Nam and throughout Indochina.

Appendix B: The Secret Nixon Letter

Testimony of Undersecretary of State Philip Habib to the House Select Committee on Missing Persons in Southeast Asia, July 21, 1976*

MR. [Benjamin] GILMAN. With regard to that high price, when we were in Hanoi there were references made to some agreements made between our Government and Vietnam with regard to postwar reparations. Can you set forth for us just where we stand with regard to those negotiations? Were there any agreements we are not aware of, secret memorandum that this committee is not aware of?

---

*Source: *Hearings*, pt. 5: 47–8.

MR. HABIB. There is no agreement or secret memorandum which this committee is not aware of in this respect. . . .

MR. [Paul] MCCLOSKEY. With all due respect, Mr. Secretary, this committee asked the Secretary of State and you the same question before we went to Hanoi last December. You did not advise us of that secret letter and we discovered its existence only when we got to Hanoi. Can you tell this committee now why we went to Hanoi without being advised of the existence of that letter which was known to the Secretary of State, especially after we asked you about it?

MR. HABIB. I don't recall that we were—were we asked specifically about the letter before you went?

MR. MCCLOSKEY. We didn't have any idea the letter existed. We asked you in November if there were any secret agreements that we should know about before we went to Hanoi and we were not advised by you or the Secretary of State of the letter's existence or of the $3.25 billion figure which we later ascertained.

MR. HABIB. That is not an agreement. . . . There is no agreement, there was no agreement, there never was an agreement as far as I know, and I think I would know at this stage. We have researched it and there is no agreement with respect to the question of aid involved in that letter. That letter was simply a letter designed to set up a Joint Economic Commission pursuant to article 21 of the Paris agreement. The truth of the matter is there was no agreement.

Complete text of the letter from President Richard Nixon to Prime Minister Pham Van Dong, February 1, 1973*

The President wishes to inform the Democratic Republic of Vietnam of the principles which will govern United States participation in the postwar reconstruction of North Vietnam. As indicated in Article 21 of the Agreement on Ending the War and Restoring Peace in Vietnam signed in Paris

---

* Sources: *The New York Times,* May 20, 1977 (the day after the declassification of this document by the U. S. State Department); *Aid to North Vietnam: Hearing before the Subcommittee on International Relations,* House of Representatives, 95th Congress, 1st Session, 1979, Appendix 2: 25.

on Jan. 27, 1973, the United States undertakes this participation in accordance with its traditional policies. These principles are as follows:

1. The Government of the United States of America will contribute to postwar reconstruction in North Vietnam without any political conditions.

2. Preliminary United States studies indicate that the appropriate programs for the United States contribution to postwar reconstruction will fall in the range of $3.25 billion of grant aid over five years. Other forms of aid will be agreed upon between the two parties. This estimate is subject to revision and to detailed discussion between the Government of the United States and the Government of the Democratic Republic [of] Vietnam.

3. The United States will propose to the Democratic Republic of Vietnam the establishment of a United States-North Vietnamese Joint Economic Commission within 30 days from the date of this message.

4. The function of the commission will be to develop programs for the United States contribution to reconstruction of North Vietnam. This United States contribution will be based upon such factors as:

(a) The needs of North Vietnam arising from the dislocation of war;

(b) The requirements for postwar reconstruction in the agricultural and industrial sectors of North Vietnam's economy.

5. The Joint Economic Commission will have an equal number of representatives from each side. It will agree upon a mechanism to administer the program which will constitute the United States contribution to the reconstruction of North Vietnam. The commission will attempt to complete this agreement within 60 days after its establishment.

6. The two members of the commission will function on the principle of respect for each other's sovereignty, noninterference in each other's internal affairs, equality and mutual benefit. The offices of the commission will be located at a place to be agreed upon by the United States and the Democratic Republic of Vietnam.

7. The United States considers that the implementation of the foregoing principles will prompt economic, trade and other relations between the United States of America and the Democratic Republic of Vietnam and will contribute to insuring a stable and lasting peace in Indochina. These principles accord with the spirit of Chapter VIII of the Agreement on

Ending the War and Restoring Peace in Vietnam which was signed in Paris on Jan. 27, 1973.

Understanding Regarding Economic Reconstruction Program

It is understood that the recommendations of the Joint Economic Commission mentioned in the President's note to the Prime Minister will be implemented by each member in accordance with its own constitutional provisions.

Note Regarding Other Forms of Aid

In regard to other forms of aid, United States studies indicate that the appropriate programs could fall in the range of $1 billion to $1.5 billion, depending on food and other commodity needs of the Democratic Republic of Vietnam.

Glossary

back seater The crew member who sits behind the pilot in U.S. fighter-bombers with a crew of two.

DOD Department of Defense.

DIA Defense Intelligence Agency. One section of this Pentagon agency—Special Office for POW/MIA—is devoted entirely to intelligence matters relating to the unaccounted for from the Indochina war and has its own intelligence team in Southeast Asia.

DRV Democratic Republic of Vietnam. The government of Vietnam which declared its independence from France in 1945 and negotiated the 1954 Geneva Agreement with France. After the U. S. government installed Ngo Dinh Diem as the ruler of Vietnam south of the 17th parallel, it began to refer to the DRV as North Vietnam, a usage that became dominant. The DRV was one of the four governments that signed the 1973 Paris Peace Agreement.

IAG The POW/MIA Interagency Group. According to an official U.S. government publication: "United States Government policy regarding the POW/MIA issue is coordinated through The POW/MIA Interagency Group (IAG). Membership in the IAG includes the Defense Department, the White House National Security Council (NSC) staff, the State Department, the Joint Chiefs of Staff (JCS), the Defense Intelligence Agency (DIA) and the National League of POW/MIA Families."

ISA Intelligence Support Activity. Supersecret Pentagon agency involved in covert operations.

Joint Casualty Resolution Center (JCRC) The joint military service organization responsible for coordinating efforts to resolve unaccounted for cases. It has a liaison office in Bangkok that works with the governments of Indochina and it oversees the U.S. Army Central Identification Laboratory in Hawaii.

KIA/BNR Killed in action/body not recovered. Included in the total of "unaccounted for" along with MIA and POW.

MIA Missing in action. Should not be confused with the much larger category "unaccounted for."

NLF National Liberation Front of South Vietnam. Founded in 1960 to coordinate the struggle against the Ngo Dinh Diem dictatorship; referred to by Diem and the U. S. government as the Viet Cong.

Operation Homecoming The Nixon administration's name for the elaborately staged and publicized reception of the 591 POWs released by the DRV, PRG, and Pathet Lao in the sixty-day period following the signing of the Paris Peace Agreement.

Pathet Lao The revolutionary forces in Laos during the Indochina war.

POW Prisoner of war.

POW/MIA Prisoner of war/missing in action. Created by the Defense and State departments during the Vietnam War, this public category lumped together two classifications that had traditionally been quite distinct and were still kept separate internally within the departments.

PRG Provisional Revolutionary Government of South Vietnam. Formed in 1969 by the NLF and other groups, it was one of the four governments that signed the 1973 Paris Peace Agreement.

PW Prisoner of war.

rallier A deserter who defects to the opposing side.

unaccounted for The combined total of those missing in action and those killed in action whose bodies have not been or cannot be recovered.

Notes

Chapter 1. Prisoners of Myth

1. *POW/MIA Flag* (Washington, DC: National League of Families of American Prisoners and Missing in Southeast Asia, [1990]); *POW-MIA Fact Book* (Washington, DC: Department of Defense, 1983, 1984, 1985, 1986, 1987, 1988, 1988, 1989, 1990); Ronald Reagan, "Remarks at a Meeting of the National League of Families of American Prisoners and Missing in Southeast Asia, January 28, 1983," *Public Papers of the Presidents of the United States: Ronald Reagan, 1983* (Washington, DC: GPO, 1984), 131; *Boston Globe*, May 13, 1984; Department of Defense and Department of State, *Final Interagency Report of the Reagan Administration on the POW/MIA Issue in Southeast Asia* (Washington, DC: January 19, 1989, Mimeographed), 16; "Role of the Uniformed Services in the POW/MIA Issue" ("Memorandum from Secretary of Defense Dick Cheney to Secretaries of the Military Departments and Chairman of the Joint Chiefs of Staff, May 26, 1990"). I am indebted to Marjorie Watson of the Dana Library of Rutgers University for obtaining a photocopy of the typescript of the *Final Interagency Report*, which is not listed in the standard indexes of government documents, directly from the State Department. Another copy, in pamphlet form, was furnished by Betsy Cox, Director of Public Relations, National League of Families, to whom I wish to express my gratitude for supplying copies of *POW/MIA Flag*, the Cheney memorandum, and other helpful documents.
2. "Gist: POW-MIAs in Southeast Asia," *US Department of State Dispatch*, December 31, 1990, 368; *POW-MIA Fact Book* (Washington, DC: Department of Defense, July 1990), 1, 7.
3. *POW/MIA Flag.*
4. The Vietnam Veterans Trivia Game; "Thunder Rolls through Liberty Park: 4,000 Motorcyclists Ride for POW/MIAs," *Jersey Journal* (Jersey City, NJ), September 17, 1990.
5. Telephone interview with David Cline, October 20, 1990. Cline became and still is a leader of Vietnam Veterans Against the War.
6. As discussed on pages 87–89, the highest total of possible unaccounted for prisoners claimed by the U.S. government was 56; by 1988 there were between 50,000 and 100,000 homeless Vietnam veterans, accord-

ing to studies cited in "Veterans of Failure: For Many Homeless, the Despair Was Born in a War Called Vietnam," *Los Angeles Times,* November 11, 1988. In 1978, a study prepared for the House Committee on Veterans' Affairs (*Presidential Review Memorandum on Vietnam Era Veterans,* House of Representatives, 96th Congress, 1st Session, 1979), estimated that 58,000 veterans were then incarcerated in state and federal prisons, with an additional 37,500 on parole, 250,000 on probation, and another 87,000 in jail awaiting trial, for a total of 432,500; at least half of these were believed to be Vietnam veterans, indicating that more than 200,000 were already in the penal system, just a few years after the war's end.

7. "Reminder of Vietnam Stays on Hand," *Los Angeles Times,* February 13, 1989. Dornan here attributes this information to "the Library of Congress"; he has not answered my requests for a more specific source.

8. *New Information on U.S. MIA-POW's in Indochina?: Hearing before the Subcommittee on Asian and Pacific Affairs of the Committee on Foreign Affairs,* House of Representatives, 98th Congress, 1st Session, March 22, 1983, 34.

9. Testimony of Mrs. Bobby Vinson, *Americans Missing in Southeast Asia: Hearings before the House Select Committee on Missing Persons in Southeast Asia,* 94th Congress, 1st Session, November 5, 11, 12, 19, December 17, 1975, pt. 2:51; testimony of Mrs. Emma Hagerman, *Americans Missing in Southeast Asia: Hearings before the House Select Committee,* 94th Congress, 2nd Session, June 17, 25, July 21, September 21, 1976, pt. 5:20–21.

10. The most important exceptions to this statement are some fine analyses of the POW rescue movies; these are cited in the discussion of these films in chapter 4. Some TV soaps about live POWs are described in "Soap Dish," *Episodes,* July/August 1991, 20.

11. The figures on total casualties are from Combat Area Casualties Current File, Record Group 330, Office of the Secretary of Defense, as of October 1989, the latest available from the National Archives. The figures of 2,273 unaccounted for, including 1,101 KIA/BNR and 1,172 POW/MIA, are from a telephone interview with Commander Gregg Hartung of the Pentagon's Public Affairs office, September 23, 1991. This represents a reduction of fifteen from the total of 2,288 unaccounted for as given in a letter to the author from Charles F. Trowbridge, Jr., deputy chief, Special Office for Prisoners of War and

Missing in Action, Defense Intelligence Agency, February 20, 1991, and *US Department of State Dispatch*, December 31, 1990, 368. A few months earlier, the State Department's "Status of the POW/MIA Issue" (September 19, 1990) gave the total as 2,296. The number of unaccounted for is shrinking because of the discovery of remains of bodies in Vietman and Laos, largely through the work of joint teams involving U.S. experts and equipment.

12. "Fatal Peacetime Accidents, Navy Combat-Type Aircraft," Naval Safety Center, Serial 394 of February 5, 1976.

13. "European Countryside Continues to Yield Remains of Yank War Dead," *Star-Ledger* (Newark, NJ), September 4, 1979; "Unfaded Memories," *Star-Ledger*, August 16, 1985; "Yank Remains Found in New Guinea Spur a Four Decade Saga," *Star-Ledger*, December 7, 1986; "Diggers Confident of Finding 28 Custer Troops," *New York Times*, June 9, 1985; "Confederate Remains Found in Mass Grave," *New York Times*, July 5, 1987; "War of 1812 Dead 'Return,'" *Star-Ledger*, July 1, 1988; "After 174 Years, 28 M.I.A.'s Return," *New York Times*, July 1, 1988.

14. *POW-MIA Fact Book* (July 1990), 3; in a letter to the author on February 20, 1991, Charles F. Trowbridge, Jr., deputy chief, Special Office for Prisoners of War and Missing in Action, Defense Intelligence Agency, reiterated that Colonel Shelton is listed as a prisoner of war merely as "a symbolic gesture."

15. *POW-MIA Fact Book* (July 1990), 9.

16. "Still Trying, Ford Says on MIA's," *Washington Post*, July 25, 1976.

17. *Americans Missing in Southeast Asia: Final Report of the House Select Committee on Missing Persons in Southeast Asia*, 94th Congress, 2nd Session, December 13, 1976, vii.

18. "Still Trying, Ford Says on MIA's."

19. Captain Douglas L. Clarke, *The Missing Man: Politics and the MIA* (Washington, DC: National Defense University, 1979), 115, 116. This invaluable source is by far the most extensive previous study of the creation of the MIA issue. Writing from personal experience as a squadron commander himself, Captain Clarke shows how the process of defining casualties is inherently heavily weighted toward declaring men missing rather than killed, because the person responsible for making the determination is their commanding officer, who is usually a personal friend of the fliers and even their families (chapter 3).

20. Department of Defense and Department of State, *Final Interagency Report of the Reagan Administration*, 13–14, 21.

21. Air Force Regulation 30–25, paragraph 1–10b(1) and Army Regulation 600–10, paragraph 8–7b as cited in Clarke, *Missing Man*, 14, 24.

22. *Final Report of the Select Committee on Missing Persons in Southeast Asia*, 65–66.

23. Ibid., 158.

24. Clarke, *Missing Man*, 17; *Final Report of the Select Committee on Missing Persons in Southeast Asia*, 200.

25. Ibid., 198–99, 202–3.

26. *Final Interagency Report of the Reagan Administration*, 20.

27. "Say Remains of G.I. 'Deserter' Lay in Army Morgue 11 Years," *Jersey Journal* (Jersey City, NJ), February 4, 1983.

28. *New York Times*, August 20, 1974; Marvin Gettleman, Jane Franklin, Marilyn Young, and H. Bruce Franklin, *Vietnam and America: A Documented History*, rev. ed. (New York: Grove Press, 1989), 315.

29. Colonel Robert D. Heinl, Jr., "The Collapse of the Armed Forces," *Armed Forces Journal*, June 7, 1971, 30–37.

30. Defense Intelligence Agency testimony, *Access to Classified Live Sighting Information concerning POW/MIAs in Southeast Asia—Is New Legislation Needed?: Hearing before the House Subcommittee on Asian and Pacific Affairs of the Committee on Foreign Affairs*, 100th Congress, 2nd Session, April 20, 1988, 192–93, 195, 201, 276–77. See also the discussion of the Garwood case on pages 113–16.

31. Testimony of Anita Lauve, *Americans Missing in Southeast Asia: Hearings before the House Select Committee on Missing Persons in Southeast Asia*, 94th Congress, 2nd Session, April 7, 1976, pt. 4:5; "Nixon Challenged on POWs: 'Frenchmen' Were Nazis," *San Francisco Examiner-Chronicle*, July 2, 1972; letter to Ethel Taylor, coordinator of Women Strike for Peace, from François Bujon de l'Estang, first secretary of the Embassy of France in the United States, July 17, 1972 (Photocopy in my possession).

32. Testimony of Anita Lauve, 4; Lauve's biography appears in the Select Committee's hearings, pt. 4:279.

33. James Bacque, *Other Losses: An Investigation into the Mass Deaths of German Prisoners at the Hands of the French and Americans after World War II* (Toronto: Stoddart Publishing, 1989), 64, 114, *et passim;* Alfred de Zayas, "'You Have No Status,'" *Military History Quarterly* (Summer

1990): 47–49. Although Bacque's estimates of the numbers of German POWs who actually died in the Allied camps seem to be wildly overstated, his controversial study, which was a best-seller in Canada and Germany, offers some important information on forced recruitment into the French Foreign Legion.

34. Anita C. Lauve, "Prisoners of War in Indochina (Geneva Settlements of 1954 and 1961–62)," as printed in *Hearings before the House Select Committee on Missing Persons in Southeast Asia*, 94th Congress, 2nd Session, April 7, May 12, 26, June 2, 1976, pt. 4:206; Dieter Dengler, *Escape from Laos* (New York: Zebra Books, 1979), 130, 170–87; narrative by Jerry DeBruin in Rod Colvin, *First Heroes: The POWs Left Behind in Vietnam* (New York: Irvington Publishers, 1987), 196–99.

Chapter 2. Prisoners of the War

1. Anita C. Lauve, "Prisoners of War in Indochina (Geneva Settlements of 1954 and 1961–62)," as printed in "Americans Missing in Southeast Asia," *Hearings before the House Select Committee on Missing Persons in Southeast Asia*, 94th Congress, 2nd Session April 7, May 12, 26, June 2, 1976, pt. 4: 202.

2. The eight missing men are listed by Rod Colvin, *First Heroes: The POWs Left Behind in Vietnam* (New York: Irvington Publishers, 1987), 287–341; for details about those captured and released in Laos see Lauve, "Prisoners of War," 204–5.

3. Lauve, "Prisoners of War," 206. See pages 29–30 for a discussion of the DeBruin case, which is one of the main examples used in the current POW/MIA myth.

4. All these points are documented with both primary and secondary sources in Marvin E. Gettleman, Jane Franklin, Marilyn Young, and H. Bruce Franklin, *Vietnam and America: A Documented History*, rev. ed. (New York: Grove Press, 1989). My own research on the Gulf of Tonkin incidents includes "How We Started Our War against North Vietnam," *Sequoia* 11 (Spring 1966): 4–12, and an extensive 1966 interview with Leonard Laskow, flight surgeon on the U.S.S. *Ticonderoga*, conducted jointly with retired Admiral Arnold True.

5. *New York Times*, November 22, 1967.

6. "Saigon under Fire," CBS News Special Report, January 31, 1968. General Westmoreland's later assessment and an opposing interpretation are presented in full in Gettleman et al., *Vietnam and America.*

7. *The Pentagon Papers: The Defense Department History of United States Decisionmaking on Vietnam,* Senator Gravel Edition (Boston: Beacon Press, 1971), 4:567. Contrary to its optimistic public statements, the administration was aware that the Pentagon had concluded by February 29 that the Tet Offensive was accomplishing its main goal, "the takeover of the countryside," and that U.S. military and political prospects in Vietnam were indeed "bleak" (*Pentagon Papers,* 4:561–62).

8. *Pentagon Papers,* 4:564.

9. For the role of veterans and GIs in the campus movement of this period, see H. Bruce Franklin, "1968: The Vision of the Movement and the Alternative Press" in *The Vietnam Era: Media and Popular Culture in the US and Vietnam,* ed. Michael Klein (London: Pluto Press, 1990), 65–81.

10. Thorne Dreyer, "Know Your Enemy," Liberation News Service, August 30, 1968. Other reports indicated that more than 160 Fort Hood soldiers had "refused to take part in riot control operations in Chicago" (*Great Speckled Bird,* August 30-September 12, 1968). Twelve paratroopers were eventually court-martialed for their refusal.

11. Richard Nixon, "Vietnam" (Speech delivered at the Republican National Convention, August 1, 1968), in *Nixon Speaks Out: Major Speeches and Statements by Richard Nixon in the Presidential Campaign of 1968* (New York: Nixon-Agnew Campaign Committee, 1968), 235.

12. *New York Times,* August 9, 1968.

13. Nixon, acceptance speech, in *Nixon Speaks Out,* 278, 281.

14. Ironically, considering his presidential policy of "Vietnamization," Nixon's 1954 argument for U.S. political and military intervention was based on his stated belief that otherwise "Indochina would become Communist-dominated within a month" because "the Vietnamese lack the ability to conduct a war by themselves or govern themselves" (Gettleman et al., *Vietnam and America,* 53).

15. Law 10/59 in *Vietnam and America,* 157–61.

16. The NLF estimated that prior to its formation, the Diem government had killed 90,000 and imprisoned 800,000, including 600,000 crippled by torture (*South Vietnam: From the N.F.L. to the Provisional Revolutionary Government, Vietnamese Studies 23,* Ed. Nguyen Khac Vien [Hanoi,

1970], 12). For primary documents on the formation of the NLF see Gettleman, et al., *Vietnam and America*, 165–92.

17. The most memorable still shot of the execution, by AP photographer Eddie Adams, filled a quarter of the *New York Times* front page of February 2, 1968. The cultural significance of the revolver, a somewhat archaic handgun associated with the American West, accentuated the grim ironies of the scene. See pages 133–35 for a discussion of attempts in the 1970s and 1980s to reverse this image in popular culture in order to help promulgate the POW/MIA myth.

18. Howard Zinn, *A People's History of the United States* (New York: Harper Colophon Books, 1980), 469–70, discusses these early accounts. The classic description is Seymour Hersh, *My Lai 4* (New York: Random House, 1970).

19. Gettleman, et al., *Vietnam and America*, 403–4.

20. Article 12 of the Geneva Convention stipulates: "Prisoners of war may only be transferred by the Detaining Power to a Power which is a party to the Convention and after the Detaining Power has satisfied itself of the willingness and ability of such transferee Power to apply the Convention"; South Vietnam was not a party to the Convention. For a description of South Vietnam's Con Son prison island, see Don Luce, "Behind Vietnam's Prison Walls," *Christian Century*, February 19, 1969, 261–4. Luce, who speaks Vietnamese, later led Representative Augustus Hawkins and William Anderson through the secret access to the tiger cages, which were then photographed for *Life* by Tom Harkin. The chief American adviser to the South Vietnamese prison system, Frank "Red" Walton (former police commander of the Watts district of Los Angeles), had first told the visiting congressional delegation that Con Son was like "a Boy Scout recreational camp"; after they found the cages, Walton angrily told them, "You aren't supposed to go poking your nose into doors that aren't your business" ("The Tiger Cages of Con Son," *Life*, July 17, 1970, 27–29).

21. *Final Report of the House Select Committee on Missing Persons in Southeast Asia*, 94th Congress, 2nd Session, December 13, 1976, 136.

22. Ibid., 106, 135; "Laird Appeals to Enemy To Release U.S. Captives," *New York Times*, May 20, 1969; Captain Douglas L. Clarke, *The Missing Man: Politics and the MIA* (Washington, DC: National Defense University, 1979), 32. Clarke notes that Henry Kissinger has alleged that Laird

initiated the campaign to boost his own political ambitions (30, 47, n. 3).

23. "Inhuman Stance on Prisoners" (Editorial), *New York Times,* May 29, 1969.

24. *American Prisoners of War in Vietnam: Hearings before the Subcommittee on National Security Policy and Scientific Developments of the Committee on Foreign Affairs,* House of Representatives, 91st Congress, 1st Session, November 13, 14, 1969, 2, 6.

25. *American Prisoners of War in Southeast Asia, 1970: Hearings before the Subcommittee on National Security Policy and Scientific Developments of the Committee on Foreign Affairs,* House of Representatives, 91st Congress, 2nd Session, April 29, May 1, 6, 1970, 2.

26. "Wives Organizing to Find 1,332 G.I.'s Missing in War," *New York Times,* July 31, 1969; Joseph Lelyveld, "'Dear Mr. President'—The P.O.W. Families," *New York Times Magazine,* October 3, 1971, 56.

27. Jim and Sybil Stockdale, *In Love and War* (New York: Harper & Row, 1984), 133–46, 206–8, 210–13, 230–31, 306–7.

28. Ibid., 310–11; testimony of Sybil Stockdale, *American Prisoners of War in Southeast Asia,* 1970, 61.

29. Stockdale, *In Love and War,* 313–14, 365–67; "Remarks following a Meeting with Wives and Mothers of Prisoners of War and Servicemen Missing in Action in Vietnam," December 12, 1969, *Public Papers of the Presidents of the United States: Richard Nixon, 1969* (Washington, DC: U.S. Government Printing Office, 1970), 1021.

30. Stockdale, *In Love and War,* 373.

31. *American Prisoners of War in Southeast Asia, 1970,* 20.

32. Ibid., 5.

33. Ibid., 27.

34. Stockdale, *In Love and War,* 375–76; Clarke, *Missing Man,* 32; Iris R. Powers, "The National League of Families and the Development of Family Services," in *Family Separation and Reunion: Families of Prisoners of War and Servicemen Missing in Action,* ed. Hamilton I. McCubbin, Barbara Dahl, et al. (Washington, DC: GPO, [1974]), 5.

35. See Clarke, *Missing Man,* 34–35, on early government connections with the League; Representative Les Aspin introduced into the *Congressional Record* of January 22 and January 31, 1972, letters proving that the Republican National Committee was actually managing the fundraising campaign of the National League and that Senator Robert Dole,

of the Republican National Committee, had placed "advisers" in the League's structure who coordinated its activities and public statements with his own.

36. *American Prisoners of War in Southeast Asia, 1970,* 79.

37. Ibid., 66–79.

38. "Exhibit to Stir Opinion on P.O.W.'s Open in Capitol," *New York Times,* June 5, 1970.

39. Jon M. Van Dyke, "Nixon and the Prisoners of War," *New York Review of Books,* January 7, 1971, 35; Richard A. Falk, "Pawns in Power Politics," reprinted in *American Prisoners of War in Southeast Asia, 1971: Hearings before the Subcommittee on National Security Policy and Scientific Developments of the Committee on Foreign Affairs,* House of Representatives, 92nd Congress, 1st Session, March 23, 24, 25, 30, 31; April 1, 6, 20, 1971, 474; Lieutenant Colonel Charles F. Kraak, *Family Efforts on Behalf of United States Prisoners of War and Missing in Action in Southeast Asia* (Carlisle Barracks, PA: Army War College, 1975), 16, 18.

40. Russell Kirk, "Students for Victory," *National Review,* May 31, 1966, 535.

41. Janet L. Koenigsamen, *Mobilization of a Conscience Constituency: VIVA and the POW/MIA Movement,* Unpublished Dissertation, Kent State University, 1987, 36, 38.

42. Ibid., 37, 77–78.

43. Clarke, *Missing Man,* 40; Koenigsamen, *Mobilization,* 65, 72; telephone conversation with Mike Sasek, Defense Intelligence Agency, October 9, 1990.

44. Koenigsamen, *Mobilization,* 44–46; "Reminder of Vietnam Stays on Hand," *Los Angeles Times,* February 13, 1989; telephone interview with Gloria Coppin, September 23, 1990. Coppin reports that at the ball Perot refused to help finance the bracelets and even refused her plea for a loan to initiate production.

45. Koenigsamen, *Mobilization,* 44–50, 78; "Unit for P.O.W.'s Has New Project," *New York Times,* February 26, 1973. Other VIVA publicity products included matchbooks, bumper stickers, "missing man" stationery, Christmas cards, T-shirts, and sweatshirts; many of these were wholesaled to other political organizations.

46. Koenigsamen, *Mobilization,* 55; "Unit for P.O.W.'s Has New Project"; "Reminder of Vietnam Stays on Hand."

47. "Reminder of Vietnam Stays on Hand."

48. *New York Times*, January 26, 1969. Lodge, who had been the running mate in Nixon's unsuccessful 1960 presidential campaign, in 1963 engineered what he called "the overthrow of the Diem government" by "a Generals' coup" even though he knew this would bring "additional risk to American lives" (Cablegram from Lodge to Secretary of State Dean Rusk, August 29, 1963, quoted in Gettleman et al., *Vietnam and America*, 225).

49. "U.S. Gives Enemy List of Missing," *New York Times*, December 31, 1969.

50. "Vietnam Unique: PWs Languish as Political Pawns," *Christian Science Monitor*, December 7, 1970.

51. "U.S. Gives Enemy List of Missing."

52. Kraak, Family Efforts, 15–16; "Borman Gives Grim Report on P.O.W.'s," *New York Times*, September 23, 1970.

53. "Washington Report," *New York Times*, December 4, 1970.

54. Jonathan Schell, "The Time of Illusion IV: For the Re-election of the President," *New Yorker*, June 23, 1975, 76; reprinted in Schell, *The Time of Illusion* (New York: Alfred A. Knopf, 1976), 231.

55. "Acting to Aid the Forgotten Men," *Time*, December 7, 1970, 18.

56. Richard Nixon, "Address to the Nation on the Situation in Southeast Asia," April 7, 1971, *Public Papers of the Presidents of the United States: Richard Nixon, 1971* (Washington: GPO, 1972), 524; "Kin of Missing and Captive GIs Urge War's End," *Washington Post*, May 29, 1971; "Missing—or Dead?—Some 'POW' Relatives Say They Are Misled by American Officials," *Wall Street Journal*, September 30, 1971; Joseph Lelyveld, "'Dear Mr. President,'" 59–60; newsletters of POW/MIA Families for Immediate Release in Committee of Liaison files. (Virginia Warner is misidentified in Lelyveld's article as Virginia Warren.).

57. "Hanoi and Vietcong Give Assurances on P.O.W. Issue," *New York Times*, June 11, 1971.

58. "Rogers Bars the Abandonment of U.S. Goals to Free Captives," *New York Times*, June 16, 1971.

59. *New York Times*, June 16, 1971.

60. Richard Nixon, in *Public Papers of the Presidents of the United States: Richard Nixon, 1971*, 541; Tom Wicker, "Illogic in Vietnam," *New York Times*, May 25, 1971.

61. "'Living Our Lives on Hold,'" *Boston Sunday Globe*, July 9, 1972.

62. *Pentagon Papers*, 4, 251–52.

63. Form letter to family members from Barbara Webster, Committee of Liaison, January 27, 1970.

64. This admirable but rather utopian document stipulated that each prisoner shall be allowed at least "two letters and four cards monthly" and "shall be permitted to send telegrams" if mail delivery is difficult. However it also recognized that the amount of mail could be much more restricted "owing to difficulties of translation caused by the Detaining Power's inability to find sufficient qualified linguists to carry out the necessary censorship," a condition that obviously pertained to North Vietnam's situation (*Geneva Convention Relative to the Treatment of Prisoners of War of August 12, 1949* [TIAS 3364], Section 71).

65. Interview with Cora Weiss, January 5, 1991, and inspection the same day of envelopes in her possession showing evidence of protracted delays within the U.S. mail system; *American Prisoners of War in Southeast Asia, 1971*, 231–33, 237–38. These congressional hearings also disclosed that the exchange of mail prior to 1969 was not nearly so poor as the Nixon administration contended, especially considering the intense bombing of North Vietnam. For example, the mother of Everett Alvarez, the first pilot captured, received twenty-eight letters by October 1968, the first of which was written a few weeks after his capture in August 1964 (p. 236).

66. *American Prisoners of War in Southeast Asia, 1971*, 231, 244–45.

67. Testimony of Cora Weiss, Ibid., 237.

68. "List of U.S. Military Personnel Missing in Southeast Asia, as Issued in Washington," *New York Times*, December 31, 1969.

69. *American Prisoners of War in Southeast Asia, 1971*, 239.

70. Cora Weiss, ". . . But It Avoided the Real Facts," *New York Times*, December 8, 1970; testimony of Cora Weiss, *American Prisoners of War in Southeast Asia, 1971*, 231.

71. *American Prisoners of War in Southeast Asia, 1970*, 20, 22.

72. "Hanoi Said to Confirm List Putting Prisoners at 334," "Names of 334 U.S. Captives Hanoi Admits Holding," *New York Times*, June 26, 1970. The 335th name, erroneously omitted from the list as printed by the *Times*, was printed the following day.

73. "Pentagon Says List of War Prisoners Is Incomplete," *New York Times*, June 27, 1970.

74. Untitled story beneath "U.S. and Egypt Manage to Get Around," *New York Times*, February 17, 1970.

75. "Hanoi Said to Confirm List Putting Prisoners at 334"; "Pentagon Says List of War Prisoners Is Incomplete."

76. Seymour M. Hersh, "The P.O.W. Story," *Journal-Herald* (Dayton, OH), February 13, 15, 16, 17, 18, 1971: February 17; also in *American Prisoners of War in Southeast Asia, 1971*, 508.

77. "6 U.S. P.O.W.'s Dead, Hanoi Reports," *New York Times*, November 14, 1970; "U.S. Information on P.O.W.'s Appears Limited," *New York Times*, November 24, 1970.

78. *American Prisoners of War in Southeast Asia, 1971*, 239–40.

79. "U.S. Information on P.O.W.'s Appears Limited" ; "Laird Reveals U.S. Planned to Keep Camp Raid Secret," "Laird Challenged on Dead P.O.W.'s," *New York Times*, November 26, 1970; Hersh, "The P.O.W. Story," February 18, 1971; *American Prisoners of War in Southeast Asia, 1971*, 510.

80. "Laird Challenged on Dead P.O.W.'s."

81. "Senators Receive Hanoi P.O.W. List," *New York Times*, December 23, 1970; "List of P.O.W. Dead," *New York Times*, December 24, 1970; "Hanoi Terms List of Captives 'Complete,'" *New York Times*, December 28, 1970; "Dates and Causes of the Deaths of 20 U.S. Pilots Captured in North Viet Nam" (Photocopy of Hanoi's mimeographed list furnished by Cora Weiss). The last document indicates that of the fifteen who died from wounds, ten had survived three days or less and only one had survived longer than ten days).

82. "The President's News Conference on Foreign Policy, March 4, 1971," in *Public Papers of the Presidents of the United States: Richard Nixon, 1971*, 389. Although White House Press Secretary Ronald L. Ziegler later stated that the figure of 1,600 referred to both prisoners and missing, the following month Secretary of Defense Laird told the crowd and the TV audience at the opening game of the major league baseball season that "some 1,600" American servicemen currently in Vietnam "have not seen a ball game in a long time" ("Missing—or Dead?," *Wall Street Journal*, September 30, 1971).

83. Telephone interview with Gloria Coppin, September 23, 1990.

84. "Agreement on Ending the War and Restoring Peace in Viet-Nam" in Gettleman et al., *Vietnam and America*, 472, 473.

85. Richard Nixon, "Remarks at a Reception for Returned Prisoners of War, May 24, 1973," *Public Papers of the Presidents of the United States: Richard Nixon, 1973* (Washington, DC: GPO, 1975), 558.

Chapter 3. The Missing of Peace

1. See Gareth Porter, *A Peace Denied:. The United States, Vietnam, and the Paris Agreement* (Bloomington: Indiana University Press, 1975), 158 ff., and Seymour Hersh, *The Price of Power: Kissinger in the Nixon White House* (New York: Summit Books, 1983), 606–32.
2. The texts of the agreements can be found in Marvin E. Gettleman, Jane Franklin, Marilyn Young, and H. Bruce Franklin, *Vietnam and America: A Documented History*, rev. ed. (New York: Grove Press, 1989), 470–87; the immediately relevant parts are reprinted in Appendix A of the present book.
3. Department of Defense and Department of State, *Final Interagency Report of the Reagan Administration on the POW/MIA Issue in Southeast Asia* (Washington, DC, January 19, 1989, Mimeographed), 21; Richard Nixon, "Fourth Annual Report to the Congress on United States Foreign Policy, May 3, 1973," in *Public Papers of the Presidents of the United States: Richard Nixon, 1973* (Washington, DC: GPO, 1975), 391.
4. For the text of the relevant articles, see Appendix A. While neither Washington nor Hanoi expressed any objection to each other's performance of Article 8(a), Hanoi and Saigon exchanged bitter recriminations based mainly on disputes about the classification of prisoners of war.
5. "Out of the 'Tiger Cages': Ex-Inmates Tell of Viet Tortures," *San Francisco Chronicle*, March 8, 1973.
6. Stephen S. Rosenfeld, "What the White House Hides: Politics and the MIAs," *Nation*, February 23, 1974; testimony of Gareth Porter, *Americans Missing in Southeast Asia: Hearings before the House Select Committee on Missing Persons in Southeast Asia*, 94th Congress, 1st Session, October 23, 1975, pt. 1:90–91.
7. "Unit for P.O.W.'s Has New Project," *New York Times*, February 26, 1973; text from advertisement in *New York Times*, February 2, 1973.
8. Janet L. Koenigsamen, *Mobilization of a Conscience Constituency: VIVA and the POW/MIA Movement* (Unpublished dissertation, Kent State University, 1987), 60–62; 69–70.

9. See Captain Douglas L. Clarke, *The Missing Man: Politics and the MIA* (Washington, DC: National Defense University, 1979), 37–44, for a balanced and sensitive discussion of these events.

10. Ibid., 39; letter to League membership from the executive director, January 21, 1974, quoted in Lieutenant Colonel Charles F. Kraak, *Family Efforts on Behalf of United States Prisoners of War and Missing in Action in Southeast Asia* (Carlisle Barracks, PA: Army War College, 1975), 53.

11. Clarke, *Missing Man*, 40.

12. I am grateful to David Burgess for this telephone interview, conducted on January 3, 1991, which provided much information and many insights beyond the province of the present book. Burgess, who now works in the Humanitarian Affairs Department of the State Department, conducted his research on the National League in 1974 as a project undertaken for the Academy in Public Service, then affiliated with Georgetown University. It was funded by the Eli Lilly Foundation, which provided money for him to fly all around the country in order to interview "hundreds" of family members involved with the League. The purpose of the research was to investigate how "a grassroots organization" had managed to transform itself into a "major national" force, able in a short time "to arrange a joint session of Congress." He never completed the study and has no idea what happened to his notes and rough draft, which were left with the now defunct academy.

13. *Hearings before the House Select Committee on Missing Persons in Southeast Asia*, 94th Congress, 2nd Session, pt. 4:58, 1st Session, pt. 3:82.

14. Testimony of George L. Brooks, Ibid., 94th Congress, 1st Session, pt. 1:75.

15. Telephone interview with David Burgess, January 3, 1991.

16. *San Francisco Chronicle*, July 28, 1973.

17. Koenigsamen, *Mobilization*, 70.

18. *Hearings before the House Select Committee on Missing Persons in Southeast Asia*, 1st Session, pt. 3:192, 2nd Session, pt. 5:37.

19. "100-Man P.O.W. Airlifts Are Expected," *New York Times*, January 26, 1973; "Hanoi Lists of P.O.W.'s Are Made Public by U.S.," *New York Times*, January 28, 1973; "Communists List 555 P.O.W.'s but Give No Data on Laos," *New York Times*, January 29, 1973; "U.S. Says 56 Prisoners Remain Unaccounted For," *New York Times*, January 30, 1973; "Laos P.O.W. List Shows 9 from U.S.," *New York Times*, February

1, 1973; "U.S. Has Cautious Hope of Finding More P.O.W.'s," *New York Times*, February 26, 1973.

20. See, for example, Paul A. Gigot, "Lost or Merely Forgotten?," *National Review*, August 17, 1979, 1036–37; Rod Colvin, *First Heroes: The POWs Left Behind in Vietnam* (New York: Irvington Publishers, 1987), 18; Monika Jensen-Stevenson and William Stevenson, *Kiss the Boys Goodbye: How the United States Betrayed Its Own POWs in Vietnam* (New York: Dutton, 1990), 4, 46, 51, 70.

21. "Unreturned G.I.'s Are Feared Dead," *New York Times*, April 13, 1973. The Stevensons attempt to discredit Shields's announcement as "a statement he would later say had been forced on him"; their evidence for this consists of claims they say they heard from two MIA family members (*Kiss the Boys Goodbye*, 4, 46).

22. Testimony of Dr. Roger E. Shields, *Hearings before the House Select Committee on Missing Persons in Southeast Asia*, 2nd Session, February 4, 1976, pt. 3:5.

23. Testimony of E. C. Mills, Ibid., 1st Session, October 9, 1975, pt. 1:67.

24. Ibid., 1st Session, pt. 3:70; 2nd Session, pt. 4:67.

25. Ibid., 1st Session, pt. 3:26. The civilian in Laos no doubt is Eugene DeBruin and the Air Force officer is either David Hrdlicka or Charles Shelton.

26. *Americans Missing in Southeast Asia: Final Report of the Select Committee on Missing Persons in Southeast Asia*, 94th Congress, 2nd Session, December 13, 1976, 62–64. Although the Committee's figures come much closer to adding up than the Pentagon's, they by no means approximate the precise accounting that has been demanded of Vietnam, Laos, and Cambodia. The list of those "definitely . . . alive in enemy hands" consists of six from the Army, three from the Navy, two from the Air Force, and two from the Marine Corps for a total stated incorrectly as 11; in a further inconsistency, the detailed explanation quoted in my text adds up to 12.

27. Michael Satchell, "Lest We Forget," Parade, May 31, 1981, 4; Edward F. Dolan, *MIA: Missing in Action* (New York: Franklin Watts, 1989), 23; Thomas D. Boettcher and Joseph A. Rehyansky, "We Can Keep You. . . . Forever," *National Review*, August 21, 1981, 960 ("2,500 MIAs" is bracketed in the original); "Dear Fellow Citizen" letter from Skyhook II Project; Jensen-Stevenson and Stevenson, *Kiss the Boys Goodbye*, 4–5.

28. *Final Report of the Select Committee on Missing Persons in Southeast Asia*, 241.

29. Ibid., 199.

30. See H. Bruce Franklin, *Back Where You Came From* (New York: Harper's Magazine Press, 1975), 115–19.

31. Statement of Lieutenant Commander George T. Coker to the Board of Directors of the National League of Families, October 27, 1973, as printed in *Hearings before the House Select Committee on Missing Persons in Southeast Asia*, 1st Session, pt. 2: 109–10.

32. *Final Report of the Select Committee on Missing Persons in Southeast Asia*, 45.

33. Lieutenant Colonel Sidney T. Lewis, "Ejection Injuries in Southeast Asia Prisoner of War Returnees," Life Sciences Division, Directorate of Aerospace Safety, September 3, 1974, printed in *Hearings before the House Select Committee on Missing Persons in Southeast Asia*, 1st Session, pt. 2:289.

34. These and the following statistics are abstracted from "Personnel Lost in Aircraft Incidents: Southeast Asia," a study reprinted in *Final Report of the Select Committee on Missing Persons in Southeast Asia*, 154–5.

35. For evidence of this intentional campaign to destroy North Vietnam's medical infrastructure, see Gettleman et al., *Vietnam and America*, 463.

36. Boettcher and Rehyansky, "We Can Keep You," 960.

37. Statement of Coker to the Board of Directors of the National League of Families, 115.

38. J. C. Pollock, *Mission M.I.A.* (New York: Crown Publishers, 1982; New York: Dell Publishing, 1983), ch. 18. This novel, which was a Literary Guild alternate selection and a Military Book Club selection, provided considerable material for the POW rescue movies discussed in the next chapter.

39. S. William Berg, "Medical Aspects of Captivity and Repatriation," in *Family Separation and Reunion: Families of Prisoners of War and Servicemen Missing in Action*, ed. Hamilton I. McCubbin et al. (Washington, DC: GPO, 1974), 98. To cite a few examples among many of medical care provided to POWs in North Vietnam: two successful operations were performed on Lynn E. Guenther, including eye surgery for an injury sustained before capture; Wilfred Abbott's broken leg was successfully operated on; Douglas B. Peterson was successfully treated in a small hospital for a broken shoulder, broken arm, severely dislocated

knee, and compression fractures of both ankles; Terry M. Geloneck had his broken and dislocated shoulder repaired; Thomas J. Klomann, who was captured unconscious and did not regain full consciousness for three weeks, was fed intravenously during these weeks while being treated for various wounds.

40. *POW-MIA Fact Book* (Washington, DC: Department of Defense, July 1990), 7.

41. *Final Report of the Select Committee on Missing Persons in Southeast Asia,* 127.

42. *Final Interagency Report of the Reagan Administration on the POW/MIA Issue in Southeast Asia,* 22. Cambodia had announced that it was releasing the crewmen of the seized ship and did actually release them before the U.S. attacks.

43. The classic account of the "secret" air war against Cambodia is William Shawcross, *Sideshow: Kissinger, Nixon and the Destruction of Cambodia* (New York: Simon & Schuster, 1979). Shawcross also details the growing contradictions and conflict between the Khmer Rouge and the DRV.

44. *Final Report of the Select Committee on Missing Persons in Southeast Asia,* 14–15, 23, 102, 127.

45. *POW-MIA Fact Book* (July 1990), 3; quotations about Pol Pot and the numbers lost in the *Mayaguez* incident are from *Final Interagency Report of the Reagan Administration,* 22.

46. *Final Interagency Report of the Reagan Administration,* 4.

47. "U.S. Experts to Seek MIAs in Cambodia," *San Francisco Chronicle,* July 14, 1990; "U.S. to Examine Remains," *New York Times,* July 24, 1990; "Cambodia Turns over Remains Thought to Be Those of U.S. Soldiers," *New York Times,* July 27, 1990; *POW-MIA Fact Book* (July 1990), 18; National League of Families Newsletter, August 7, 1990; "Status of the POW/MIA Issue," Department of State, September 19, 1990; "MIA Experts Ready Mission to Cambodia," *Star-Ledger,* July 30, 1991.

48. "Where Is David Hrdlicka?," VIVA advertisement, *New York Times,* May 22, 1973.

49. "Where Is David Hrdlicka?"

50. See testimony of Ernest Brace, March 31, 1976, *Hearings before the House Select Committee on Missing Persons in Southeast Asia,* pt. 3:63–78.

51. (1) Bo Gritz, interview with Ben Bradlee, Jr., *Penthouse,* March 1982,

152; he modified this slightly in his prepared statement in *New Information on U.S. MIA-POW's in Indochina?: Hearing before the Subcommittee on Asian and Pacific Affairs of the Committee on Foreign Affairs*, House of Representatives, 98th Congress, 1st Session, March 22, 1983, 30: "[N]early 700 airmen were shot down over Laos during the Vietnam War. Not one has been returned."(2) Charles G. Patterson, *The Heroes Who Fell from Grace* (Canton, OH: Daring Books, 1985), 22. (3) "Missing," *Life*, November 1987, 113. (4) Jensen-Stevenson and Stevenson, *Kiss the Boys Goodbye*, 4.

52. Statistics abstracted from "Personnel Lost in Aircraft Incidents: Southeast Asia," 154–55.

53. Statement of Coker to the Board of Directors of the National League of Families, 117–19.

54. *Final Report of the Select Committee on Missing Persons in Southeast Asia*, 160.

55. Interview with David Burgess, January 3, 1991.

56. "Bombing in Laos Confirmed by U.S.," UPI story datelined Saigon, August 13, 1967; "The Air Force's War over Laos—Open 'Secret,'" *San Francisco Chronicle*, October 7, 1968.

57. See pages 158–61 for details about how U.S. drug complicity in Laos works into the thesis of Bo Gritz's 1988 book *A Nation Betrayed* and the Stevensons' *Kiss the Boys Goodbye*, which discusses the CIA campaign against McCoy's book (pp. 19– 20).

58. *Final Report of the Select Committee on Missing Persons in Southeast Asia*, 24–5; *Final Interagency Report of the Reagan Administration*, 21.

59. Prepared Statement of General Vernon Walters, *Hearings before the House Select Committee on Missing Persons in Southeast Asia*, 1st Session, pt. 3:207.

60. "Marine in Hanoi May Face Inquiry in Return to U.S.," *New York Times*, March 4, 1979.

61. "Return of Marine Buoying Hopes on the Missing in Southeast Asia," *New York Times*, May 25, 1979.

62. Winston Groom and Duncan Spencer, *Conversations with the Enemy: The Story of PFC Robert Garwood* (New York: Putnam's, 1983), 321ff.

63. Ibid., 301, 321.

64. "Robert Garwood Says Vietnam Didn't Return Some American POWs," *Wall Street Journal*, December 4, 1984. Paul has since published at least six other major articles in *The Wall Street Journal* propagandiz-

ing about live POWs and is frequently cited as an authority. He works closely with ex-Representative LeBoutillier and was LeBoutillier's conduit for the Reagan administration's 1985 "leak" discussed on page 157.

65. Groom and Spencer, *Conversations with the Enemy*, 307.

66. Zalin Grant, *Survivors* (New York: W. W. Norton, 1975), 110–11.

67. *Final Report of the Select Committee on Missing Persons in Southeast Asia*, 21, 44.

68. Testimony of Ernest C. Brace, March 31, 1976, *Hearings before the Select Committee on Missing Persons in Southeast Asia*, pt. 3:182.

69. "List of Captive Soldiers Proves a Fabrication," *New York Times*, October 20, 1984.

70. "Detainees to Be Released," *New York Times*, November 12, 1988; "Freed Pair Convinced Some MIAs Are Still Alive," *Star-Ledger* (Newark, NJ), November 15, 1988.

71. *Access to Classified Live Sighting Information Concerning POW/MIAs in Southeast Asia—Is New Legislation Needed?: Hearing before the House Subcommittee on Asian and Pacific Affairs of the Committee on Foreign Affairs*, 100th Congress, 2nd Session, April 20, 1988, 192–93, 195, 201, 276–77.

72. Ibid., 195.

73. See, for example, Socialist Republic of Vietnam, Ministry of Foreign Affairs, *On the Question of Americans Missing in the Vietnam War* (Hanoi, 1980), 24–27.

74. "Excerpts from *CAIB*-Scott Barnes Interview," *Covert Action Information Bulletin 17* (Summer 1982): 34.

75. "Agent Exposes Secret Mission"; "Excerpts from *CAIB*-Scott Barnes Interview"; Kevin Cody, "Scott Barnes: Spook or Spoof"; Ellen Ray, "Mystery in Bangkok: Yellow Rain Skeptic Found Dead," *Covert Action Information Bulletin* 17 (Summer 1982): 32–46; Scott Barnes, with Melva Libb, *Bohica* (Canton, OH: Bohica Corp., 1987).

76. Letter to Prime Minister Pham Van Dong from President Richard Nixon, February 1, 1973, reproduced in Appendix B.

77. See Gareth Porter, "The Broken Promise to Hanoi: Kissinger's Double-Cross for 'Peace,'" *Nation*, April 30, 1977, 519.

78. Gerald R. Ford, "Remarks and a Question-and-Answer Session . . . , April 23, 1976," in *Public Papers of the Presidents of the United States: Gerald R. Ford, 1976–1977* (Washington, DC: GPO, 1979), II, 1166;

"Ford Denies Plans for Ties with Hanoi," *New York Times*, April 24, 1976.

79. *Hearings before the House Select Committee on Missing Persons in Southeast Asia*, pt. 5:47–8; see Appendix B for relevant excerpts from Habib's testimony.

80. Gettleman et al., *Vietnam and America*, 487–88.

Chapter 4. Mythmaking in America

1. Gerald R. Ford, "Remarks at the Annual Convention of the National League of Families of American Prisoners and Missing in Southeast Asia, July 24, 1976," in *Public Papers of the Presidents of the United States: Gerald R. Ford, 1976–1977* (Washington, DC: GPO, 1979), 2:2085; "Ford Vows To Aid Search for G.I.'s," *New York Times*, July 26, 1976.

2. Gerald R. Ford, "Remarks on Administration Efforts To Account for Americans Missing in Action in Vietnam, September 7, 1976," in *Public Papers of the Presidents of the United States: Gerald R. Ford, 1976–1977*, 2:2211; "U.S. Decides to Veto Vietnam's Request for U.N. Membership," *New York Times*, September 14, 1976; "Transcript of Foreign Affairs Debate between Ford and Carter," *New York Times*, October 7, 1976.

3. "Wrong Veto," *New York Times*, November 17, 1976.

4. *Americans Missing in Southeast Asia: Final Report of the House Select Committee on Missing Persons in Southeast Asia*, 94th Congress, 2nd Session, December 13, 1976, vii, 209.

5. Captain Douglas L. Clarke, *The Missing Man: Politics and the MIA* (Washington, DC: National Defense University, 1979), 99.

6. Jimmy Carter, "Presidential Commission on Americans Missing and Unaccounted for in Southeast Asia: Remarks at a News Briefing on the Results of the Commission's Trip to Vietnam and Laos, March 23, 1977," in *Public Papers of the Presidents of the United States: Jimmy Carter, 1977* (Washington, DC: GPO, 1979), 1:489.

7. Quoted in Clarke, *Missing Man*, 109.

8. "President Indicates That He Will Pursue Tie with Vietnamese," *New York Times*, February 12, 1977.

9. See page 119.

10. For a detailed discussion of this cultural and political context, together with sources on the Committee on the Present Danger and its role, see H. Bruce Franklin, *War Stars: The Superweapon and the American Imagination* (New York: Oxford University Press, 1988), Chapter 15.

11. See Marilyn Young, "Revisionists Revised: The Case of Vietnam," *Newsletter of the Society of Historians of American Foreign Relations*, Summer 1979, 1–10.

12. "How Helicopter Dumped a Viet Captive to Death," *Chicago Sun-Times*, November 29, 1969; "Death of a Prisoner," *San Francisco Chronicle*, November 29, 1969.

13. In *P.O.W.: The Escape* the replay of the execution comes as a flashback to the one less-than-heroic American POW, persuading him to give up his greed, cowardice, and sexual lust in order to become a true hero. The cover of *The 'Nam* literally reverses the original image by showing the execution scene from a position behind the participants. This offers a frontal view of the photographer, whose deadly camera conceals his face and occupies the exact center of the picture. The prisoner appears merely as an arm, shoulder, and sliver of body on the left. The only face belongs to the chief of the secret police on the right: it displays the righteous—even heroic—indignation that has led him to carry out this justifiable revenge against the treacherous actions of the Viet Cong described in the story.

14. For an excellent analysis of other aspects of the mythic and psychological content of *The Deer Hunter*, see Leonard Quart, *"The Deer Hunter: The Superman in Vietnam,"* in *From Hanoi to Hollywood: The Vietnam War in American Film*, ed. Linda Dittmar and Gene Michaud (New Brunswick: Rutgers University Press, 1990), 159–68.

15. Quoted in Charles J. Patterson and Colonel G. Lee Tippin, *The Heroes Who Fell from Grace: The True Story of Operation Lazarus, the Attempt to Free American POW's from Laos in 1982* (Canton, OH: Daring Books, 1985), 102. Patterson, who was Gritz's second in command during the first raid, published an account in *Soldier of Fortune* magazine while Gritz was still in Southeast Asia, leading to a break between the two, who had fought together in the Special Forces in Vietnam. Getting to the truth about Bo Gritz's adventures is a formidable task, especially since each of the three participants who have written extensively about them—Gritz, Patterson, and Scott Barnes—accuses the other two of being inveterate liars.

16. "Daring Search for POWs Told," *Los Angeles Times*, January 31, 1983; "'Star-studded' Raid Fails to Free POWs," *Star-Ledger* (Newark, NJ), February 1, 1983; "Private Raid on Laos Reported," *New York Times*, February 1, 1983; Patterson and Tippin, *Heroes Who Fell from Grace*, 52. Most of the stories about the Gritz raids were broken by the *Los Angeles Times*, which received a series of oral and written messages from Gritz in January and February.

17. "Daring Search for POWs Told"; Patterson and Tippin, *Heroes Who Fell from Grace*, 50, 70, 92–107.

18. Patterson and Tippin, *Heroes Who Fell from Grace*, 146; the less theatrical version is reported in "Eastwood Told Reagan of Planned POW Raid," *Los Angeles Times*, February 25, 1983.

19. Patterson and Tippin, *Heroes Who Fell from Grace*, 128–29, 147, 176; Scott Barnes, with Melva Libb, *Bohica* (Canton, OH: Bohica Corp. 1987), 34.

20. *New Information on U.S. MIA-POW's in Indochina?: Hearing before the Subcommittee on Asian and Pacific Affairs of the Committee on Foreign Affairs*, House of Representatives, 98th Congress, First Session, March 22, 1983, 32–33; "Gritz Has No POW Evidence, Pentagon Says," *Los Angeles Times*, March 4, 1983.

21. *New Information on U.S. MIA-POW's in Indochina?*, 71.

22. Ibid., 29.

23. Department of Defense and Department of State, *Final Interagency Report of the Reagan Administration on the POW/MIA Issue in Southeast Asia* (Washington, DC, January 19, 1989, Mimeographed), 2, 16.

24. Ibid., 1–2; *POW/MIA Fact Book* (Washington, DC: Department of Defense, July 1990), 13. The ascendancy of the Interagency Group and the rising role of the National League within it are suggested by the evolution of the wording of this statement. Prior to the 1986 edition—the first to be issued after *Rambo: First Blood Part II* (1985) had changed the public climate—the IAG coordinated the government's "efforts," not "policy.".Every edition prior to 1990 included in the IAG "House and Senate staff members from the respective Foreign Affairs and Foreign Relations Committees"; evidently the Congress of the United States either no longer participates or is no longer worth mentioning.

25. *Final Interagency Report of the Reagan Administration*, 14.

26. Ronald Reagan, "Remarks at a Meeting of the National League of Families of American Prisoners and Missing in Southeast Asia, January

28, 1983," in *Public Papers of the Presidents of the United States: Ronald Reagan, 1983* (Washington, DC: GPO, 1984), 131.

27. Headline for review by Richard Freedman, *Star-Ledger* (Newark, NJ), December 16, 1983.

28. Aljean Harmetz, "2 Holiday Movies Turn into Surprise Successes," *New York Times*, February 13, 1984. An opposing view was offered in *The Wall Street Journal* by Julie Salamon, who argued that the antimilitarism and liberalism of "the critics" had blinded them to the great aesthetic merits of this "solid adventure film well worth seeing" ("The Movie the Critics Missed at Christmas," January 19, 1984).

29. Rob Edelman, "Uncommon Valor," *Cineaste* 13 (no. 3, 1984): 47.

30. *New Information on U.S. MIA-POW's in Indochina?*, 30.

31. Patterson and Tippin, *Heroes Who Fell from Grace*, 14–15, 16, 27, 35, 37, 195, 206; Monika Jensen-Stevenson and William Stevenson, *Kiss the Boys Goodbye: How the United States Betrayed Its Own POWs in Vietnam* (NY: Dutton, 1990), 190, 239, 308; "Mercenaries Sent to Laos Seeking MIAs: U.S. Financed Team That Tried in Vain to Find Americans in Laos," *Washington Post*, May 21, 1981; "Daring Mission, Dashed Hopes: CIA Finds No P.O.W.s in Laos, but M.I.A. Families Keep Hoping," *Time*, June 1, 1981, 31.

32. Ben Bradlee, Jr., "For Him, POW Rescue Is a Mission Not Accomplished," *Boston Globe*, July 7, 1981.

33. *New Information on U.S. MIA-POW's in Indochina?*, 22–3; Jensen-Stevenson and Stevenson, *Kiss the Boys Goodbye*, 309.

34. "Mercenaries Sent to Laos Seeking MIAs"; "Daring Mission, Dashed Hopes"; Steven Emerson, *Secret Warriors: Inside the Covert Military Operations of the Reagan Era* (New York: Putnam's, 1988), 78.

35. For an incisive analysis of the protofascist content of the POW rescue films and other movies, see J. Hoberman, "The Fascist Guns in the West: Hollywood's 'Rambo' Coalition," *Radical America* 19 (no. 6, 1985): 53–61, which also appeared in a revised form in *American Film*, March 1986.

36. My analysis of the role of gender in the POW rescue movies owes a considerable debt to Susan Jeffords's brilliant study *The Remasculinization of America: Gender and the Vietnam War* (Bloomington: Indiana University Press, 1989).

37. Ibid., 148.

38. See Tony Williams, "*Missing in Action.*: The Vietnam Construction of

the Movie Star," in *From Hanoi to Hollywood*, 129–44, for an excellent analysis of the creation of Norris's persona in the *Missing in Action* films. Louis J. Kern, "MIAs, Myth, and Macho Magic: Post-Apocalyptic Cinematic Visions of Vietnam," in *Search and Clear: Critical Responses to Selected Literature and Films of the Vietnam War*, ed. William J. Searle (Bowling Green, OH: Bowling Green State University Popular Press, 1988), 37–54, offers an exceptionally insightful overview of the psycho-social significance of what he calls "the POW-MIA/Avenger subgenre," tracing its cinematic history back to Norris's 1978 (not 1977, as indicated by Kern) film *Good Guys Wear Black*.

39. Smith's memoir, with an introduction and epilogue by Special Forces veteran and anti-war activist Donald Duncan, was published by Ramparts Press. The best bibliographies of these POW writings are both by Joe Dunn: "The POW Chronicles: A Bibliographic Review," *Armed Forces and Society* 9 (Spring 1983), 494–514; "The Vietnam War POW/MIAs: An Annotated Bibliography," *Bulletin of Bibliography* 45 (no. 2, 1988), 152–57.

40. Dunn, "The POW Chronicles," 501.

41. Jeremiah Denton, *When Hell Was in Session* (Mobile, AL: Traditional Press, 1982), 30. This is one of several editions reprinted by Denton himself in the early 1980s.

42. For evidence and sources see Marvin E. Gettleman, Jane Franklin, Marilyn Young, and H. Bruce Franklin, *Vietnam and America: A Documented History*, rev. ed. (New York: Grove Press, 1989), 461–69.

43. "Reagan Cites 'Rambo' as Next-Time Example," *Star-Ledger* (Newark, NJ), July 1, 1985; "Reagan Gets Idea from 'Rambo' for Next Time," *Los Angeles Times*, July 1, 1985.

44. "'Machismo' on Capitol Hill," *New York Times*, July 14, 1985.

45. "Iraq Spurns 'U.S.-imposed' Council Solution; Saddam Vows Fight for Kuwait," *Star-Ledger* (Newark, NJ), December 1, 1990.

46. "War Is Swell?," *San Francisco Examiner*, October 9, 1985; letter to Michael P. Felker from Barbara C. Wruck, vice president for corporate communications, Coleco Industries, August 13, 1985.

47. Richard Slotkin, *Regeneration through Violence: The Mythology of the American Frontier, 1600–1860* (Middletown, CT: Wesleyan University Press, 1973), 5. Any exploration of the role of the frontier myth in American culture, including mine, owes much to this classic work, together with Slotkin's *The Fatal Environment: The Myth of the Frontier*

in the Age of Industrialization, 1800–1890. (New York: Atheneum, 1985). John Hellman, *American Myth and the Legacy of Vietnam* (New York: Columbia University Press, 1986), cogently relates the frontier myth to the imagined role of the Green Berets in Vietnam. My analysis is also indebted to Gaylyn Studler and David Desser's fine essay "Never Having to Say You're Sorry: *Rambo's* Rewriting of the Vietnam War," *Film Quarterly* 42 (Fall 1988): 9–16. Other important writings on the cultural implications and effects of *Rambo* include Don Kunz, "First Blood Redrawn," *Vietnam Generation.* 1 (Winter 1989): 94–111, and Gregory A. Waller, "*Rambo:* Getting to Win This Time," in *From Hanoi to Hollywood,* 113–28.

48. See Ralph E. Friar and Natasha A. Friar, *The Only Good Indian: The Hollywood Gospel* (New York: Drama Book Specialists, 1972).

49. Slotkin, *Regeneration through Violence,* 21.

50. Ibid., 418–22.

51. Waller, "Rambo," 115.

52. Jacket copy, Jack Buchanan, *M.I.A. Hunter* (New York: Jove, 1985). By mid-1991, Jove had published a total of fifteen of Buchanan's *M.I.A. Hunter* novels. After various bloody adventures elsewhere (*M.I.A. Hunter* numbers 8, 9, 10, 12, and 13, respectively, *Escape from Nicaragua, Invasion U.S.S.R., Miami War Zone, Desert Death Raid,* and *L.A. Gang War*), Mark Stone returned to Vietnam in the 1990 *Back to Nam* (number 14).

53. "McFarlane Tells Group He Believes Some U.S. POWs Remain in Indochina," *Wall Street Journal,* October 15, 1985. McFarlane's remarks, which were supposedly made "off the record," were leaked to *The Wall Street Journal* by former Republican Representative John Le-Boutillier, who had taped the proceedings.

54. "Convention on MIAs to Open Amid Dissension; High Hopes, Stronger Action Sought on Missing U.S. Servicemen," *Washington Post,* July 18, 1985; "Laos Agrees to Search Crash Site; Bush Details Plan to Look for MIAs," *Washington Post,* July 20, 1985.

55. Jensen-Stevenson and Stevenson, *Kiss the Boys Goodbye,* 9–10 *et passim.*

56. James "Bo" Gritz, *A Nation Betrayed,* 2nd ed. (Boulder City, NV: Lazarus Publishing Company, 1988; 2nd edition 1989), v, vii, 147, *et passim.*

57. Jensen-Stevenson and Stevenson, *Kiss the Boys Goodbye,* 87, 142, 411.

58. Ben Bradlee, Jr., "For Him, POW Rescue Is a Mission Not Ac-

complished," *Boston Globe*, July 7, 1981; Ben Bradlee, Jr., "Pentagon Confirms It Has Formed a Task Force to Combat Terrorism," *Boston Globe*, February 11, 1982.

59. *New Information on U.S. MIA-POW's in Indochina?*, 10, 23–25.

60. Raymond Bonner, "Secret Pentagon Intelligence Unit Is Disclosed," *New York Times*, May 11, 1983; Seymour M. Hersh, "Who's in Charge Here?," *New York Times Magazine*, November 22, 1987; Emerson, *Secret Warriors*, 80 *et passim.* Gritz had evidently first divulged the name "the Activity" a year earlier in an interview with Kevin Cody printed in the April 15, 1982, issue of (Hermosa Beach, CA) *Easy Reader* and reprinted in *Covert Action Information Bulletin* 17 (Summer 1982): 40.

61. Jensen-Stevenson and Stevenson, *Kiss the Boys Goodbye*, 20. An updated and greatly expanded version of McCoy's 1972 book was published in 1991 as *The Politics of Heroin: CIA Complicity in the Global Drug Trade* (Brooklyn, NY: Lawrence Hill Books).

62. Jensen-Stevenson and Stevenson, *Kiss the Boys Goodbye*, 415.

63. Ibid., 91–92.

64. *Wall Street Journal*/NBC News Poll reported in "Minor Memos," *Wall Street Journal*, August 2, 1991.

Chapter 5. Still Missing

1. The following sources were used to reconstruct this story: "U.S. Team in Hanoi for MIA Search," *Star-Ledger* (Newark, NJ), November 14, 1985; UPI story datelined Yen Thuong, November 18, 1985, story tag "MIA-scene," time 8:08 PS; UPI story datelined Yen Thuong, November 18, 1985, story tag "MIA," time 10:14 PS; UPI story datelined Yen Thuong, November 18, 1985, story tag "MIA-scene," time 13:26 PS; "U.S., Viet Begin Search for American War Dead," *Star-Ledger*, November 18, 1985; "U.S. Experts Arrive to Probe Viet MIA Site," *Los Angeles Times*, November 18, 1985; "Digging Set in Vietnam for 4 MIAs," *Philadelphia Inquirer*, November 18, 1985; UPI story datelined Yen Thuong, November 19, 1985, story tag "fornbriefs," time 2:02 PS; UPI story datelined Yen Thuong, November 19, 1985, story tag "MIA," time 4:59 PS; UPI story datelined Yen Thuong, November 19, 1985,

story tag "MIA," time 9:49 PS; "MIA Dig Raises Bitter Past," *Star-Ledger*, November 19, 1985; "U.S. Experts in Vietnam to Excavate Crash Site," *New York Times*, November 19, 1985; UPI story datelined Yen Thuong, November 21, 1985, story tag "MIA," time 6:46 PS; UPI story datelined Yen Thuong, November 21, 1985, story tag "MIA," time 11:07 PS; "Americans, Vietnamese Find Pieces of Downed U.S. Plane" (AP), *Washington Post*, November 21, 1985; "American Hurt in MIA Search," *San Jose Mercury News*, November 21, 1985; UPI story datelined Yen Thuong, November 23, 1985, story tag "MIA," time 4:18 PS; UPI story datelined Yen Thuong, November 23, 1985, story tag "MIAs," time 8:37 PS; "Bomber Adds Little to MIA Hunt," *Star-Ledger*, December 1, 1985; UPI story datelined Yen Thuong, December 2, 1985, story tag "MIA"; "Joint Effort Completed at Vietnam Crash Site," *New York Times*, December 2, 1985; "Vietnam: The Hunt for MIA's," *Newsweek*, December 2, 1985, 60; "Americans Take Home 7 Caskets from Hanoi," *Philadelphia Inquirer*, December 5, 1985; "MIA Excavation Ended," *Facts on File*, December 20, 1985; UPI story datelined Bangkok, June 11, 1986, story tag "MIA"; UPI story datelined Bangkok, November 2, 1986, story tag "MIA"; autobiographical statements by Paul L. Granger and Thomas J. Klomann in Captain and Mrs. Frederic A. Wyatt, eds., *We Came Home* (Toluca Lake, CA: P.O.W. Publications, 1977).

The crucial *Star-Ledger* reports were found, clipped, and filed by Jane M. Franklin, whose letter "Funding for MIA Operations," *Star-Ledger*, June 29, 1988, inspired much of this book. Ann Mills Griffiths responded with her own letter "Hope for MIAs," *Star-Ledger*, July 21, 1988, which dismissed the Vietnamese grief because "there is no lingering uncertainty for Vietnamese families."

2. Personal statement of Thomas J. Klomann, *We Came Home*, n.p.

Chapter 6. "The Last Chapter"?

1. "Kicking the 'Vietnam Syndrome,'" *Washington Post*, March 4, 1991.
2. "'Road Map' to Renew Ties with Hanoi Could Lead to Some Trade by Year End," *Wall Street Journal*, April 15, 1991; "Concerned Citizen Newsletter," *National League of Families of American Prisoners and Missing in Southeast Asia*, May 31, 1991.

3. U.S. Senate Committee on Foreign Relations Republican Staff, *An Examination of U.S. Policy Toward POW/MIAs*, May 23, 1991, p. 5–8.

4. Ibid., November 1991 edition, p. 5–8.

5. Testimony of Carl Ford, November 15, 1991, *Hearings Before the Senate Select Committee on POW/MIA Affairs*, Part I of II (Washington, DC: GPO, 1992), 641.

6. *Hearings before the Senate Select Committee on POW/MIA Affairs*, Part I of II, November 5, 6, 7, and 15, 1991, 443–47.

7. "Panel's Top G.O.P. Staff Is Dismissed by Helms," *New York Times*, January 8, 1992.

8. Telephone conversation on July 21, 1992, with Senate Foreign Relations Committee staff member who declined to give her name.

9. Poll reported in "Minor Memos," *Wall Street Journal*, August 2, 1991.

10. "Lawmakers Pledge Cash to POW Reward," *Los Angeles Times*, July 16, 1987; *Report of the Select Committee on POW/MIA Affairs, United States Senate* (Washington, DC: GPO, 1993), 319. McDaniel acknowledged raising "several million dollars . . . in addition to the $2.4 million" thanks to his appearances on the *Morton Downey, Jr., Show* ("POW/MIA Debate," *Vietnam*, February 1992, 56).

11. Telephone interview with Commander Gregg Hartung, Public Affairs Office, Department of Defense, September 23, 1991. Since then, the Lao highlander has been extensively interviewed and photographed.

12. Interview with James Bamford, the investigative reporter who led the ABC team that exposed the fraud, February 28, 1992. Bamford played for me the extensive videos showing the bird sanctuary, the bird smuggler, and the unmasking of the scam.

13. Defense Department press conference, July 2, 1992; "U.S. Is Sure Photo of Missing Is Fake," *New York Times*, July 19, 1992.

14. "Baker Presses Vietnam on MIAs, Cambodia," *St. Louis Post Dispatch*, July 25, 1991; UPI story datelined Olney, IL, story tag "mia-borah," July 22, 1991; *Report of the Select Committee on POW/MIA Affairs*, 319.

15. Peter Jennings's *World News Tonight*, ABC, February 11 and February 12, 1992.

16. "Trouble on the MIA Committee," *Time*, May 4, 1992, 13. Even fellow POW/MIA crusader John LeBoutillier had presented evidence of Hendon's possibly illegal activities to the National League of Families (Monika Jensen-Stevenson and William Stevenson, *Kiss the Boys Goodbye* [New York: Dutton, 1990], 139–40).

17. "Bui Tin: My 'Detention' at Dulles," *Washington Post*, October 20, 1991.
18. "The Avenger. Love Him or Hate Him, Senator John Kerry Has Always Been a Man on a Mission," *Boston Globe Sunday Magazine*, February 9, 1992.
19. Memorandum from H. R. Haldeman to General Hughes, April 26, 1971, and "POW/MIA Wives," memorandum from General James D. Hughes to Haldeman, April 29, 1971, Nixon Presidential Materials Project, National Archives and Records Administration, Alexandria Annex, White House Special Files, Haldeman, Box 77, General Hughes Folder.
20. My own efforts to testify, which persisted from February to December 1992, were officially rebuffed not only by the staff and in letters from Senator Kerry but also by Senators Kerry and Grassley when I appeared with each of them on national television.
21. Confirmation hearings of Dr. Henry Kissinger as secretary of state, September 7, 10, 11, and 14, 1973, as reprinted in "Americans Missing in Southeast Asia," *Hearings before the House Select Committee on Missing Persons in Southeast Asia*, Part 5, June 17, 25, July 21, and September 21, 1975, 175.
22. "Long Shadow of the M.I.A.'s Still Stalks a Pentagon Official," *New York Times*, September 20, 1992.
23. Richard Nixon, "Fourth Annual Report to the Congress on United States Foreign Policy. May 3, 1973." *Public Papers of the Presidents*, 1973, Document 141.
24. *Report of the Select Committee on POW/MIA Affairs*, 164.
25. Ibid., 221.
26. Ibid., 302.
27. Ibid., 155.
28. Ibid., 310.
29. Ibid., 305–310, 334–35.
30. Ibid., 221, 276–80.
31. Ibid., 334.
32. Letter from Boris Yeltsin to Senate Select Committee, June 12, 1992.
33. Telephone interview with John LeBoutillier, June 25, 1992.
34. John Taylor, "Commando-in-Chief," *New York*, June 15, 1992, 27–29.
35. "Veterans Raise Perot Banner," *New York Daily News*, June 11, 1992.
36. Interview with LeBoutillier, June 25, 1992.

37. David Jackson, "MIAs' Kin Want Perot as President," *Dallas Morning News*, May 19, 1992; interview with David Jackson, May 18, 1992; interview with LeBoutillier, June 12, 1992; "It's Businessman Perot and Not War Hero Bush Who Attracts a Following among U.S. Veterans," *Wall Street Journal*, July 2, 1992.

38. Telephone interview with Dolores Alfond, July 5, 1992; telephone interview with Jeffrey Donahue, June 23, 1992.

39. "Money Talks," *Newsweek*, December 8, 1969, 57; Fred Powledge, "H. Ross Perot Pays His Dues," *New York Times Magazine*, February 28, 1971, 22, 24.

40. Lawrence Wright, "The Man from Texarkana," *New York Times Magazine*, June 28, 1992, 40, 43; "Road to the White House" (transcript of interview with Perot on C-Span), May 17, 1992, 14.

41. Richard Nixon telephone log, White House Special Files, Peter Flanigan File, Box 9.

42. Memorandum from Office of Arthur Burns, April 9, 1969, White House Special Files, Haldeman File, Box 133, Ross Perot Folder.

43. "Richard Nixon Foundation," White House Special Files, Haldeman File, Box 133, Perot Folder; "Nixon Worth Put at $596,900," *New York Times*, May 13, 1969.

44. "Agenda for Ross Perot Meeting with the President, May 16," White House Special Files, Haldeman File, Box 133, Perot Folder.

45. "H. Ross Perot," Memorandum from Gordon Strachan to H. R. Haldeman, January 12, 1971, White House Special Files, Haldeman File, Box 133, Perot Folder.

46. Robert Fitch, "H. Ross Perot: America's First Welfare Billionaire," *Ramparts*, November 1971, 42–51.

47. Memorandum from Peter Flanigan, June 30, 1969, White House Special Files, Haldeman File, Box 133, Perot Folder.

48. "POW Policy in Vietnam," Memorandum for the President from Henry A. Kissinger, October 2, 1969, White House Special Files, President's Office Files, Series A: Documents Annotated by the President, Box 3. In response to the first edition of this book, Sybil Stockdale and Richard Capen alleged that the government was not involved in their activities in creating the National League of Families. The Nixon Archives prove the opposite. The first major media event using the wives was a methodically planned meeting to be held on December 12 between the president and a carefully selected delegation led by Sybil Stockdale. "Dick Capen and his people have worked hard to put

together the package," Alexander Butterfield wrote to fellow White House staffer Colonel Hughes on December 4, but "a final decision has been made that there will be no fathers among those invited so wives and mothers must be substituted for the 2 sets of parents," the "demographic spread" must be widened, and "there must be at least 1 and preferably 2 more enlisted men represented, without exceeding a total of 23 ladies" (Memorandum from Butterfield to Colonel Hughes, December 4, 1969, White House Special Files, Haldeman File, Box 55, Hughes Folder). Lyn Nofziger asked Butterfield for "a brief bit on each POW wife we might be able to make use of . . . on the Hill" (Nofziger to Butterfield, December 4, 1969, White House Special Files, Butterfield File, Box 8). Butterfield asked Hughes to forward the president's preplanned answers to possible questions from the press "so that I can complete the required scenario" (Butterfield to Hughes, December 8, 1969, Haldeman File, Box 55, Hughes Folder).

49. "Projects Proposed by Ross Perot," Memorandum from Butterfield to Haldeman, Ehrlichman, Kissinger, and Harlow, October 24, 1969, White House Special Files, Haldeman File, Box 133, Perot Folder.

50. Script for *United We Stand*, list of TV stations, and "Perot's Project" (November 14 memorandum from Butterfield to Haldeman), White House Special Files, Haldeman File, Box 133, Perot Folder.

51. Memorandum from Colson to Butterfield, December 3, 1969, White House Special Files, Butterfield File, Box 8.

52. White House Special Files, Presidential Office Files, Memoranda, Box 79.

53. White House Special Files, Haldeman File, Box 55, John Brown Folder.

54. "Message from Perot," Memorandum for the President from Alexander Butterfield, White House Special Files, President's Handwriting Files, Box 4. Nixon has written a big double-underlined "Good!" on this.

55. Interview with Jeffrey Donahue, June 23, 1992; interview with LeBoutillier, June 25, 1992.

56. "Bush Sees Gain in Vietnam Ties," *Los Angeles Times*, October 24, 1992.

57. "Corporations Ask Bush to Lift Vietnam Ban," *New York Times*, May 9, 1992; "Vietnam: The Big Buildup Begins," *Washington Post*, December 9, 1992.

58. "Nixon Opposing U.S.–Vietnam Normalization Policy: He Could

Influence Any Move by Bush Administration to End Trade Embargo," *Los Angeles Times*, January 9, 1993.

59. "U.S. Firms Gear Up for Vietnam Business Once Trade Ban Ends," *Wall Street Journal*, February 9, 1993.

60. "President Clinton, Normalize Ties with Vietnam," *Wall Street Journal*, March 8, 1993.

61. "U.S. Firms Line Up to 'Invade' Vietnam," *Star-Ledger* (Newark, NJ), March 15, 1993.

62. "U.S. Businesses Turning to Vietnam," *New York Times*, February 8, 1993; "Heading for Hanoi: U.S. Firms Gear Up for Vietnam Business Once Trade Ban Ends," *Wall Street Journal*, February 9, 1993; "U.S. Firms Losing Out in Emerging Vietnam," *Chicago Tribune*, March 7, 1993.

63. "U.S. Won't Heed Mitterrand Plea to Rush Vietnam Trade," Reuters, February 10, 1993.

64. "Clinton Prepares to Relax Policy on Vietnam as U.S. Business Urges Access to New Market," *Wall Street Journal*, April 12, 1993.

65. "U.S. to Press Hanoi to Explain '72 P.O.W. Report," *New York Times*, April 13, 1993.

66. *MacNeil/Lehrer NewsHour*, April 13, 1993.

67. *Washington Times*, April 12; *USA Today*, April 12; *Washington Post*, April 15; *Jersey Journal*, April 18, 1993 (respectively).

68. References are to a photocopy of the English- language text sent by fax from the Moscow bureau of the *New York Times* to the *Times* foreign desk with a cover letter referring to it as a "Sept 15, 1972 Vietnamese Top Secret report, recently discovered in Soviet Communist Party archives—confirming that Vietnam was holding on to far more US POWs than it had pubicly [sic] admitted." I am grateful to *Times* reporter Steven A. Holmes for this copy.

69. The history of all thirteen camps, together with aerial photos of each, is given in "Americans Missing in Southeast Asia," *Hearings before the House Select Committee on Missing Persons in Southeast Asia*, Ninety-fourth Congress, First Session, Part 3, February 4–March 31, 1976, 313–37.

70. "War Foes to Bring 3 Prisoners Home," *New York Times*, September 3, 1972.

71. Gareth Porter, *A Peace Denied: The United States, Vietnam, and the Paris Agreement* (Bloomington: Indiana University Press, 1975), 128.

72. *Wall Street Journal*, April 23, 1993.

Index